TELEPEN

6 00 171822 4

D1610041

with all good wishes
from
Lula Reynolds
Xmas 1909

MODERN STUDIES

[All rights reserved]

Modern Studies

By Oliver Elton

Professor of English Literature
in the University of Liverpool

UNIVERSITY COLLEGE NOTTINGHAM

London
Edward Arnold
1907

c

PREFACE

THE articles in this volume are reprinted with many changes and enlargements. *Giordano Bruno in England, Recent Shakespeare Criticism, The Meaning of Literary History,* and *The Novels of Mr. Henry James* first appeared in the *Quarterly Review* ; *A Word on Mysticism* in the *Fortnightly Review* ; *Mr. George Meredith* and *Living Irish Literature* in the *Tribune,* but the pages on the Irish drama in the *Manchester Guardian* ; *Mr. Swinburne's Poems* in the *Speaker* ; *Colour and Imagery in Spenser* and *Literary Fame* in *Otia Merseiana.* I have to thank the authorities of these journals for courteously granting the use of published material.

The appendix of notes contains some pieces of evidence, quotations, or titles that would have burdened the text.

I venture to dedicate the book to the makers of the University of Liverpool ; for amongst them are many of the friends with whose help and goodwill the articles were written. One of these, Mr. John Sampson, has given most valuable counsel throughout.

O. E.

LIVERPOOL,
August, 1907.

CONTENTS

GIORDANO BRUNO IN ENGLAND

I. Interest of the Topic.   II. Bruno at the French Embassy.   III. Oxford.   IV. 'La Cena de le Ceneri'. V. The Italian Dialogues: the Legend of a 'Club'; Other Notices of England.   VI. Silence of English Records; Suggested Influence of Bruno on Shakespeare and Spenser; Allusions in Seventeenth-century English Writers.   VII. Allusions to Bruno in the Age of Anne.

I

'The prophetic soul of the wide world dreaming on things to come'—these words of Shakespeare in his darkest sonnet have been read as a stray echo from the theories of Giordano Bruno. At least they may serve to denote Bruno himself, with his presentiment of the ethics and pantheism of a later day. One of the divining, representative minds of the later Renaissance, full of its clashing elements of animal will and ideal aspiration, he remains, with his vision upon distant things, rather solitary in its midst. His work has been much investigated, above all since his monument rose in Rome upon the place of his martyrdom. His biography has been built on the standard researches of Berti, begun more than half a century ago. His ideas are chronicled in every history of thought. The patient and solid expositions of scholars like Tocco have prepared the ground, and, in our own language, the book of Mr. McIntyre, published four years

B

ago, and following on the earlier account by Miss Frith,
worthily inaugurates inquiry.[1]   But there is more human
nature in Bruno than in almost any philosopher.   He is
never quite impersonal; few lives have been more
dramatic ; he should be the subject of a great tragedy
with broad and buoyant interludes; and this side of him
has received little justice.   He has left the materials for
it himself, though often in a turbid form.   Pater's little
essay reveals some of the subtler fires of Bruno's temperament, but hardly prepares us, when we open Bruno
himself, for his fever and his boisterous richness.   To
bring all this home, a critical English version is required
of the Italian dialogues, and of some of the Latin verse
and prose.   Here a single episode of his life is sketched
once more, so far as may be in his own words.   It tells
us something of his temper, and claims the more attention
as it has often been mistold.   It is his narrative of his
stay in England, where the dialogues were written and
printed.   The unexplained silence of contemporary
records, the possible traces of his influence upon Spenser
and Shakespeare, and his contrast with those poets, open
curious problems; and further interest attaches to the
fitful allusions to his name and works in the English
literature of the seventeenth and early eighteenth
centuries.

II

Bruno was in England some two years and a half, like
a man waiting in harbour between two violent voyages,
enjoying a peace that for him could only be comparative.
He came, not more than thirty-five years old, with a
passionate mental experience already behind him.   In
the shade of the Dominican life at Naples he had read
freely, and the irritant, original quality of his thought

had soon brought adventures. He had been threatened by the Church, had put off the religious habit and fled. Thus he started on his long, unquiet, missionary pilgrimage, joining the assailants of Aristotle and those of the old astronomy, and adding theological heresies of his own. He could not rest in Italy, nor yet in the city of Calvin, which would only harbour a convert; although, luckily for Bruno, Calvin was dead. He lectured boldly in Toulouse, one of the homes of the Inquisition, and next, to the credit of Henry III, found shelter and a reader's platform in Paris. Here he spoke and wrote much on the art of mnemonics; and also, in the same breath, and in the way of the neo-Platonists, on the *Shadows of Ideas*, or the deceiving shows of sense—to him faint copies of the eternal realities or Ideas, which in turn emanate from the supreme Idea of all. About the spring of 1583 he quitted Paris 'because of the disturbances', bringing letters from Henry to the French ambassador in London.

Michel de Castelnau de Mauvissière, whose valuable memoirs[2] only reach to 1569, had held his post for nine years. He had watched the drama of Mary Stuart, but was to leave England before its completion. He was much at court, he was a man of reading and culture, and to be his guest was an introduction. He was therefore an apposite guardian for such a visitor as Bruno. Old cuts are to be seen of the low-hung and narrow-windowed mansion in Butcher's Row, leading from Wych Street to the Strand, with the fleur-de-lis on its outer walls, and then or later called Beaumont House.[3] The place is now cleared to purge the thoroughfares of London. Here, probably, Bruno wrote some of the most explosive books of the sixteenth century. He lived as the 'ambassador's gentleman', perhaps a kind of secretary, under the roof

of a staunch Roman Catholic, and safe by privilege from
the arm of any Church.   His inconvenient estate as an
unfrocked priest was made easy by a special exemption
from mass.[4]   During his whole stay he 'did not go to it
when it was said indoors, or out of doors, neither to any
sermon'.   He was on intimate and happy terms with his
host, who ' welcomed him with such largesse to a notable
position in his own household', and who earns our thanks
even if unaware that he entertained the chief thinker
that had visited England since Erasmus.   For Bruno his
bounty 'turned England into Italy, and London into
Nola'.   To him is inscribed the recondite *Exposition of
the Thirty Seals*, printed apparently in London soon after
Bruno's arrival, and also three of the far more notable
Italian dialogues.   The vehement gratitude of the exile
rings true amid the ebullient superlatives.   Hatred and
calumny are the lot of ruthless reforming philosophers,
and Bruno runs over with complaints against the ignorant tale-bearers and caitiffs who assailed him.   From all
such Castelnau is his only rock of shelter.   The note is
sounded of that superlative pride, which saves Bruno's
language from our ridicule, because it carried his unpaci-
fied spirit through to martyrdom.   The higher accent of
the age is caught in his words to the ambassador :—

   In having one who is in any wise worthy of your
furtherance, protection, and aid, you show yourself, as
ever, conformable to the princes great of soul and to the
gods and heroes who have appointed you and those like
you to be guardians of their friends. . . . For while your
betters in fortune can do nothing for you, who exceed
many of them in virtue, you can do for others something
that shall outlast your walls and tapestries, and shall
straightway be written in the book of eternity, whether
that which is seen upon earth or that which is supposed
in heaven.[5]

Another passage begins by loading the female sex, in Bruno's way, with thirty-nine separate epithets, the lightest of which are 'frailty' and 'imperfection'; and they are also quaintly contrived to fit his other aversion, the 'first matter' of Aristotle; but he ends, by way of exception, with a compliment—so sudden and vehement are the turns of his tongue!—to the wife and child of Castelnau. His hostess is endowed with 'no mediocre bodily beauty' and with courtesy and discretion. Maria, though only six, might, for her speech, be either Italian, French, or English, and will so 'handle musical instruments that you cannot tell if she is of bodily or incorporeal substance'; while her 'ripe and goodly bearing makes a doubt whether she has come down from heaven or is merely born of earth'.[6] This tone is in the English as well as the Italian taste of the time, and might remind us of some passionate praise of a child in a play of Shakespeare, or of Fletcher afterwards.

III

Soon after his arrival Bruno had made his only known excursion to an English seat of learning. Before the *Thirty Seals* he had set a Latin letter, conceived in the language of an enemy, and addressed to the University of Oxford. Its heady self-praise and reviling are pitched even above Bruno's ordinary shout of exultation or disdain. He has not a quiet style. The dust of his advance and the flaming and creaking of the axles of his chariot are hardly credible. He accumulates epithet and synonym as though something were to be gained by them, until we hardly know what he is saying. At his best he is steadily noble, sometimes full and ample like Rabelais, turning his thought over and over, as

though loth to let it fall till he has shown its last facet ;
while at moments he is inspired by Plato, and is not
unworthy to recall him.   His own ideal of writing he
tells in a sentence: 'Let me not deal in petty, delicate,
curt, cramped, and concise epigram, but in a broad and
affluent vein of prose, which is large and long, firm and
flowing.'   And with due affluence he writes [7] :—

To the most excellent Vice-Chancellor of the Academy
of Oxford ; to its illustrious Doctors and famous Masters;
greeting from Philotheus Jordanus Brunus of Nola, doctor
of a more careful divinity, professor of a purer and a
more harmless wisdom ; known in the chief academies of
Europe ; a philosopher approved and honorifically welcomed ; a stranger only amongst churls and savages ;
the awakener of nodding spirits, the queller of insolent
and kicking ignorance, in all his actions betokening
a general love of mankind; affecting Briton as much as
Italian, woman as much as man, alike the wearer of
crown and mitre, and of gown and sword, the cowled
and the uncowled ; but most affecting him whose
converse is peaceful, humane, loyal, and profitable :—he
who looks not to the anointed head, the crossed forehead,
the washen hands, and the circumcision, but to the spirit
and the cultivation of the wit, whenever he is suffered to
see the face of a true man ; is hated by spreaders of folly
and petty humbugs (*hypocritunculi*), but loved by men
of proof and zeal and applauded by the nobler spirits.   All
greeting to the illustrious and excellent Vice-Chancellor,
and to the chief men of his University.

After all, this was true in substance, and Bruno was
only carrying far the principle of Flaubert's high
counsel, 'Soyons plus fiers!'   He goes on to advertise
his philosophic wares with a ferocious politeness that is
always breaking down, and intimates his readiness to
dispute with any one whom he can answer without
disgracing himself.

Bruno thus invited himself to lecture at Oxford and dispute against all worthy opponents. Naturally no reply of the Vice-Chancellor, Thornton, is on record. There is no trace of any permit being granted, nor is Bruno named among the foreigners who were incorporated in the University. The silence of all the English chronicles but one contrasts with his own loud volubility. Much as he liked, in his own comedy, to pillory pomposity, he might have posed as another stock personage therein. The 'Miles Gloriosus' of the anti-Church militant speaks aloud in every allusion that he makes to his Oxford visit. Somehow he attained his wish to be heard. He had made the acquaintance of Philip Sidney already, and probably also of Fulke Greville, Lord Brooke ; both their names were soon to resound through his pages. From them he may have taken letters to their own House, Christ Church, of whose Dean, the elder Sir Toby Matthew, as well as of Dr. Martin Culpeper, Warden of New College, he speaks with ardour as exceptions to the ruck of Oxford doctors. He lectured, or disputed, on the two matters that filled his mind and were sure to exasperate discussion. He assailed Aristotle's theory of immortality, and also, in discourses 'De Quintuplici Sphaera', the still received astronomy. About one of these themes he may have spoken on the public and festal occasion which is also noted (though without mention of Bruno) by Camden and Anthony à Wood.[8] So Nietzsche, three centuries later, might have left little mark after haranguing a company of Oxford dons. Yet one Oxonian has alluded to Bruno's oratory. No passage is yet known in which any other Englishman of the time refers to Bruno's presence in England. Samuel Daniel, the poet, was then an undergraduate at Magdalen Hall, and, as it appears,

heard him speaking in the Schools. In a preface to
a translation by Daniel from Paulus Jovius, it is remarked
by N. W.:—

You cannot forget that which Nolanus (that man of
infinite titles amongst other phantastical toys) truly noted
by chance in our Schools, that by the help of translations
all sciences had their offspring ; and in my judgement it
is true.[9]

Even such a fragment points to Bruno having won
a certain reputation. The 'toys' may be an allusion to
his works, already mentioned, on mnemonics. The *De
Umbris Idearum,* the latest of them, had already found
one English follower in Alexander Dicson, the ' Dicsono '
of the *De la Causa,* and Dicson had found an opponent
in print. Otherwise we have only Bruno's own word
for the part he played. His remark on translation proved
ironical ; for the first English version of any of his books
was William Morehead's of the *Spaccio* (1713).

On June 10, 1583, a political visitor, Albert Lasco, or
Alaski, prince of Poland, a soldier, scholar, and mathe-
matician, 'his personage proper, utterance sweet, nature
facile, and wit excellent,' was received by a pomp of
scarlet doctors and baillies, entertained with orations and
fireworks, and lodged in Christ Church. Among his
hosts were Matthew and Culpeper ; and he passed three
days in a whirl of banquets, speeches, and other de-
monstrations, 'hearing exercises in the Bible Schools to
his great content'; and on the evening of June 11,
'several of that House disputed before him in their
common hall.' It may be guessed that Bruno made
himself at home in the House, and was allowed speech
by Matthew ; or he may have spoken at St. Mary's,
where the customary fencing-match on divinity and on

natural and moral philosophy was held ; or again, on
the morrow, in the Schools. For on the latter occasion
his friend, Matthew Gwinne, of St. John's, a recent
Master of Arts, a doctor, musician, and linguist, who
recurs in Bruno's chronicle, contested, on that ancient
and husk-laden threshing-floor, the questions ' whether
males live longer than females', and whether ' divination
is possible through the stars'. Leyson, the senior proctor,
was moderator, and may have been the disputant whom
Bruno says that he perplexed. There is no sure
evidence ; and Wood describes more such spectacles on
the next and last day of Alaski's visit. The whole scene,
with its endless gowned formality and loquacity, bursts
into froth ; the doctors go back to cloister, and the
celebrated person with his ' very long beard and seemly
raiment' departs from Oxford amid more compliments,
but from the country in a cloud of debts, and is last
' seen by an English gentleman in Cracow, very poor
and bare '.

The obscure Italian, who remained unnoticed, thought
himself the centre of all beholders. We have his
words :—

Go there and let them tell you of what befell the
Nolan, when he publicly disputed on theology with
those doctors, before Prince Alasco the Polack, and
others, noblemen of England. Hear how they could
answer his reasonings, and how that unhappy doctor
stuck fifteen times, like a chicken in the stubble, amidst
the fifteen syllogisms he propounded to us as Coryphaeus
of the University on that momentous occasion ! Hear
how rudely and discourteously that swine went on, and
how humanely and patiently spoke that other, showing
he was indeed Neapolitan born and reared under a
kinder sky. [10]

If the Church had taught Bruno language, the profit

of it was that he knew how to curse.   Thus he pictures
the sixteenth-century doctors :—

They were clad in velvet, and one of them had two
chains of shining gold on his neck, and the other, *per dio*,
twelve rings on two fingers of his precious hand, like a
jeweller . . . and they showed acquaintance with beer as
well as with Greek.

Two of them re-appear in *The Ash Wednesday Supper*,
where this sharp review of Oxford can be found.   But he
felt he had gone too far, and in his next work, *On the
Cause*, there is a long recantation.[11]   He was able to
disown the slur of being ' an odd, impatient, and fantastic
featherhead ', who has insulted a whole city and kingdom.
For Oxford is the nurse of Greville and Sidney and many
other keen and gentle spirits ; and its well-ordered studies
and solemn ceremonies make it, we now hear, one of the
first academies in the world.   Thus, in one of his quick
revulsions, Bruno furls a little sail.

IV

He had retreated, we know not when, from Oxford
to the embassy, and doubtless had occasion to thank
Castelnau for saving him ' from these doctors and
from hunger '.   For seven months no more is heard ; but
on Ash Wednesday, February 15, 1584, occurred the
scenes described in *La Cena de le Ceneri*, published in
that year.   There is no other such picture of the time.
The astronomical discussion, in which Bruno defended
the motion of the earth, is of less note than the frame-
work of half-intended comedy.   The heresy put forth
forty years before by Copernicus, not as physical truth, but
as the best mathematical explanation of the phenomena,
was still the subject of endless dispute and could serve

for an evening's baiting. There is some gap at the beginning of the tale. Bruno receives two messengers from a 'royal esquire' [*regio scudiero*] saying that his conversation on this topic is desired. Then suddenly (after another gap in the dialogue) he is found conversing with Lord Brooke, already a close acquaintance, who asks him for the grounds of his belief.

To which he replied, that he could not have given him any reason without knowing his capacity ; and not knowing how far he might make himself understood, he feared to do like those who reason with statues and go on parleying with the dead . . .

But, he adds, he was ever ready to answer worthy questioners. Bruno often violently contrasts the incivility of the English lower orders with the courtesy of the upper. Greville earned the praise by his reception of such a reply ; for it

greatly pleased the Signor Fulke, and he said, You do me a most pleasing service. I accept your offer, and would fain settle a day, when you will be opposed by persons who perchance will not fail to give you cause to display your forces. Wednesday week will be Ash Wednesday, and you will be invited with many gentlemen and learned personages, in order that after meat there may be debate on sundry and noble matters. I promise you, said the Nolan [Bruno], that I will not fail to be there at the hour, yea, and whenever a like occasion presents itself. . . . But I pray you not to make me come before persons who are ignoble and miscreate and of little understanding in such speculations. . . . The Signor Fulke replied that he need not doubt, for those that he proposed to have would be men of the best learning and behaviour.[12]

This is true good manners, and the supper is arranged. But Ash Wednesday comes, and sunset, and neither boat nor horse nor equipage is sent by the host to carry

Bruno through the lampless mire of London. It is an insult ; and he departs to spend his time with some Italian friends. Returning late, he finds two messengers awaiting him. One of them, John Florio, already domesticated in England, who was afterwards to be the client of Shakespeare's friend Southampton and to make Montaigne an English classic, doubtless served as interpreter. For Bruno scorned to learn more than a few words of English. All Englishmen of rank, he says,

know that their own tongue is only used in their own island, and would think themselves barbarians if they could not speak in Latin, French, Spanish, and Italian.

The other companion was the Welsh physician, Matthew Gwinne,[13] who had disputed on astrology and lectured on music at Oxford, and was also a maker of Latin plays. They tell Bruno that a company of knights, gentry, and doctors are waiting supper for him and will by no means miss him. He consents, and the route then taken by the three can partly be followed. Greville cannot have been at his mansion, Brooke House, in Brooke Street, near Holborn, but was apparently lodged in or near Whitehall. Eight years later Bruno, when questioned by the Holy Office,[14] said that the debate of *La Cena* occurred in the French embassy and was attended by certain physicians. He cannot well have forgotten. Either there was another debate, or it seemed best to have aired the alleged heresy under the roof of an unimpeachable Catholic. In *La Cena* a curious journey is described. It was the statelier as well as easier way to go to Westminster by water. But, on quitting Butcher's Row, instead of descending from St. Clement's to the Temple Stairs, the travellers for some reason turned eastward first, and got to Dorset Stairs, leading down from Dorset House, the abode of

Lord Buckhurst, the poet of the 'Induction' and Elizabeth's trusted councillor.   Here they hailed a boat ; and
what follows is like a sudden interlude from Chapman's
or Porter's comedy, save that instead of the British joy
in farce and blows we feel the fierce nerves and quick
intolerant senses of Italy.

There we shouted and called *oares, id est gondolieri* ;
and stayed a long time, in which we could easily have
got to our appointed place by land and have done some
small business withal.   At length, from afar off, two
boatmen answered, and right slowly they came to shore-
ward as though to put in ; and then, after much question
and answer about the whence, and the where, and the
why, and the how, and the when, they brought up their
bows to the lowest step of the stairs.   And lo, there were
two ; and one of them, who looked like the ancient mari-
ner of the realm of Tartarus, put out a hand to the Nolan ;
and the other, who I think was his son, though he was a
man of some sixty-five years, received the rest of us.[15]

The boat creaks and leaks, *accepit rimosa paludem*, and
might 'safely rival Noah's ark in age, for it seemed a
relic of the Flood'.   In this rotten craft they go painfully forward, the two Italians singing, and Florio doing
it 'as though thinking of his loves'.   The boat seems to
be made of lead ; and at length the boatmen, instead of
hurrying, turn into shore, and this when they have not
gone a third of the way, being only just beyond 'the
place that is called the Temple'.   They will go no
farther, for hereabouts they live.   After vain entreaties
the passengers pay the fare, and land, it would seem,
somewhere about the Temple Stairs, not in comfort.
They plunge perforce through a terrible *tenebroso Averno*
of low-tide Thames ooze,

one of them hissing with fury, another whispering, another

snorting with his lips, or throwing a sigh and stopping a little, or cursing under his breath.

At last, after reaching shore, they come to a slough with a dry narrow margin or side-lane, and thence somehow make their way up towards the Strand. And behold, they find themselves some twenty steps from Bruno's house, back near Temple Bar. They debate whether to go on; and, though they have been maltreated, they prefer to conquer by courtesy, and not to baulk the hopes of so many knights and noble personages. Moreover, Bruno is ever anxious to 'learn men's natures, to see manners, and, if it might be, to acquaint himself with some novel truth'.

They go forward, and the adventures begin again, though the route becomes less traceable. Near 'the pyramid by the mansion where three roads meet', Bruno is mobbed, and is thankful (answering *Tanchi, maester* —'thank ye, master') because he is merely hustled, and does not receive the sharp-pointed boss of the ruffian's buckler. The English populace is a mere 'sink' in Bruno's eyes, and the most raw and barbarous folk ever born upon the earth. The scene is alive, and we feel the hot breath and clamour of Elizabethan London at nightfall.

The artisans and shopfolk, who know you to be in some fashion a foreigner, snicker and laugh and grin and mouth at you, and call you in their own tongue dog, traitor, and stranger, which with them is a most injurious name, qualifying its object to receive every wrong in the world, be he young or old, in citizen dress or armed, noble or gentle. And now, if by evil chance you take occasion to touch one of them, or lay hand to your arms, lo, in a moment you will see yourself, for the whole street's length, in the midst of a host that has sprung up quicker than the men-at-arms, in the fiction of the poets, sprang from the teeth sown by Jason.

They seem to come out of the earth, but in truth they
issue from the shops, and give you a most lordly and
noble view of a forest of sticks, long poles, halberds,
partisans, and rusty pitchforks ; and these things, though
the sovereign has given them for the best of uses, they
have ever ready for this and like occasions.   So you will
see them come upon you with a peasant fury, without
looking where, or how, or why, or upon whom, and none
of them thinking of any other ; every one discharging
the natural despite he hath against the foreigner ; and,
if he is not stayed by the heels of the rest who are
carrying out a like intent, you will find him taking the
measure of your doublet with his own hand or his own
rod, and, if you are not wary, hammering your hat upon
your head withal.[16]

After such adventures they reach Greville's door.

The various people and servants in the hall, without
giving way, or bowing the head, or making any reverence, and showing scorn by their gesture, did us the
favour to point us to the right door.   We go in and
upstairs, and find that, after waiting for us long, they
have sat down to table in despair.[17]

This behaviour of the great man's retinue accords
with Bruno's curious and acute digression on the various
classes of English dependants—gentlemen's needy gentlemen who wear a badge, bankrupt merchants, runaway sailors, and rogues, who all enter service.   Then
the supper-party is described in the same vivid, excited,
often distorted style.   What eyes, what a memory, what
a passion of learned hatred are needed for a picture like
this of the Oxford doctor !   It might be drawn by an
exasperated candidate of his examiner in the schools :—

With an emphatic visage—like that wherewith *Divum
pater* is described in the ' Metamorphoses ' as sitting in
the midst of the council of the gods, to fulminate that
harsh judgement against the profane Lycaon—after

looking at his golden necklace—*torquem auream, aureum monile*—and then, having glanced at the breast of the Nolan, where he might rather have missed a button, he sat up, took his arms off the table, shook his shoulders a little, snorted somewhat with his mouth, set his velvet cap straight on his head, twirled his moustache, put his perfumed visage into gear, arched his brows, expanded his nostrils, glanced behind him and adjusted himself, and leaned his left hand on his left side.[18]

The two doctors, called here Torquato and Nundinio, sat on each side of an unnamed knight who took the head of the table.   Florio, after some polite parleying, sat at the foot, with Greville on his right and Bruno on his left.   Portraits of the day help to sharpen the outline of the scene.   Bruno, spare, short, with a wide persistent gaze and endless vitality, probably not yet bearded, careless of dress and copious of words ; Greville, with smallish clear-modelled features, high-bred, dignified, and dressed like a courtier, with, as we may imagine, a halting, fastidious utterance ; Florio, another dark Italian face, full of cheerful affectations of speech ; the cavalier, possibly Sidney, with more distinction than beauty ; the excited rampant doctors ; the Latin shouting and arguing over diagrams, the philosophers crying out while the gentlemen keep their heads ; the ceremony, so disgusting to Bruno, of passing round the loving-cup ; the break-up of the party in confusion ; the doctors departing without salutation, having been easily silenced and refuted ; and all this about the motion of the earth :— surely few scenes of older England have been rescued so clearly from the darkness of time !   The conclusion is in keeping.   The entertainers, still unperturbed, beg Bruno not to be vexed with the doctors, but to pity the poverty of the land, which has been 'widowed of all good literature so far as touches philosophy and mathe-

matics'. Then, after courtesies, Bruno returns in the
dark 'without coming on any of those butting and kicking beasts who had molested our advance'.

V

The years 1584–5 were the most fruitful of Bruno's
life. In the leisure and shelter of the embassy he wrote the
Italian dialogues that show the full compass of his style
and the early maturity of his philosophy. Apart from
the Latin poems subsequently published, they contain
almost every seminal thought which Bruno left for posterity. It is wholly certain that they were issued from
a British press, though *La Cena* bears imprint of no place,
while the others bear the imprint of Venice or Paris.
Long after, at his trial,[19] Bruno explained that all the
books which were dated from Venice, and also those dated
from Paris, were really printed in England, in the hope
that a foreign imprint would increase the English sales.
It may not have been easy to find a publisher for works
that Anglican and Puritan and Romanist would alike
repudiate. A tradition of some age, resting on a note
of Thomas Baker the antiquary, steadily asserts that
Bruno applied to one of the most courageous and let-
tered printers in London, Thomas Vautrollier, the
learned Huguenot, who had already been checked and
fined for producing Lutheran pamphlets, and who fled
to Scotland (where he introduced a new era in printing)
because, according to Baker, he had been printer to
Bruno. The whole tradition is doubtful; for these
works, though all from one London press, are said by
experts to bear no likeness in type or decorations to
Vautrollier's issues. Who produced them is unknown.[20]
Thus, when England was barren of philosophy, at

least ten years before Hooker's treatise and twenty
before the *Advancement of Learning*, the Italian refugee
had brought out in London the dialogues he had written
within a bow-shot of Temple Bar. Each of them shows
his temperament colouring a different problem. *De la
Causa, Principio et Uno*, seeks the final, single, and
divine principle of things, which is infused into all matter.
De l'Infinito, Universo, e Mondi refutes the current
notion of the physical universe as bounded by fixed walls
or 'flaming ramparts'. In *Spaccio de la Bestia trion-
fante*, with its parasitic *Cabala del Cavallo Pegaseo*, a
fresher code of human excellence is propounded, and the
current social ethics are revised. In *De gli eroici Furori*
(*Of the kinds of Heroic Rapture*) the upward journey of
the soul towards illumination is portrayed. Bruno wove
no system, but passed on to further developments in his
Latin poems, which expound his view of the monad, or
constituent unit of all things and thoughts.

In these Italian books there is endless Vesuvian reek
and fulmination. There is little trace of the serenity
that crowns the talk of the Platonic Socrates, though
there is subtlety to spare. There is no lack of sardonic
declamation and noise; and the speakers who disagree
with Bruno are too soon, and with too little slyness,
made foolish. But the style, so various, often so high,
always alive and never satisfied, animates the formal
metaphysics, even disguising the outline of the novel
thoughts to which it gives an impetus. One of
Bruno's needs is to seek and absorb as much of the
picturesque manifold of life as possible. He will grasp
and devour everything before he feels ready to seek the
unity that binds the pageant together. And his other,
his co-equal need, is to seek for that unity in life itself,
in spirit, in divinity, whose omnipresence he guesses and

passionately asserts rather than approaches by steps of
proof. The dialogues quiver, as in noonday heat, with
this play of two intellectual passions—so real can the
metaphysical desire of 'finding the one in the many' be
when thus taken to heart! To such a quest the widen-
ing of knowledge in his own day, and the corresponding
liberation of human dreams and passions, gave reality.

We now take up the narrative, often mistold, of
Bruno's life in London.

There is no other record of his visiting Fulke Greville,
nor is there anything to demonstrate that the 'cavalier'
at the supper was Sidney. There is no reason why
Sidney should not have been named, if present; but
Bruno seldom names him before the later dedications—
those of the *Spaccio* and the *Furori*; though then we
learn that Sidney (of whom he had first heard at Milan)
had been among his first English acquaintances. A passage in the dedication to *La Cena* may be given in full,
as it is the main source of what must be called the
Bruno legend :—

What is the drift of this banquet, this supper? Not
merely to muse on the disposition of the right noble and
well-conditioned Signor Fulke Greville, in whose honoured
dwelling we met; nor on the honourable bearing of
those most courteous gentlemen who were there present
to see and hear. But our desire is to see how far nature
can go in compounding two fantastic bugbears, dreams,
shadows, and quartan agues [these are the two Oxford
doctors]. And while the historic sense of this matter is
first sifted and then tasted and digested, there are drawn
out aptly certain speculations, some topographical, some
geographical, or ratiocinatory, or moral, or again metaphysical, or mathematical, or natural.[21]

Bruno merely says in his rapid way that all kinds of
digressions may be looked for in his dialogue; and on

this remark appears to rest the time-honoured fiction of a 'club', or periodical gathering, of which Sidney, Greville, and Bruno were the leaders, and which met to 'discuss', as it is usually put, 'moral and philosophical speculations.' This notion seems to be traceable to a remark of Joseph Warton [22] in a note upon a line of Pope. He says that Sidney was 'in a secret club with' Bruno 'held in London' in 1587 (sic). Prosy Zouch, the biographer of Sidney, added the detail that 'philosophical and metaphysical subjects of a nice and delicate nature were there discussed, and the doors of the apartment in which they met kept shut'. Later writers have seized the hook, which is baited by the authentic records of the secret 'atheistical' sittings that were charged first against Marlowe and then against Sir Walter Raleigh. There is proof that various loose counterparts of the Italian Academies existed in Elizabethan London. The 'impact of hot thought on hot thought' in a time of mental ferment always leads to their formation. The so-called 'Areopagus' of Sidney, Greville, Dyer, and Spenser, have been occupied with the ephemeral craze of adapting English metre to classic prosody. But of any club, numbering the same writers, and concerned with speculative discussions, no trace has yet been produced. For some reasons it is unlikely to have existed. Sidney was not a man to deal in philosophic heresy. No sign is alleged of his knowing Bruno's ideas, or of his caring for high metaphysic or freethinker's ethics. Nor do the pensive poems of Greville, even though their stoicism is tinged with Platonic allusion, visibly resemble anything in Bruno.

It has often been said that Bruno was widely known in London society, and was acquainted—so the list often runs—with Dyer, Spenser, Bacon, Temple (the translator of Ramus), and, it is sometimes added, with Walsingham and Leicester.   The evidence is still to seek.   The first four of these names he never mentions.   Leicester he says, in 1584, that he neither knew nor expected to know. To Walsingham he alludes in terms that might be used by an admiring stranger.   The unfounded tradition is repeated not only in the popular Italian accounts of Bruno, which run over with mistakes, but by writers of standing.[23]   From these must be excepted Mr. Symonds, in his *History of the Renaissance*, and Dr. Höffding, whose *History of Modern Philosophy* contains the best short account of Bruno in existence and can be read with pleasure by the man of letters as well as the philosopher.   To ascribe an unverified prominence to Bruno is to hide the most curious problem of his life in England, namely, why he was ignored.   From what he further relates of his visit not much can be gleaned towards a solution.

In the dedication of the *Spaccio* there is fervent praise of Sidney ; his wit and manners and his truly heroical disposition and merits were ' shown to me at my very first arrival in the British isle ' ; and Bruno adds that he would not turn his back on that fair and fortunate land before saluting Sidney in gratitude ; a remark which points to the *Spaccio* having been issued shortly before his departure.   With this greeting he couples another to Greville,

who resembles you in his many inward and outward perfections, being allied to you in the long and strait friendship wherein you have been reared and have grown together ; and, for myself, he was the next to proffer me his services after you, who were first ; and I should have taken and he accomplished them, if the jealous Erinnys of mean and malignant persons concerned had not sprinkled its arsenic betwixt him and me.[24]

He adds that though some unnamed slanderer had estranged Greville, he keeps another book in reserve to inscribe to him. The promise was not kept. We do not know what the calumny was; but Bruno was waspish and sensitive, and his prefaces run over with complaints of being misconstrued and defamed. Perhaps, after the exhibition in *La Cena*, Greville had politely dropped him. In *De la Causa* he represents himself as a victim of general hatred, envy, and persecution, and Castelnau as his one protector. It might be fair to think that he is really angry at not being noticed. He hints also at another side of his experience. Among his troubles, and the last drop in his cup, was a 'mad, malicious, and discourteous feminine scorn'. But the *Furori*, perhaps a year later, opens with an indifferent sonnet to the 'fair and delectable nymphs of England', and ends with a long confused lyrical parable in honour of those ladies, 'the graces of the Thames,' and their queen.[25] Perhaps the nymphs are the same referred to later still in the *De Immenso*, where Bruno likens himself to the hairy Pan— *setosum quia me natura creavit*—well enough, if we think of his large, indiscriminate zest for life and his fierce buoyancy of temper. His tone is like that of Whitman ; he is strenuous, he says, and invincible, and male ; and if he is reproached he has his answer ready for the Narcissi —*peramarunt me quoque nymphae*.[26] Such an attitude may serve to show why his ethics did not appeal to Spenser or to Sidney, the sons and singers of chivalry. For of chivalry he had little enough. Crossing his Platonic strain, and at last overpowering it, is the decisive, positive spirit of a Southerner. Sidney may have scrupled to admire one tirade in the *Furori* which Shakespeare might have been glad to invent. Taxed long after by the Inquisitors concerning his attitude to

women, Bruno gave conventional answers ; but the passage in question recalls the tone of his early, rampant
comedy, *The Candle-holder* :—

What ?   Am I, perchance, a foe of generation ?   Do I
hate the sun ?   Am I vexed that I and others have been
put into the world ?   Am I the one to bar the holy
institute of nature ?   God forbid. . . . I do not think that
I am cold, and doubt if the snows of Caucasus or
Riphaeus could allay my heat. . . . What then do I con-
clude ?   This, O eminent knight, that we should render
unto Caesar the things that are Caesar's, and unto God
the things that are God's . . . I mean that women should
be loved and honoured—as women should be.[27]

Bruno had also to own to the Inquisition that he had
been guilty of praising heretical sovereigns.   But he
pleaded that he had praised them, not as heretics, but
for their moral virtues.   He admits his error in applying
the word *diva* to Elizabeth.   'But I was all the
readier so to call her, because she knew me, as I went
constantly with the ambassador to Court.'[28]   This is his
only reference to his personal knowledge of the Queen.
Yet in *De la Causa* he falls into the strain of high but not
absurd fancy familiar in Spenser and Drayton.   He does
not merely dole out the requisite compliment ; he has
stayed long enough in England to catch the rising tone of
patriotic hope and triumph.

With the glory of her eyes, for twenty-five years and
more, she has pacified the great ocean, who with perpetual
ebb and flow quietly receives into his bosom his beloved
Thames ; and he without fear and annoy goes on gay
and secure, creeping to and fro along the grassy shores.[29]

The 'rocks unscaleable and roaring waters' of England
stayed in Bruno's memory.   Part of his Lucretian poem,
De Immenso, must have been written here ; and we seem

to trace him staying near Dover. He argues that the eye
is deceived by the seeming nearness to one another of the
fixed stars, as compared with the distance of the planets,
'just as a corner of this house seems, from the height of
Calais, to be further from the other corner than one
distant end of Britain from another.'[30]   Later in the same
work, which was printed in 1591, we catch a far-off echo
of the journeys of Drake, and a kind of naturalized pride
in the English fleet, which represents so much toil, so much
of *nimis imperterrita virtus*, triumphant over obstacles,
yet bringing sometimes, so he adds, the pests and mala-
dies of other lands.[31]   It was in the late summer of 1585
that Bruno left England for good. There is no reason to
think that the slanders about which he is eloquent
shortened his stay. It ended naturally with that of the
ambassador, who took him back to the French court.
He resumed his wanderings, which ceased fourteen years
later, in February 1600, with his martyrdom on the
Campo dei Fiori ; not dust unto dust, but flame unto
flame—a death of which any thinker might be jealous.

VI

But for the passing phrase of Daniel's friend, every
mention of Bruno's life in England comes from himself,
and no allusion to his name has yet been traced in the
English writings of the sixteenth century. Neither Sidney nor Greville speaks of him. It has been suggested
that the phrase ' sweet enemy ', which comes in Bruno's
sonnets in the *Furori*, and in a famous phrase of Sidney,
is a recollection ; but it is simply one of the paradoxical
felicities, like Romeo's ' cold fire, sick health', that swarm
in the verse of the time. Bruno's books were not
reprinted for two centuries in the original, and became

disregarded rarities. The other great Italians were freely translated; Vautrollier himself issued Fenton's version of Guicciardini. Tasso, as well as Ariosto, Castiglione, and many lesser men, were in an English dress. There are constant allusions to the presence, or signs of the influence, of other visitors from Italy, as Mr. Lewis Einstein well shows in his work on *The Italian Renaissance in England*. But no written word of Bruno's appears to have been quoted as his until the days of the *Spectator* and Toland. All this throws discredit on the fancy that he was a recognized focus of thought and culture in London, or that he left a deep impression on the English mind. As Dr. Höffding puts it,

There is no ground for supposing that there was any real comprehension of his views even in small and select circles ; at any rate no trace of it can be pointed out . . . Philosophical interest in England ran in quite another direction from that taken by Bruno, both then and in the following age.

Yet we may ask more narrowly, not only why so keen and rare a spirit was neglected, but whether the neglect was total after all. There was so much 'celestial thieving' among the Elizabethans—Spenser seized whole stanzas of Tasso silently—that it would be rash to deny such a possibility.

Bruno's system never reached cohesion ; his style was foreign to that of all contemporary English prose ; the nearest analogue, strange as it may sound, being that of Thomas Nash. His vanity and suspiciousness were not endearing, and he may have seemed to the superficial a bundle of pretensions and fantasies. He did not speak English. But the causes of his being soon forgotten lay deeper. On one side he was not very original : much of his Platonism was part of the common stock of the

Renaissance. On another side he was far too original and prophetic to be understood by any of his hosts. During his stay there was little true philosophical life in England, and the rise of Hooker or Bacon could only deepen the oblivion which had overtaken the strange, vehement visitor, so soon become a rumour. It is among the poets, if anywhere, that we must seek his influence. Had he any upon Shakespeare, or upon Spenser?

In 1585, when Bruno left London, Shakespeare is not known to have reached it. Florio, we saw, had met Bruno; and both he and Shakespeare became clients or friends of Southampton. Shakespeare read Florio's version (1603) of Montaigne. This is the sole personal channel through which we know definitely that Shakespeare might have heard of Bruno. The language of the Italian dialogues is much harder than that of Cinthio or the other tale-tellers whom Shakespeare may have read in the original. Many scholars [32] have insisted on finding Bruno's thoughts in *Hamlet* or the *Sonnets*, but all such attempts have brought misfortune. The philosophical ideas which recur in Shakespeare—not as a doctrine but as an intermittent *motif* (if we seek for more we are led as by Ariel's music into many traps and pools)—are usually incompatible with those of Bruno. Beyersdorff proved this in detail in 1889; and everything confirms his sceptical treatment and refutes the rakers-up of dubious parallels. Bruno would have said that even Alexander's dust had its share of the *anima mundi*, despite the 'progress of a king through the guts of a beggar'. Hamlet refers purely to physical change, and no one can see any affinity to Bruno's theory who does not confound his pantheism with atomic materialism. Hamlet, too, could 'count himself a king of infinite space', without the poet being driven to the *De Infinito* for the idea. Shakespeare shows no sign of abjuring the old astronomy which Bruno had risen to subvert. His imagery is firmly tied to the orbs and spheres, even as his sun 'rises on the earth'. It is their music that is heard quiring by Lorenzo, it is their pre-dominance over human fates that is doubted by Edgar. There is no sign of his following Bruno's daring excursion through the legendary outer sphere, in which the fixed stars are 'pegged, panelled, and plastered' as in a kind of cupola.[33] Bruno's conception, which acts on his fancy like a drug extending the apparent range of vision, is that of endless room for innumerable worlds, in one of which the sun is central; and it was not used by our own poets till long afterwards. Indeed, we know Shakespeare all the better if we see that he is not, after all, at the centre of the new philosophy, any more than the earth, with all its riches, tempests, and entertainments, of which he is the master and presenter, is at the centre of the new heavens. And other fancied echoes of Bruno fail to stand analysis. One sceptical phrase of Hamlet, 'There is nothing good or bad but thinking makes it so,' is more likely to be a following of Montaigne than of Bruno. Again, the 'shadow' and 'substance' in Shakespeare's *Sonnets* have been compared with Bruno's *Umbrae Idearum*, but the usage is not the same. Add to this that no contrast or criticism of the current religions is to be safely traced in Shakespeare, while it was Bruno's task to deride many of the doctrines common to the old faith and the new. What a quick-sand the study of verbal parallels may be, is shown in those who compare the allusion in *Hamlet* to an external providence, or the 'divinity that shapes our ends' with Bruno's profoundly pantheistic sentence, that 'we have

a divinity close to us, nay, it is more within us than we
are within ourselves'.[34]   The thought in Shakespeare's
reference to 'the prophetic soul of the wide world' is
different once more.

It would be natural to seek for some intellectual contact between Bruno and Spenser, who drank far more
deeply than Shakespeare of Italian thought and poetry.
Both of them drew from the same sources of neo-Platonism—partly from Plato himself, or Plotinus, but more
immediately from the recognized expositions by Ficino,
Pico, and Benivieni.[35]   From Pico, for instance, could
be learned the several stages, each purer than the last,
by which the soul rises to the apprehension of a beauty
divine and absolute.   By others the contrast of vulgar
and Platonic love was developed in a way that is familiar
through the *Four Hymns* and *Comus*.   There are passages in Bruno to match anything in those poems, but
it does not follow that Bruno was the creditor of the
English poets.

Love is not a ravishment by the snares of bestial
affection, bound under the laws of an unworthy destiny ;
but it is a rational impulse, which follows on the intellectual apprehension of the Good and Fair, which are known
to it, and whereto it would fain conform itself; so that
it comes to be kindled by their light and nobleness—
comes to be invested with a quality that makes it seem
worthy and noble. . . . It does not go stumbling and
dashing now into one ditch, now another, or upon a
rock, as though drunken with Circe's cups ; neither does
it change from aspect to aspect like a vagrant Proteus ;
but it conquers and controls the monsters of terror without any jar to harmony.   The affection that is well-
conditioned loves bodies and bodily beauty as a token of
the beauty of the spirit.   Nay, what enamours us in the
body is a certain spiritual quality that we see therein
and call beauty.[36]

Certainly Bruno's Platonism misses the note of chivalry. His Rabelaisian fullness of life, which utters itself in his spendthrift eloquence, carries him far from his contemporary Tasso. He lacks Shakespeare's human conception of love, just as he misses the strain of saintliness that is heard in Spenser. Love to him is now a gaily Lampsacene appetite, now a purely intellectual rage, and is identical with the philosophic thirst for immersion in the supreme unity. The scheme of morals in the *Spaccio* is lofty ; but it is naturalistic and positive, designed for men at large, and it lays little emphasis on spiritual love, in the sense that descended from far sources to Dante Gabriel Rossetti. The *Eroici Furori*, however, is a guide, not for the multitude, but for elect and thinking souls. Bruno shields himself in that dialogue from the charge of blindness to the price that must be paid for moral progress, although his rarer and his week-day mood are hardly in keeping. The *Furori* is a dream of the path by which the soul may ascend to behold the highest object possible. The ' heroic fury ' is a choice kind of spiritual passion, calling for a prefatory culture of the will as well as for a practised exaltation of the contemplative powers. At moments Bruno feels the pain and sacrifice of such an ascent, the dangerous ease of staying in that world of sense, to which he is himself so excitably alive.

Disordinate love carries in itself the principle of its own punishment. Freed therefrom by an act of conversion (*atto di conversione*), the soul rises into the rarer world, with a gaze bent singly upon the only worthy aim.[37]

And then the soul chases its quarry, the quarry of Actaeon, until it sees its Diana unveiled at last—but only to be absorbed in what it sees, in the highest fountain of the ideas, in the ocean of all truth and all goodness.

Rare indeed are such spirits; they are at last transformed, they become, like Actaeon, stags; they are 'no longer the hunters, but the hunted now'.[38] They are part of that highest reality which in turn becomes the quest of other men. This reality is spirit, but not spirit in separation; for it is infused in the whole world of matter, which thus, as we return to it, catches a glow of divinity which was not there (Bruno might seem to say) when first we left it. Rarely has the adapted Platonism of the Renaissance been taken more in earnest; perhaps only by Michelangelo, in his far different fashion. Bruno makes more of it than any Englishman of his time, more than Spenser in the *Hymns*, or than Shakespeare in his *Sonnets*; more, even than Donne, his likeness and unlikeness to whom it would be fascinating to explore. Of the happiness of mystical attainment he uses much the same words as Spenser makes his tempter, Despair, use of the mere quiet of death:—

There is the fruit of toilsome virtue, there is joy, there the river of delights . . . there is the term of tempestuous labours, there peace and rest, there quiet undisturbed.

The parallel is doubtless again an accident. And the turn which Bruno gave to his Platonism removes it far from that of Spenser or of our later Cambridge divines. It was but a single affluent of his monism or pantheism, which was far beyond his own age. But there are other elements in his thought whose presence it is less hazardous to detect in Spenser.

It has been noticed [39] as a possibility that Spenser read Bruno's strangest and best-hated book, the *Spaccio*, which has a fitful history in English literature afterwards. It soon passed out of knowledge, or was misknown. Scioppius, whose virulent letter is our chief authority

for Bruno's martyrdom, thought that the 'Triumphant
Beast' was the Pope. Leibniz, with all his vast reading,
may never have handled the book, and he confused the
word *spaccio*, dispatch or rout, with *specchio*, a mirror.[40]
Even now the work is often ill understood, owing to the
cumber and diffuseness of the allegory. It shows in a
parable Bruno's vision of a new society on earth, which
is preceded by a great, vague catastrophe. The reigning
vices and poltrooneries are superseded by justice and
truth. This new earth Bruno's ironic and Lucianic fable
shows under the guise of a new heaven. The scene is
the pagan Olympus. Jove feels old; he cannot descend
any more to earth to misbehave in bestial disguises, and
he dreads to suffer from the universal law of change.
Perhaps he may die into something which has no memory
of Jove. Like a man, he prays to Fate,[41] whilst knowing
that it cannot alter, and resolves on a reformation that
shall begin with others. The god turns pious, rebuffs
Ganymede, and taunts Venus with the physical omens of
the dowager condition. On the anniversary of the fall
of the giants he assembles the gods, who are to show
repentance by instituting a wholly fresh chart of the
firmament. There follows every kind of guerilla warfare
against Jewish and anthropomorphic theology; but the
aim is to construct a new ideal of human ethics. The
old stars and constellations merely blaze out the amours
and rapine of the gods. So the sign of Hercules is a
witness of Jove's adultery, and the sky is filled with
symbols of squalid vices, moral and intellectual. All
together these make up the 'Triumphant Beast' who has
now to be dispatched. Jove goes steadily through the
work of degrading each of them and promoting its
contrasted excellence.

The ethical ideal that results is one of the most signifi-

cant produced by the Renaissance, and is a corrective to
that set forth in the *Faerie Queene*. It is one of noble
daring, magnanimous free-thinking, and frank respect
for human needs and passions. It is naturalistic, like that
of Telesio, while Spenser's is mediaeval and chivalrous.
Though Bruno's fable is confused and crowded, his exposition is instinct with that sense of the infinite which
is his birthright, and he intimates much that we are even
now imperfectly trying to express. The cardinal virtues
are Truth, 'the purest and divinest of things, nay their
essential purity and divinity, which is not stirred by
violence, marred by age, wrinkled by time, or veiled by
darkness;' and Wisdom, with the various sciences in her
train; high Prudence, her mundane counterpart; Law
and Justice; Courage, which is described in Aristotelian
manner as midway between the extremes of Weakness
and Meanness on one side, and Insolence and Savagery
on the other; Indignation which is just and well regu-
lated; Love of the Commonweal, and many more.
Sometimes the turn given is a quaint one. The de-
thronement of Cruelty suggests a tirade against the
hunting of game—a pursuit only worthy of butchers, and
fit to be banished to England, or at least to Corsica.[42]
The sign of the Cup must disappear and be given to the
chief tippler produced by high or low Germany, where
gluttony is 'renowned among the heroic virtues, and
Drunkenness among the heavenly attributes'.[43] This
ancestral foible of the North had been taxed for centuries; yet we find a modern pedant tracing a debt to
Bruno in Hamlet's allusion to the 'heavy-headed revel'
of the Danes. As a whole, Bruno's ethics, though he is
not methodical, and has no understanding of the Christian
virtues, rank as high, clear, and prophetic.

With all this difference of spirit, we seem to find an

echo of Bruno in Spenser's verse. During these years
Spenser was in Ireland; but we do not know when the
broken cantos *On Constancy* were written, and Sidney, to
whom the *Spaccio* was dedicated, may have made it
known to his friend. The fragment certainly recalls part
of the *Spaccio* in its machinery, and some other works of
Bruno in its ruling idea. Both writers play with large
conceptions of change and recurrence. Here also is a
conclave of gods led by Jove and discomfited by the
feeling of decay. Mutability is a ' Titaness' who makes
a struggle to revive her dynasty. She pleads before the
gods her right of conquest. So far the scenery closely
recalls that of the *Spaccio*; but the sequel differs. Nature
sits in judgement, and before her, in proof of the endless-
ness of Change, passes the pomp of the Seasons, Months,
and Hours.

> For who sees not that Time on all doth prey?
> But times do change and move continually,
> And nothing here long standeth in one stay.

But Nature pronounces that if all things change, they
change in a fixed cycle (so that change and order imply
each other) ;

> And turning to themselves at length again
> Do work their own perfection so by fate.
> Then over them Change doth not rule and reign,
> But they rule over Change, and do their states maintain.

The notion is an old one, but it had been phrased
recently in the *Eroici Furori*, though without Spenser's
Christian application.

> Death and dissolution do not befit this entire mass, of
> which the star that is our globe consists. Nature as a
> whole cannot suffer annihilation ; and thus, at due times,
> in fixed order, she comes to renew herself, changing and
> altering all her parts ; and this it is fitting should come

D

about with fixity of succession, every part taking the place of all the other parts. . . . Thus all things in their kind have the vicissitudes of lordship and slavery, felicity and infelicity, of the state that is called life, and the state that is called death; of light and darkness, and of good and evil. And there is nothing which by natural fitness is eternal but the substance which is matter.[44]

The notices of Bruno in English are fitful for more than a century after his death. Those by Bacon[45] are cursory and show no sign of study or appreciation. But the *Spaccio* is suddenly traced in a masque played at Whitehall by Charles I and his court and set to music by Henry Lawes. It is unknown how Thomas Carew came to use a work so rare and so discredited for the fabric of his *Coelum Britannicum*, an incoherent show produced in the same year as *Comus* (1634). He had visited Venice, where the tale of Bruno may have lingered. He does not own his debt (which was first noted by Dr. Robert Adamson[46]), nor does he use it with any notion of its grandeur, but he has taken Bruno's setting and dipped into his episodes. Mercury and Momus, the satiric god, a Thersites of Olympus, play their parts. Mercury advances King Charles and his queen into the place of the usurping stars, which are plucked down as in the *Spaccio*. A dozen heavenly signs are saddled with the same vices that Bruno assigned to them; the original harangues of Riches, Poverty, and Fortune are diluted. Further traces of Bruno in Stuart or Commonwealth writings are yet to seek. There are a few casual words upon him in the *Anatomy of Melancholy*.[47] Burton alludes to his physical theories, and untruly calls him an atheist. But the stigma helped to cancel his name in England, and the thought of Hobbes and Locke proceeded on other lines than his.

VII

The deistical movement caused a ripple of interest
in Bruno. Copies of the *Spaccio* rose at book-sales[48]
to £30 or £50 ; than which, writes Eustace Budgell in
the *Spectator*,[49] 'nothing has more surprised the learned
world.' The work, he says, might have been thought
alarming, being by 'one Jordanus Brunus, a professed
atheist, with a design to depreciate religion'. Budgell
read it, and found it so little perilous that he ventured,
hazily, to mention its contents. Bernard de Mandeville,
in the *Remarks*[50] on his own *Fable of the Bees*, speaks of
the *Spaccio* as 'that silly piece of blasphemy', and couples
Bruno with Vanini as a person 'executed for openly pro-
fessing and teaching of atheism'. This event Mandeville
twists into an example of the vanity of martyrs, in order
to refute 'the simplicity of some good men' who will
have it that no one could be constant at the stake unless
'supported by some miraculous assistance from Heaven'.
On the contrary :—

Some men of firm constitution may work themselves
up into enthusiasm, with no other help than the violence
of their passions ; it is certain that there have been men
who, only assisted with pride and constitution to maintain
the worst of causes, have undergone death and torments
with as much cheerfulness as the best of men, animated
with piety and devotion, ever did for the true religion.

This flank attack upon the orthodox, with its lip-service
to the 'true religion', reminds us that we are in the age
of Bayle, and is much in Bayle's disconcerting manner.
Mandeville doubtless knew the *Spaccio* through Morehead's
version,[51] published in 1713, which remains the only one
in English ; and Morehead may well have been inspired
by John Toland, who knew more about Bruno than any
Englishman of his day. Toland, with airs of secrecy,

summarized the work in a letter to Leibniz[52] explaining that 'the matter is not to be communicated to every one'. Also, in a tract, he cites and corrects Scioppius' story of the burning, names the *De la Causa*, adds a fuller note on the more harmless *De l'Infinito*, and translates its preface. The Ptolemaic astronomy had receded even from poetry, and the infinity of space was now no heretical tenet. But how little Toland understood may be seen from his imputing the opinion to Bruno that spirit is 'only a more movable and subtle portion of matter'. More than fifty years later Jacobi and the German idealists began to redress the neglect of Bruno's shade. But it was only in the nineteenth century that he took his commanding place in the perspective of modern thought, and his rank among the stars, like some radiant figure in his own allegory.

LITERARY FAME

A RENAISSANCE NOTE

I. THE LOVE OF FAME, ITS NATURE. II. SOME CLASSICAL NOTICES. III. DANTE AND PETRARCH. IV. RONSARD AND DU BELLAY. V. SPENSER, SHAKESPEARE, DRAYTON, DANIEL. VI. SIR T. BROWNE AND OTHERS.

I

NOW that the printing-press has overreached itself, and the cure for vanity is to consider, not the frailty of parchment, but the hugeness of libraries and the pressure of oblivion upon books, we talk less than our ancestors of the eternal fame that is given or obtained by poetry. The passion of men to outwear time and conquer distance by their writings, and so to survive the death of the body, has not been equally strong in all civilized periods. In its train there is one illusion hard to banish. We wish our work to remain when we have gone : yet we half think we shall be there to see it honoured. Our shade, though it cannot speak, shall attend the scholar who digs our inscription from the red earth, or the lover on the hillside who reads our sonnet with its self-promise of eternity. The relish of this foretaste lies in the deception. And we write carefully on the vanity of fame, hoping posterity will read the words. 'Ceux qui écrivent contre la gloire veulent avoir la gloire d'avoir bien écrit' (Pascal). And some of them have their desire: for the best things in derogation of glory were said by those who have gained it and who have also praised it best—the writers of classical antiquity. They left little to add, but their arguments awoke again at the Renaissance, with their rediscovered works for a chief example; and the love of glory became a conscious and vehement motive, a tenet of faith, and an inspiration to writers, escorted by doubts and revulsions new or old. At many a moment between Petrarch and Milton this past mood of the world-spirit is fanned into utterance, afterwards to fade with the usual caprice; as a few chance passages can show. They come, with a classical note for preface, from two or three critical periods in the history of letters; from the fourteenth century, with the late middle ages and the first Renaissance side by side; from the verse of the Pléiade, in the sixteenth; and from Spenser, Shakespeare, and their successors. They are only torn pages of the book which is left for some historian to write upon the struggle of the artist against oblivion, on his cry of hope and his misgiving.

The desire for glory is but one form of our passion for our own identity. Like the desire for children, which is another form, it is rooted in our stubborn wish to stamp ourselves, before we go, upon something, and so to prolong our real essence after our individual existence. It may be rare that great ideas are conceived, any more than human beings, with this purpose clearly in view. It is an afterthought, a comfort, and a good warrant. The hoped-for result is much more surely attained in works of art, which really express a man's personality, than in sons and daughters, who often do not do so; but, as if in recompense, the power of founding a family is more widely spread than the power of expressing ideas. Yet

in either case witness is borne, as Plato puts it, to man's
'share in immortality'. In the *Laws* (721 B) he says :—

A man shall marry between the ages of thirty and
thirty-five, considering that the human race naturally
partakes of immortality, of which all men have the
greatest desire implanted in them ; for the desire of
every man that he may become famous, and not lie in
the grave without a name, is only the love of continuance.
Now, mankind are coeval with all time, and are ever
following, and will ever follow, the course of time ; and
so they are immortal, inasmuch as they leave children
behind them, and partake of immortality in the unity of
generation.   (Jowett's tr.)

The same feeling drives a minority to leave children of
the brain.   More than one mind of the first rate has
used the figure of procreation for the immortal thoughts
of the philosopher and the eternal forms of the artist.
Schopenhauer, in the following passage, is thinking of
the former, but his admirable words hold good of the
latter equally :—

The begetter of a truly great idea becomes aware, at
the very moment of his conceiving it, of his community
with future generations ; he feels therewith the extension
of his existence through centuries ; and so he lives *with*
posterity as well as *for* it.   Take the other side ; we, in
our admiration for some great spirit, whose works have
engrossed us, are seized with the wish to summon him to
us, to see him, to speak with him, to have him for our
own amongst us ;—well, this longing is not quite unsatisfied.   For he, too, has longed for the recognition of
a posterity, which should pay him the love, the thanks,
and the honour, refused to him by the envy that filled
his own generation.[53]

Such thoughts as this only become fully articulate
after many centuries and long gaps of silence.   But
they go back to the classic world, and we find, here as

so often, that if they begin in Greece, Latin is their
messenger.

II

The wish for fame in general, which all men and
nations feel, was marked strongly in the Greek and
Roman world.   The wish for the posthumous fame that
is won by the written word was only its intenser utterance, implied in some of the literary forms that came in
Greece to their first perfection.   The drama, the satire,
the philosophic poem or dialogue, and the oration, do not
look avowedly to the future.   But the epic aims at
keeping the past, and therefore itself, in memory, above
all when it becomes, as in Virgil, racial and imperial.
The purpose of history is the same ; yet Pericles, praising
the dead, does not find the treasury of their honours in
poems or chronicles, but in inscriptions and monuments,
still more, like Abraham Lincoln, in the hearts of men.
So too Plutarch in his patriot biographies :—

Surely it is a common thing, that happeneth unto all
good and just men, that they are far more praised and
esteemed after their death, than before, because that envy
doth not long continue after their death, and oftentimes it
dieth before them.[54]

But in the ode, whether triumphal or funeral, national
or personal, in the elegiac idyll, and in the lyrical epitaph
or epigram, a name is preserved by the power of verse ;
and the mere existence of such noble forms of art goes to
prove that the aspiration is a sound one.   In lines like
those of Simonides and Tyrtaeus fame is offered to the
Spartan and Athenian heroes.   So in the promise of
Theognis to Cyrnus ; and Pindar returns again and
again to the theme.   To have a fair fortune, he says, is
the first of prizes : good fame is the second ; and the

highest garland is his who lights upon both and wins them. Words are longer lived than deeds, and to leave a fair name to a fortunate family makes black death more beautiful. A word well said never dies, it passes, continually bearing fruit, over land and sea; like a ray of noble deeds, unquenchable for ever.[55]

This is in praise of persons; but the Roman poet was exalted by the sense of belonging to a great single state or empire with an indestructible language. He cordially believed in glory and thought it worth winning and worth promising and in his power to bestow. His motto is the 'volito vivo' per ora virum ' which is found in the saved fragments of Ennius. Horace, Ovid, and Propertius[56] saw the material splendours of the city which their verse was to outlive, and their strain was to be harped on again to the end of the Renaissance. Propertius' lines forecast Spenser or du Bellay:—

Nam neque pyramidum sumptus ad sidera ducti,
    nec Iovis Elei caelum imitata domus,
nec Mausolei dives fortuna sepulcri
    mortis ab extrema condicione vacant.
aut illis flamma aut imber subducet honores,
    annorum aut ictus pondera victa ruent.
at non ingenio quaesitum nomen ab aevo
    excidet; ingenio stat sine morte decus.

In ushering forth a great work the Roman liked to adopt some such lofty formula, like a last rite at the opening of a temple.[57] To the humanist Petrarch, who felt warranted in echoing their accents[58] when he wrote *Africa*, many centuries seemed to bear out their confidence, for he found their Latin still fresh amidst the material changes of Rome.

Cicero speaks less of literary (*gloria*) than of civic, and less of posthumous than of contemporary fame (*bona fama*), of which he treats variably. Commonly he

vindicates the love of glory and sets it high in his
ethical programme.   Sometimes it is an absolute good ;
oftener, as the more liberal Stoics allowed,[59] it is derivative and desirable, though not a good of the highest kind ;
at other times it is almost vanity.   The fair reputation,
which makes a public man more useful in his lifetime, is
analysed into the love, the admiration, and the confidence
of his fellows ; nor can anything win it but real service.[60]
In general, fame is a kind of parasite, echo, or reflection
of virtue, and is only for that reason to be coveted.   The
context [61] suggests that the two books *De Gloria*, which
Petrarch says that he lent to his teacher Convennevole
and so lost, were on the subject of a public man's contemporary repute.[76]   The adoration of Cicero by the
humanists helped, on the strength of such passages, to
consecrate the cult of fame.   But one of his stateliest
utterances is in the contrary sense, and fell in better with
the tone of the Middle Ages, to which it was well known
through the commentary of Macrobius.   Most of his
De Republica was only found in the nineteenth century [62]
—a curious comment on our theme.   But the *Somnium
Scipionis* was familiar to Chaucer and his world.   It sets
forth, through the mouth of Africanus, the enemy's case.
Deluge and fire destroy all monuments.   The great
tracts of desert in the earth limit the scope of glory in
space, as the short memories of men limit it in time.[63]
How long will those who talk of you have for talking ?
The wise man must look to his eternal home and stake
his hopes upon no human rewards.   Virtue must draw
us by her own charm.   The peroration echoes down late
in literature and well expresses the stricter view of the
ancients.

Quid de te alii loquantur ipsi videant : sed loquentur
tamen.   Sermo autem omnis ille et angustiis cingitur iis

regionum, quas vides, ne unquam de ullo perennis fuit, et obruitur hominum interitu et oblivione posteritatis exstinguitur.[64]

Seneca thought the matter out closely from the Stoic's point of view, and, despite some coldness of form, he had weight before as well as after the revival of letters. He makes many concessions to the love of glory, and promises, not altogether flatteringly, to preserve the name of his friend Lucilius by mentioning him in his correspondence.[65] It is striking to find the official philosopher of Latin Stoicism falling into 'that last infirmity'. But he makes distinctions : first, between the praise of the good and wise and that of the many, and then between the praise of posterity and that of contemporaries. Then he identifies the two distinctions ; and in a touching and magnificent passage utters his belief in the final judgement of history. Democritus, Socrates, and Cato seemed madmen to their time. Though all those of our own age are instructed by envy to keep silence, men will come hereafter who will judge without rancour or favour ; and this is the only undying reward of goodness.[66] Yet the praise (*laus*, not *laudatio*) of a single worthy man, though it be unuttered in public, suffices.[67]

This view, so high and sane, seems to have been less to the liking of the Middle Ages than the more rigid one represented in Boethius, whose contempt of every worldly good fitted in with gloomy theological theories, while his consolations were adjusted, possibly in his own mind, certainly by his readers, to those offered by Christianity : in so far, at least, as he preached an eternal order of excellence and love, which it was the work of the good man to reflect as in a small mirror. More than any writer, he stood to the centuries before the Renaissance for the higher thought of the old world. In his reflections on fame [68] he follows and quotes the *Somnium Scipionis*. The earth, he repeats, is only a spot in the universe; much of it is uninhabited; much is inhabited by nations of alien tongue, whom our glory never reaches: and the rest may be given in Chaucer's English, so heartfelt and vivacious:—

But how many a man, that was ful noble in his tyme, hath the wrecchid and nedy foryetynge of writeris put out of mynde and doon awey; al be it so that, certes, thilke wrytynges profiten litel, the whiche writynges long and dirk eelde doth awey, both hem and ek hir auctours? But yow men semeth to geten you a perdura-blete, whan ye thynken that in tyme comynge your fame schal lasten.

But natheles yif thow wolt maken comparysoun to the endless spaces of eternyte, what thyng hastow by whiche thow mayst reioisen the of long lastynge of thi name? ... And forthi is it that although renome, of as longe tyme as evere the list to thynken, were thought to the regard of eternyte, that is unstaunchable and infynyt, it ne sholde nat only semen litel, but pleynliche ryght noght (si cum inexhausta aetate cogitetur, non parva sed plane nulla esse videatur).[69]

The accompanying 'metre' of Boethius sums up this matter, and ends:—

Quod si putatis longius vitam trahi
    mortalis aura nominis,
cum sera vobis rapiet hoc etiam dies,
    iam vos secunda mors manet.

The 'second death' of a man, or the speedy forgetting of his name, is a sharp phrase, expressive of the sterner ancient opinion on the subject of glory. It is easy to see how it chimed in with mediaeval religious sentiment, which could ignore and despise the second death on earth, when the second life beyond it was everything.

III

For the value of a man's soul in the eye of heaven is a totally distinct conception from that of the value of his personality to himself; the first is Christian and mediaeval, the second is classical and secular and belongs to the Renaissance. The passion for fame we saw rooted in the conviction that a man's personality is valuable to himself. The feeling, indeed, that his personality is best expressed and best preserved in forms of art, and that form alone endures, is hardly more than implicit until much more recent times. With the comparative apathy to fame in the Middle Ages may be connected the anonymity of most mediaeval art, the lack of a personal stamp in so much of the great body of Romance, and that general weakness of the sense of 'copyright', which lasted even after printing came, and made unowned borrowing no theft. Chaucer, in the *Knight's Tale*, perfectly expresses the chivalrous feeling about honour. There is no thought of fame being ensured by verse, for Theseus merely speaks of the praise of dying well and not too late :—

And certeinly a man hath most honour
To dyen in his excellence and flour
Whan he is siker of his gode name ;
Than hath he doon his freend, ne him, no shame.
And gladder oghte his freend been of his deeth
Whan with honour upyolden is his breeth
Than whan his name apalled is for age ;
For all forgeten is his vasselage.
Than is it best, as for a worthy fame,
To dyen whan that he is best of name.

But in his *House of Fame* Chaucer thinks of the vanity and caprice of the goddess : it is such that sometimes, though from no right motive, she even makes a right award. She will hardly give a man what he wants, be it even oblivion, unless he expects that she will not do so. This humorous and sad-ironic treatment is coloured by the teaching of Boethius. Chaucer disowns with a shrug of amusement any expectation of glory for himself. Yet, while so little touched by the new learning, he so far approaches it as to make, no doubt upon Italian models,[70] one of those lists, so common at the Renaissance, of the poets who have made their names endure. The actual range and choice of these names is mediaeval. The prototype of Fame is not *Gloria* but the Ovidian goddess, who is akin to the *Fama* of Virgil. The term ' mediaeval ' is to be defined not by dates but by feeling, and Dante in this matter is more modern than Chaucer, though neither stands within view of the new learning.

But Dante's usual attitude may be described as that of Stoicism wrought into Christianity ; and it is very different from Petrarch's, although the two views, we shall see, are still struggling in Petrarch. Burckhardt,[71] in his excellent pages on ' The Modern Idea of Fame ', treats Dante too much as a man of the Renaissance, on the strength of his stately appreciation [72] of glory : but well says of him : ' In his great poem he firmly maintains the emptiness of fame, although in a manner which betrays that his heart was not set free from the longing for it.' In the sphere of Mercury are the souls who have been active in order that honour and glory may come to them, and the rays of the divine love rest less fully upon those whose desires are stayed upon such things. Elsewhere in Dante [73] the desire of fame is a form of pride, and is punished in purgatory by the pain inherent in its own nature. Dante finds that the ' grand passion for excelling ' defeats itself, because one reputation is soon displaced by another, and that again

by a third. The strain of the *Somnium Scipionis* and
Boethius is in his mind : and Mr. Shadwell's version,
done in Marvell's measure, is the best to quote :—

> What if from thee thy flesh thou shed,
> Outworn with length of days, instead
>   Of dying a child, before
>   Thy baby prattle o'er ;
> Will any fame be thine at last,
> After a thousand years are past ?
>   A thousand years, how small
>   A space, when matched with all
> The period of eternity !
> 'Tis but the twinkling of an eye
>   To orb that tardiest rolls
>   About the heavenly poles.

Thus Dante and Chaucer stop short of the new feeling
towards literary fame, which is proclaimed at length by
Petrarch.

A recent historian, Prof. Volpi, says, not too
strongly [74] :—

Petrarch was the first man in the Middle Ages to have
formed clearly and precisely this conception of surviving
by notable works in the memory of men ; a conception
which belongs to the peoples of old and which Petrarch
drew from his study of the classics, where he so often
found the longing for renown. . . . The works of Roman
art, both plastic art and the art of words, which were
more familiar to him than the Greek, what were they
but a consecration of noble enterprises ? Is it not one of
the noblest tasks of art to save fair and great things
from oblivion ? Glory was a spur which never left
Petrarch at rest.

Petrarch was the first man to whom the ancients, as
newly rediscovered, were the principle of his intellectual
life, the star of his literary passion, and the model for his
style. His large acquaintance with the Latin classics

quickened his feeling that in poetry lay the way to immortality. His lists of old authors in *Trionfo della Fama*, so much fuller than those of Dante or Chaucer, show that the proof positive for the stability of fame must have seemed to him far more extensive than it could to them; although, in that sonorous, somewhat dry poem, the abstractions of the Middle Age are still playing their part. The Triumph of Love is shortlived; Laura dies; that is the Triumph of Death. But over Death triumphs Fame; and a procession defiles past, as on a frieze, of the great men of old,—warriors, generals, and at last writers and thinkers whose names are glorious. But over Fame triumphs Time, and nothing prevails over Time but Divinity, or true religion. The Triumph of Divinity is Petrarch's homage to his faith. But in Petrarch the conception of the triumph of Time over Fame takes a new shape, which is destined to bulk large among the humanists. It is more than a revival of the old reflections of Boethius. It represents a mediaeval revulsion against that classical pride and confidence in glory, which wrought itself out to its utmost and defied Time the conqueror. This conflict of feelings was stimulated by the new interest in the ruins of ancient buildings and ancient art in Rome. Down to the late sixteenth century one or other can be seen paramount, according as the written record or the marred masonry is the object of attention. Meantime Petrarch drinks to the full of the old Latin hope, now in its hour of resurrection. *Africa*, his Latin poem on the Second Punic war, is written while he is rising on a wave of such exaltation. And his sketch of his own life [75] he dedicates to Posterity, with a wistful doubt, as though to seize the stray chance, which he yet secretly hopes is not a mean one, of his name surviving.

Suppose that perchance thou hear something about me; doubtful as it may be whether my slender and obscure name can reach any distance either in time or in space; perhaps thou wilt care to know what manner of man I was, or what was the upshot of my works, especially of those whose fame may have reached thee or of whose unsubstantial name thou mayst have heard. The voices of men will vary, for almost every man talks as he is moved by his pleasure, not by truth; nor is any measure observed in dealing out either praise or infamy.

But Petrarch's desire of a lasting name seldom becomes a full assurance; for he strove to be free, but he was not born free, and in this he is like most men. He underwent a revulsion to the ascetic feeling in which he had been reared, and some of his Latin works are written under its influence. He lets us trace the conflict of currents in his mind, for he is one of the first masters and publishers of subtle self-analysis. We can see the strife within him of the fever and of what, as he came half to think, was the antidote. In a brief dialogue [76] between Reason, who represents the saving religious monitor, and Hope, whose voice is that of the secular man, the issue is contested. Hope stubbornly ignores the words of Reason, and keeps repeating:—

Famosus ero . . . famam inveniam post mortem . . . si famosus sum dum vivo, cur non famosior sim post mortem?

Reason preaches, that many like Ovid and Statius have promised themselves renown. Yet many famous men are forgotten after death, who owed their living fame to their behaviour, their 'clear brow', their kindly greeting, their sheltering goodness to those near them and their clients. Neither noble deeds nor writings will guarantee survival, for knowledge and eloquence vanish into vapour. Fame is often the death of the possessor; it so fell with Cicero

E

and Demosthenes. And 'what will it profit you to be praised by those who would not know you if they were to see you?' *Famosus ero*, replies the poet.

In another work, one of his most intimate, *De Contemptu Mundi*, Petrarch introduces St. Augustine, whose *Confessions* [77] did so much to change his frame of mind, playing the part of confessor, and eliciting, as at a shrift, every weakness of his pupil. It is well written, for he was one who hoped posterity would see his acquired scorn of its opinion. He is full of these shifting and equivocal moods. The voice of the father of the church is that of Petrarch's own over-sharpened conscience, of the misgivings which sway him more and more as he dissects the hope of fame. [78] Who detest the deeds and the opinions of the vulgar more than he does? Yet in their voices fame consists, when it comes at all. How, then, place the summit of happiness in their little discourses (*sermoniunculi*)? Petrarch, says the saint, has begun both a history of Rome and his great *Africa*; what if death interrupt them? Yes, replies the poet, this has nearly taken place; and in his extreme danger, finding *Africa* unfinished, he has had an impulse to burn it, rather than trust the last improvements to any of his friends.

Africa, which lies eternally under the blaze of the sun, and had also thrice been burned up by the Roman torches, was nearly consumed in my flames as well; but enough of that bitter recollection.

But what, then, is it, pursues the confessor, that you really wish to create? 'A work that is illustrious, choice, and notable.' Not one, of course, that has the divine kind of immortality. 'Human glory is enough for me, I am a mortal, and mortal things,' says the natural man, letting himself slip, 'are what I really crave'. The confessor instantly falls upon him: suppose—what you cannot be sure is not the case—that you had only a year to live, how would you spend it? Would you spend it in the business of merely tickling the ears of men, in the vain hope of fame, which has mocked thousands, in putting off the occasion for making your soul to the last moment? Augustine then adds some other arguments which are more those of a secular pessimist than of a divine. Let the poet think of the continual growth of new men, each anxious for his own glory, and of envy (*invidia, Schadenfreude*), which pursues even the dead. Let him think (the plea is of the days before printing) of the possible destruction of all books by some material catastrophe. Petrarch is not convinced; he clings fondly to vanities, and in the true humanistic spirit he rejoins: 'Yet dignity of language, and an orderly narrative, and the weight and worth of the speaker, count for much '— *multum valet*. What, he adds, is the father's final judgement? Is he to stop working or is he not? Shall he not make haste to put the finishing touches, so that he may be free of care and give the rest of his days to greater spiritual matters? So speaks the incorrigible poet; but Augustine is relentless, and bids him think of his end, and drop his history and his poem, by which he will never, after all, enhance the glory of his hero Scipio. The dialogue closes in the gloomier mediaeval strain, with an image taken from Aristotle. The life of men is like that of certain little beasts on the river Hypanis, who are born in the morning, come to their prime at noon, and die at sunset.

These ideas are now commonplaces: but in Petrarch we are back at the moment when they were new and passionately felt. *They* lived their life, longer than that of the flies on the Hypanis; they were turned and tested this way and that, for nearly three hundred years, fitfully enough, until it was seen how much life they had left in them, what forms of art and emotion they could disengage. If they are commonplaces now, it is not that they are too obvious, or that they are too much part of our consciousness; but that they are not, in their old form, a living part of it at all; that art has said its last word, for the present, to them in their classic shape; that they are now only part of the history of ideas. But their life was long, and may revive.

IV

Two hundred years later, when the true Renaissance had risen and declined in Italy and had passed to France,[79] we find the love of personal glory dominant in the chief poet of the middle sixteenth century. There are none of Petrarch's scruples left, and any doubts are only due to the weariness of a moment. The individualism that was a chronic fever of Renaissance rulers and poets found in the passion for fame its natural voice. An emphasis almost frantic, and louder than anything heard even in the Latin poets, is laid on the hope of making an immortal name. As conceived by Ronsard and du Bellay his lieutenant, the ideals of the Pléiade [80] lent themselves to the theme, which was now linked with the doctrine that a modern language is a worthy casket for the highest and most enduring verse. The destined means for achieving this end is the imitation in French of ancient forms and models. Ronsard meant to be as sure of glory as the old poets whom he followed, by using his own language as highly as they had used theirs. French was to be trained and ennobled into a classic speech by study of the Pindaric ode, the elegy, or the epic—forms which had proved their title to endure, and

were, as we have seen, specially devoted to challenging
the power of Time. This conquered, it was right to imitate
one thing more, the formal boastings of antiquity. After
the way of the Renaissance, the tradition or sentiment
of the old writers is repeated so often that it becomes
a kind of dogma; so often, too, that at last the poet
swings back from it into a misgiving. But not for long:
the last word is one of pride and hope. So Ronsard in
his *Odes* (1550), *Hymnes* (1555-6), and *Elegies*, translates
Pindar and Horace and domesticates their feeling:—

> Ne pilier, ne terme dorique
> D'histoires vieilles décoré
> Ne marbre tiré d'Afrique
> En colonnes élaboré
> Ne te feront si bien revivre
> Après avoir passé le port
> Comme les plumes et le livre
> Te feront vivre après ta mort.[81]

In another Pindaric, addressed to du Bellay, he gives
voice to the same assurance, and the verse has a clang of
classic bronze:—

> Mais ny les ans
> Ny l'audace des vents nuisans
> Ny la dent des pluyes qui mord
> Ne donne aux vers doctes la mort.[82]

But, he adds, the writings even of some who wrote in
Greek have been lost. Even though Ronsard may win
a century or two of renown, any writer in a modern tongue
is liable to oblivion. Perhaps it is better after all to
spend one's life in trafficking and making money.[83] In
another and finer passage Ronsard declines from the
severe Senecan ambition for posthumous fame upon the
applause of contemporaries, which he will, after all, be
there to enjoy. His reasoning is not of the sublime kind,

but probably it represents the sincere wish of most poets
except the very greatest :—

> Ainsi notre escriture
> Ne nous profite rien : c'est la race future
> Qui seule en iouyst toute et qui juge à loin
> Les ouvrages d'autrui et s'en donne plaisir,
> Rendant, comme il luy plaist, nostre peine estimée.
> Quant à moy, i'aime mieux trente ans de renommée
> Iouyssant du soleil, que mille ans de renom
> Lorsque la fosse creuse enfouyra mon nom,
> Et lorsque notre forme en une autre se change,
> ' L'homme qui ne sent plus, n'a besoin de louange'.

We might think we heard La Fontaine speaking here,
and a different age—one of chastened, rather incredulous
worldly sense. It is a relief after the monotony of the
official Renaissance attitude, to which we return, though
the tone is more plaintive, in Ronsard's lieutenant
Joachim du Bellay. The *Défense et illustration de la
langue françoise* (1549) just preceded Ronsard's first
Odes (1550); but du Bellay, for our purpose, falls into
line behind Ronsard, whose direct sway in England was
smaller. Du Bellay, as we shall presently find, left his
mark on the early, questing talent of Spenser. Speaking
of the 'long French poem', or epic, which is to vie like
Petrarch's with those of old, he writes, in an outburst
of assurance, what may serve as a motto for the whole
epoch :—

Et à la vérité, sans la divine muse d'Homere, le mesme
tombeau qui couvroit le corps Achille eust aussi accablé
son renom. Ce qui advient à tous ceux qui mettent
l'assurance de leur immortalité au marbre, au cuivre, aux
colosses, aux pyramides, aux laborieux édifices et aux
autres choses non moins subjectes aux injures du ciel et
du temps, de la flamme et du fer, que de frais excessifs
et perpetuelle sollicitude. . . . Or néantmoins quelque
infelicité de siècle ou nous soyons, toy, à qui les dieux et

les Muses auront esté si favorables, comme j'ay dit, bien
que tu sois dépourveu de la faveur des hommes ; ne laisse
pourtant à entreprendre un œuvre digne de toy, mais
non deu à ceux, qui tout ainsi qu'ils ne font choses
louables, aussi ne font-ils cas d'estre louez : espere le
fruict de ton labeur de l'incorruptible et non envieuse
posterité : c'est la gloire, seule eschelle par les degrés de
laquelle les mortels d'un pied leger montent au ciel et se
font compagnons des dieux.[84]

In his verses *De l'immortalité des poètes* du Bellay,
in his light firm way, is sure that his better part does
not fear the hand of Fate, and that the Muses have
promised him a tomb which can face the winds and the
centuries.   In his *Regrets* he is less sure, and refuses
to emulate those who boast that they will live by their
writings,

> Et se tirent tous vifs dehors des monuments.

He is not like Ronsard, who enjoys his glory already
in his lifetime.[85]   Ronsard need not fear the crowd of
other writers of the day, the Maevii of France : for those
of Rome are forgotten—unhappily indeed, since the
humanist would like to have seen the rimes that served
the ancients for a *passe - temps*.   The master alone
survives :—

> Tout œuvre qui doit vivre, il a dès sa naissance
> Un dæmon qui le guide vers l'immortalité :

—a guardian 'spirit that keeps' it.   The great event of
du Bellay's life, next to his meeting with Ronsard, was
his journey to Rome, which only quickened this mood.
In one of the sonnets of his *Antiquités de Rome* he wishes
that he had the harp of Amphion to rebuild the city, or,
failing that, a pen like Virgil's to raise the edifice for which
his hands are too weak.   Then he regains a doubtful
hope, and asks his verses if they can aspire to be read by

later times. The monuments of which he sings would have lived, if anything could live. Nevertheless he continues to chant, lowly as his lyre may be. Much of all this sentiment is found directly passing into his English translator, Spenser.

V

We pass over forty years, to England, to another great springtide, or *Floréal*, of poetry.

Into our Elizabethan verse the ideas connected with the love of poetic glory are found streaming somewhat late. They are not prominent in Wyatt, Surrey, Gascoigne, or the miscellanists who come in their wake. They are hardly avowed in Sidney's verse,[86] or in the *Apology for Poetry*, or the more conventional manuals of poetic in England. The lowering and dreary goddess who presides over the *Mirror for Magistrates* is Fortuna, herself of true classical descent. She is essentially mediaeval in cast, although she is most to the fore in those chronicle lists of unfortunate great persons which were inspired by early humanism, and which Petrarch and Boccaccio made the mode. Perhaps the earliest English mind on which the conception of the combat of Fame with Time (who to us is a mere figure on a clock-case) left a clear impress is Spenser's. In the youthful translations published in Van der Noot's *Theatre of Voluptuous Worldlings* (1569), Spenser drew both from Petrarch and from du Bellay, who himself drew from Petrarch.[87] Here, however, Time has his will, and the emblematic pictures of his power, rudely set forth in Van der Noot's woodcuts, sank into the fancy of Spenser and may have given the first shape to his characteristic imagery. When these poems were reprinted in the

Complaints of 1591, together with the *Ruins of Rome*
and the *Visions of the World's Vanity*, the emblematic
habit and the sentiment associated with it were rooted
in Spenser. *The Ruins of Rome* are translated from
' Bellay ', and No. 32 :—

> Hope ye, my verses, that posterity
> Of age ensuing shall you ever read ?

supplies the transition to that notion of poetical glory
which du Bellay had harped on not always conventionally.
The full idea is apparent in *The Ruins of Time*, which is
in the same volume.   Indeed this is the first and, but for
Shakespeare, may be the loftiest expression in our poetry
of the peculiar kind of hope we are here chronicling.
The contesting powers of Time and Glory had seemed
to the humanists to hover round the masonry of Rome.
Spenser transfers the scene to his ' Verulam '—the house
of Dudley, which had sheltered him and seemed in danger
of perishing out of life and memory.   His lines gather
up all the pessimism which besets the Renaissance itself,
in the pauses of its exultation and energy, like a deep
musical wail amidst the jubilation of a marching army :—

> All is but feigned, and with ochre dyed,
> That every shower will wash and wipe away :
> All things do change that under heaven abide,
> And after death all friendship doth decay.

And then, retorting on himself, Spenser gives the turn
—call it Stoical or Christian—which comes so easily to
him :—

> Living, on God and on thyself rely :
> For, when thou diest, all with thee shall die.

Leicester is doubly dead, for no poet, not even Colin
Clout or Spenser himself, has yet honoured him. Sidney

is also gone ; but he shall live in heaven, a blessed spirit :
amongst

> Heavenly poets and heroes strong,
> So thou both here and there immortal art.

Immortal in both worlds! what could show more
clearly that wonderful companionship, without union, of
the secular and the doctrinal point of view, which faces
us everywhere in the Renaissance! Spenser, though a
sound believer, after thus acquitting himself, turns and
speaks with the unreserved pagan bitterness that is always
welling up in him and that makes him so fascinating :—

> But such as neither of themselves can sing,
> Nor yet are sung of others for reward,
> Die in obscure oblivion, as the thing
> That never was, ne ever with regard
> Their names shall in the later age be heard,
> But shall in rusty darkness ever lie
> Unless they mentioned be with infamy.

But there is one cure :—

> For deeds do die, however nobly done,
> And thoughts of men do as themselves decay,
> But wise words, taught in numbers for to run,
> Recorded by the muses, live for ay :
> Ne may with storming showers be washed away,
> Ne bitter-breathing winds with harmful blast,
> Nor age, nor envy, shall them ever waste.

From the mood of the *Ruins* Spenser passed away :
it lost hold on him, when he was busy with the great
poetical construction of the *Faerie Queene*, though it
recurs there also, and is found in the midst of his solemn
invocation to Chaucer while continuing the *Squire's
Tale*.[88] But the contemplation of mere waste, only
redeemed here and there by the saving power of verse,
becomes itself wasteful. Spenser, in the dedication of
his poem, regains confidence ; in set terms and as though

without lifting his voice he gives immortality to the High Admiral of England, Lord Charles Howard, and to others, with the assurance of an ancient Roman. The tone is that of Tibullus addressing Messala. In his *Amoretti* (27) he promises the like to his bride; the Romans were not so ready with that kind of offer. But the handling of this theme in the sonnet form is best seen in Shakespeare; he has the fullest right to harp on it, he does so most loudly, and he has the widest metaphysical background for his ideas.

It is known from Meres that some of Shakespeare's *Sonnets* were in private circulation before 1598, and it is hard to think that the majority of the twelve or thirteen numbers dealing with poetical fame do not belong to the first five or six years of that decade, when Spenser, Drayton, Daniel, and many more were touching on the same motive in the same metre. Mr. Wyndham's description of this 'verse-loving society divided by emulous coteries,[89] if exaggerated, is true in the main. To Drayton and his fellows I return; but their and Shakespeare's attitude to fame has this feature in common—that the spirit of the humanist is now superseded by that of the lover or friend. In their sonnets, at any rate, they are not pensive scholars like du Bellay or Petrarch, full of poetical reading and overpowered by the thought of Rome. The ideas of those scholars pass into them and are transformed; they are thinking only of themselves and the person they love. In the scholar Ben Jonson[90] the double strain, personal and historical, is present, while the historical is the stronger. But Shakespeare here as elsewhere manages while using an old topic to shake off the burden of the past.

The *Sonnets* need not be studied in their traditional order, which may be due to the bookseller Thorpe or the vendor of the manuscript. In 15 to 19 the dominant image is that of Time the Enemy, who has to be conquered, now by the progeny of the youth celebrated, now by the verse of Shakespeare, but best of all by both—the desire of continuance being at the root of both modes. Sonnets 55 (which most resembles the usual historic strain) and 60 follow up this vein of thought. Time corrodes things of beauty, and 'feeds on the rarities of nature's truth', but Verse arrests his power (64 and 65). But the thought has become more intricate in Shakespeare's hands than it had ever been before. In 81 he seems to say that his verse will eternize his friend, but not himself; he regards, in 18 and 22, the passing of youth in himself and in his friend (the first being accomplished, the second inevitable) as mystically arrested; in the case of the friend, by the power of poetry. Its business is to countervail not so much the death of the body as the previous death of youth and beauty. Had Shakespeare used Petrarch's form of pageant, he would have presented the Triumph of Time over Beauty, and then the Triumph of Fame, or of Love, over Time. And the whole conception of Time at odds with Verse is woven up with the conception of Beauty and its transcendental relation to Truth, Verse being considered as a kind of balsam or preservative for both. This strain of thought is clearly connected with Renaissance Platonism. Those two streams, of distant origin, meet in the *Sonnets*, and Shakespeare once more stands free of philosophical system and of the learned past, while its thoughts are gathered into his verse to 'suffer a sea-change'.

The topic of glory is twice treated in the *Sonnets*, and at two distinct stages of the drama. There is good cause to think that 100–26 all refer to a season of reconciliation between the poet and his friend, both of whom have in diverse ways offended. If so, it is natural to read the series addressed to the dark woman, 127–52, before the series 100-26 ; and this great displacement is only one of the arguments for rearranging the *Sonnets* much more freely than has hitherto been orthodox. In any case, the contest of Time and Verse is reopened in 100–26. Time has passed ; for 104 names a space of three years. 107, the obscurest number of all, closes on the familiar note that Love, through the power of Verse, conquers Time : in 122–3 the poet says that he needs no tablets of his friend to make him remember that Time is nothing :—

Thy pyramids built up with newer might
To me are nothing novel, nothing strange (123).

But the emphasis is soon changed, for it is now no longer Verse, but Love, that is the conqueror over Time ; 'Love's not Time's Fool' (116). Mr. Wyndham has well shown how this theme of the 'unreality of Time' besets Shakespeare, though it is more a fitful and hovering fancy than an article of doctrine. The *Sonnets* of Shakespeare are greater poetry in their execution than any others of the time ; but they owe much of this power of style to the mighty pressure of philosophic thought behind—the thought of a poet, which comes in phrase and image, not in logical sequence. To go back to Shakespeare's contemporaries is to discard these complexities : we find ourselves in a plainer and more traditional order of ideas at once.

Many of Drayton's sonnets are, as often noted, strangely Shakespearean in ring. He may, of course, have seen Shakespeare's poems ; but he is not for that a plagiarist or a maker of exercises ; he was truly inspired by what he read. Let those who doubt it try to play the 'sedulous ape' as follows :—

Whilst thus my pen strives to eternize thee,
Age rules my lines with wrinkles in my face,
Where, in the map of all my misery,
Is modelled out the world of my disgrace.
Whilst in despite of tyrannising times
Medea-like I make thee young again,
Proudly thou scorn'st my world-outwearing rhymes,
And murther'st virtue with thy coy disdain.
And though in youth my youth untimely perish,
To keep thee from oblivion and the grave,
Ensuing ages yet my rhymes shall cherish,
When I, entomb'd, my better part shall save :
And though this earthly body fade and die,
My name shall mount upon eternity.[91]

But in *Poly-Olbion* Drayton goes back to a less
personal strain. He uses the power of verse in the
service of England. At his back, giving him much of
his story, he has Camden, whose *Britannia* (1586) was
an effort to restore to Britain a knowledge of her antiquities. The archaeologists, English as well as Italian, felt
they were in a kind of league to outwit Time by pre-
serving the memory, if they could not the existence, of
his victims. Such was the spirit that passed into
Drayton and nerved him for his long ungrateful task,
which has been repaid with a partial success. The
passion of the antiquary could hardly be better
worded :—

O Time, what earthly thing with thee itself can trust,
When thou in thine own course art to thyself unjust ?
Dost thou contract with Death, and to oblivion give
Thy glories, after them yet shamefully dar'st live ?

(Song 21.)

Again :—

So, when injurious Time such monuments doth lose,
(As, what so great a work by Time that is not wrackt ?)
We utterly forgo that memorable act :

But, when we lay it up within the minds of men,
They leave it their next age ; that leaves it hers again.

(Song 10.)

Lastly :—

Even in the aged'st face, where beauty once did dwell,
And nature in the least but seemed to excel,
Time cannot make such waste, but something will appear,
To shew some little tract of delicacy there.

(Song 1.)

In Samuel Daniel, Drayton's companion in poetry,
but the master of a more even style, quiet, felicitous, and
grey, we feel once more what the revival of learning
meant to the graver thought and fancy of the time.
Daniel is a Stoic, deep in Seneca, whose plays he imitated,
and whose ethics he studied. He echoed the now conventional strain in his sonnets, the first of which came out
in 1592. But he has left also the curious *Musophilus*
(1599), in which the nature of poetical fame is the matter
of a set debate. The disputants are Philocosmus, who
chills the hopes of literary fame, and Musophilus, who
defends them and expands his defence, after the usual
way of Renaissance 'Apologies' for Poetry, into a vindication of the English tongue and its future and of the
whole of learning. This line of argument rested on the
plea, which proved too much, but was then so constantly
heard, that the poets from Homer onward are the
greatest purveyors of information and edification. Seldom
were the native claims of literature as an art frankly
recognized. Dr. Saintsbury, in his *History of Literary
Criticism* (vol. ii), has discovered the few exceptions to
this rule, and they seldom come from England. In
Daniel's poem, if the true charter of Poetry is not clearly
stated, many noble things are said by the way in her
honour. Musophilus assigns her the power to give the
poet a second life, 'where others have but one' :—

> Short-breath'd Mortality would yet extend
> That span of life so far forth as it may,
> And rob her Fate; seek to beguile her end
> Of some few lingering days of after-stay,
> That all this little All might not descend
> Into the dark, a universal prey.

Philocosmus tells him to quit his ambition, which is made so vain by the stings and confusions of criticism, and to follow the taste of the hour. Musophilus spurns these vulgar ideals, derides the quick and fading vanity of earthly honours and palaces, and points to the freshness of Chaucer's name amidst the wreck of those coarser monuments. Then Philocosmus, in the old strain of Africanus, which Daniel may perhaps remember here, descants on the narrow geographical boundaries of glory, and on the thousands who

> Never heard the name
> Of Sidney, or of Spenser, or their books.

But he is not loth that the 'great historical deserts of brave renowned spirits' should be sung, and seems to limit his protest to elegiac and esoteric poetry 'begot in shades'. The defendant, however, has his stoical answer. Fame to him is not general glory:

> If only one allow
> The care my labouring spirits take in this,
> He is to me a Theatre large enow
> And his applause only sufficient is;

—the retort not only of the philosopher but of the true artist in all ages. The rest is a general and stately eulogy on knowledge, virtue, and the English tongue. Daniel's pensive, silvery felicity of style is different from the fuller strain of Shakespeare or Drayton. His poem is a kind of judicial charge to clear the character of Fame.

VI

Ce que Malherbe écrit dure éternellement.[92]

So wrote Malherbe, and this line at least endures, with a few more. The censor of the Pléiade, he thus far inherits their strain ; but, in the century he inaugurates, it is to die down. We hear it in Corneille, but not in Molière or La Fontaine. To their age such *bravura* may have seemed unmeasured and a little absurd, a subject for irony, not even to be quickened by the pride or conceit of their nation in its own achievements. The sentiment was undermined as the sway of reason and versified rhetoric increased, and we can trace the change in France and England. In the masters of our prose, from Ralegh to Barrow, can be heard the sombre revulsion that declares itself from the buoyant expectancy of the sonnet age. Literature becomes more solemn and devout, both in prose and verse. The deeper Anglican or philosophic eloquence speaks more of the vanity than of the permanence of glory. The *Urn-Burial* (1658) is almost the burial, in England, of the old hope.

Time hath spared the epitaph of Adrian's horse, confounded that of himself. In vain we compute our felicities by the advantage of our good names, since bad have equal durations, and Thersites is like to live as long as Agamemnon without the favour of the everlasting register. Who knows whether the best of men be known, or whether there be not more remarkable persons forgot, than any that stand remembered in the known account of time ?

This pensive psalm is on the futility of monuments, not of poetical honours, but it avails against them also ; and we are back with Chaucer's notion, now become graver and larger in presence of so many visible wrecks of our mortality, that Fame is capricious, is ignorant of the elements of justice. But our poets hold out long. They begin, it is true, to be more engrossed with Platonic or Christian consolations than with posthumous honours. But some of them still return to the Latin feeling. Cowley rings hollow enough in the *Motto* to his *Miscellanies*, and Drummond's sonnet to Fame is artificial. But Herrick, in *His Poetry his Pillar*,[92a] makes Horace or Jonson his model for a phrasing as light and durable, for a design of just such Cellini-like perfection, as Gautier's ' Sculpte, lime, cisèle '. And Milton, in his *Lines to Shakespeare*, and his sonnet *When the Assault was Intended*, is a pure humanist and Elizabethan. The classical allusion in his Latin lines [93] on the House of Fame is half-Chaucerian. He is most himself in *Lycidas*, where the spur of winning fame contends as an inspiration with the heavenly vision, and the two ideas are blended in the faith that the final meed is awarded

> By perfect witness of all-judging Jove.

Dryden later, in his tender modest lines *To Mr. Congreve*, simply cares that his memory may last a little longer in those pious hands.

The treatment of these ideas in romantic poetry and thought would open another lengthy chapter. The cruder and older challenges to Time are seldom heard, but their essential idea revives. Renewed value has been given to artistic form as the surest if not the only kind of personal immortality. Amongst others, the theorists of pessimism laid hold of this truth, which was, perhaps, only felt and uttered with perfect clearness in the nineteenth century.

COLOUR AND IMAGERY IN SPENSER

I

BEFORE Blake and Keats, a sense for the stranger
modulations of colour is uncommon in the English
poets.

> Through their paly flames
> Each battle sees the other's umber'd face.

That night-watch in Shakespeare, which carries us at once
to Rembrandt's vast picture, is an exception, like the
' dusk faces with white silken turbants wreathed ' which
floated before the inner eye of Milton.   Spenser, like both
his great successors and all good poets, cared more for
sound, the medium of poetry, than for colour, which
poetry can only mention.   His hues are often bright and
violent, and are often drawn from luxury or the crafts ;
he likes gold and ermine (*F. Q.* iii. 1. 59), silver and
satin and purple (iv. 11. 11 ; v. 5. 2).   He pays honour
to the standard face of rose and lily, like the neo-Latin
and Italian poets ; and once he uses and betters an old
likeness when he compares the blood rising in the cheeks
to fair vermilion overlaying ivory (ii. 9. 41).

But Spenser is eminently sensitive to varied and
mysterious degrees of light and darkness.   Void blackness he does not know, yet he ranges from all but

F 2

unaltered night—'a little glooming light, much like a shade' (i. 1. 14)—through the twilight of morning and evening, or starlight mirrored in water, or sunlight glancing off it, up to daybreak or fullest noon. Most of these indications are embodied in his formal similes and come in the *Faerie Queene*. In clear and full light, though he often describes it vaguely, he is not at home, as Dante is throughout the *Paradiso*. The sun he uses for ceremonial commonplace, comparing to its blaze the aspect of Artegall, Lord Grey, unhelming. Britomart in the act of blushing is like the dawn (iii. 3. 20). But he is not happiest in the beating rays of the morning; and his more favoured element is sudden vibrating light, sometimes curious or ominous. A different blush of Britomart is said to 'flash through her face' like 'a *flake* of lightning through bright heaven fulmined' (iii. 2. 5); and in another passage (vi. 7. 7) a knight who misses his thrust at the tilt and is carried past his adversary is likened to the 'heavenly spark' or meteor that flits over the sky. The only true point of comparison in this fantastic image is the sudden motion; but we are forced to think, first of all, of the flash coming between two periods of darkness; and that does not touch the comparison at all. There is reparation in the famed passage (iv. 1. 13) where the golden hair winding round Britomart is illustrated by the auroral streamers, by which the sky

Is creasted all with lines of firie light,
That it prodigious seemes in common people's sight.
Here surely is a lawful and splendid use of the superfluous in simile. The imagination is satisfied first by the visual likeness of the bright scattered hair to the crossing streaks of light. Then it rides away safely on the unavoidable associations of a meteor with a note of

prodigy or doubtful omen. There is nothing ill-omened about Britomart. But that does not matter, the imagination has been satisfied first.

Spenser sees many things *sub luce maligna*, in a chary half-light; and his images of this kind are his own, they are very seldom taken from the classics or from Ariosto or Tasso. The cave of Mammon (ii. 7. 29) is lighted with a 'faint shadow of uncertain light', or *reflet*, like that cast by a fading lamp or the moon in cloud. And as the moon, on a foggy night, may still be seen to be herself, so may the face of Radigund the Amazon, deformed as it is with the toil and sweat of battle (v. 5. 12). The colour of a gentler heroine, Pastorella (vi. 11. 3), who has fallen into evil hands, is like that of the morning still swathed in mist. Acrasia (ii. 12. 78) is graced, after a manner utterly alien to her allegorical significance, with images of purity and quiet, for her glance is

> Like starry light,
> Which, sparckling on the silent waves, does seeme
> more bright.

The poet's favoured atmosphere, in his own words, is

> A continual candle-light which dealt
> A doubtful sense of things not so much seen as felt.

Spenser freely uses all the decorations of Italian heroic verse, including the deliberate simile. There are more than 150 such similes in the *Faerie Queene*. What he borrowed, adapted, or serenely translated from *Orlando Furioso* and *Gerusalemme Liberata*, the dredging of Upton and other editors of the last century may help to show. It is not much out of the whole mass of Spenser's imagery, and his use of it only shows how long the mediaeval notion lasted that all matter of the imagination was owned in common. But he learnt from Ariosto and

Tasso, what he could not learn from the ancient hexameter epics, how to fill the spaces of a stanza, which are already ruled and distributed more or less clearly by the metre. Spenser's verse, a more involved one than the *ottava rima*, has its natural rise, and its pause in the middle, and the crash or climax comes either in the alexandrine or just before. In making a set comparison, he either allots a whole verse to it, or poises the opening quatrain or six lines, which contain the image, against the remainder, which contain the thing compared. The Italians oftener give their entire stanza, which is one line shorter than Spenser's, to the image. Here are two typical arrangements of the same figure. The possible original from Tasso (*Ger. Lib.* iii. 4) may be given first. Even as the Christian army beholds Jerusalem :—

> Così di naviganti audace stuolo
> Che mova a ricercar estranio lido,
> E in mar dubbioso e sotto ignoto polo
> Provi l' onde fallaci e 'l vento infido,
> S' alfin discopre il desiato suolo,
> Il saluta da lunge in lieto grido
> E l' uno al altro il mostra ; e in tanto obblia
> La noia e 'l mal della passata via.

Now Spenser (*F. Q.* i. 3. 31) :—

> Much like, as when the beaten marinere,
> That long hath wandred in the Ocean wide,
> Ofte soust in swelling Tethys saltish teare,
> And long time having tand his tawney hide
> With blustring breath of heaven that none can bide,
> And scorching flames of fierce Orion's hound ;
> Soone as the port from far he has espide,
> His chearfull whistle merily doth sound,
> And Nereus crowns with cups : his mates him pledg
>   around :
> Such joy made Una. . . .

All the life of this image is in the latter lines; but

Spenser is indistinct by the side of Tasso, who sees the men on deck pointing out the holy city to one another. Yet he disposes the matter in the same way, through a complete verse. Elsewhere (*F. Q.* vi. 11. 44) the simile is panelled in the last four lines :—

> But when as Calidore was comen in,
> And gan aloud for Pastorell to call,
> Knowing his voice, although not heard long sin,
> She sudden was revived therewithall,
> And wondrous joy felt in her spirits thrall :
> Like him that being long in tempest tost
> Looking each hour into deathes mouth to fall,
> At length espyes at hand the happie cost,
> On which he safety hopes that earst feard to be lost.

II

Without the similes, the world of the *Faerie Queene* would be vaguer and more lifeless. It is full of the sound of running waters, and its ovals of faint sunshine are tempered by the forest branches. But the flowers and creatures are poorly described, except in the similes ; otherwise, they rely on their book associations and their emblematic values. Una's lion and lamb might be in Berlin woolwork ; they do not move ; or they might have walked out of a Bestiary, where beasts have only moral meanings and fabulous customs. Spenser uses his reading without mercy. Cicuta, or hemlock, was the death of an ancient Athenian, who, as he is the earliest authority to tell us, was the 'belamy' of Socrates. In the Garden of Adonis are found all the seeds of eternal life and beauty ; but we do not see the garden, except for a grove of myrtle and entwining 'eglantine and caprifole'. No wind ripples over the beds of flowers, no bees hum about them ; it is like some dim airless pleasance—under glass. We are told the stories of Hyacinthus and Narcissus, or the uses of the trees:—

> The Birch for shaftes: the Sallow for the mill.

Now and again there is a sweet mysterious scene, like one in a tapestry, as the knight passes

> By a beaten path
> Unto a garden goodly garnished.

But no curious life patters through the silent undergrowth of Spenser's enchanted wood. It is the similes that make amends, by their freshness and definition, for this want of motion. And he cares to put into these delicate inlaid designs the feeling and humanity that are denied to most of his phantom knights and abstract women. We can look at his similes as they stand, to learn some of the finer workings of his fancy, and some of the facts of his experience. No need to ask what he borrows; it is enough to see what he writes.

One class of these comparisons will show, if it need be shown, that the supposed poet of dreams and languors was filled with images of energy and sinister combat ; he had seen an Irish war and perhaps helped to draft death-warrants. Rain and wind, fire and deluge, sometimes (iii. 4. 13) express a tempest of grief or vengeance, but more naturally the rage of onset. Pyrochles (ii. 8. 48), windily wasting his blows, checks the cloud of Arthur's anger which falls on him when his own is spent. Guyon (ii. 11. 19) routs the temptations as the 'wroth western wind' strips the withered leaves from the stock. Scudamour (iv. 1. 45) keeps in his wrath like an overblown cloud that cannot fall in rain but still darkens the sky. The explosion of hindered fire or water is often suggested by the burst of delayed fury. Arthur (ii. 11. 32) breaks out against the hags of Maleger ' with furious

unrest', like a fire long kept in a hollow cave.   Calidore's
violence is released like a millstream (vi. i. 21).

There are also vehement or tender images drawn from
the sea, from great ships, and from the home-coming of
the sailor.   The great poem itself (vi. 12. i) is like a ship
that still keeps for home while wandering amidst ' counter
wind and tide '.   For an Englishman who wrote when he
did, Spenser is strangely impressed with the hostility of
the sea, and its ghastliness, and the remarkable bravery
of seafaring.   In *Colin Clout* he commends those who
hate their lives and wish for a sight of death to take a
voyage ; and admires the ' huge great vessel', a hardy
monster, that had brought him over the Irish Sea.   Ships
are usually named to illustrate a combat or disaster, like
creatures that shatter on one another or on the elements.
They are all but alive, and add something of animal and
deadly volition to their mere destructive bulk.   One
warrior, fighting against odds, is a vessel flung between
contrary billows (ii. 2. 24 ; iv. i. 42).   Another is a
dismasted ship veering before the storm, and glad of the
aid of a fisher-boat (vi. 4. i).   The Red Cross knight
combats for a whole canto with one of the dullest dragons
of romance ; but in one overpoweringly close similitude
the creature's ' flaggy wings ' are like bellying sails, and
' the pens that did his pinions bind ' are the ' mainyards
with flying canvas ' (i. 11. 10).

The great poem is a series of duels between good and
evil champions.   Hence the free and natural use of
similes drawn from animals fighting ; some are nobler,
some baser, but all are bent on mutual extirpation.
Beasts, like men, have their natural ranks ; and Spenser,
that inveterate and simple-minded champion of the social
hierarchy, uses such distinctions to the full.   The eagle
must conquer the kite, the lion the wolf, the mastiff the

cur, the nobler the baser, the gentleman the churl, the Protestant the Papist, and Lord Grey Desmond. Any momentary reversal of this order is unnatural and must be corrected by force. The animal similes in the *Faerie Queene* outnumber all the others in the poem, and their range is wide. In one of the most triumphant (i. 11. 34), the Red Cross knight rises from the well of life as the fabled eagle comes 'fresh out of the ocean wave' with new pinions,

And marveiles at himself still as he flies.

There are a dozen comparisons from hawking. The falcon is a noble knight on the right side ; the goshawk varies ; the kite or puttock is a carrion-feeder, and a low or predatory person. The heron is a victim of the falcon, but still is a noble enemy, wary to avoid the souse, and sometimes able to impale the pursuer with a wicked back-stroke (ii. 11. 43 ; iv. 3. 19 ; vi. 7. 9). The image of a bird may be used contemptuously. Braggadochio crawls out into the presence of Belphoebe like a 'fearful fowl' that has fled into a cave from a hawk (ii. 3. 36). Florimell runs from Arthur like a dove from a tassel-gentle (iii. 4. 49) (unlike Juliet, who wished to lure her tassel-gentle back again), and is afraid of Proteus, her rescuer, even as a partridge who has escaped the hawk fears the spaniels. There is the mythical natural history of the unicorn (ii. 5. 10), and of the weeping crocodile (i. 5. 18), whom Spenser takes so solemnly as to make us wonder about the quality of the lost 'nine comedies'.

The bears, bulls, lions, wolves, and goats in these similes are literary and conventional. Half classical, half homely are the references to the steer, brushing away the gadflies, or staring at the intruder in the herd, or held down by the yokel in the shambles ; or in the field

(iii. 4. 17), where he stands dight for sacrifice and garlanded, and then falls under the stroke. 'So fell proud Marinell'; but nothing is alike in the two falls except that Marinell fell and also the bull. The imagination, once more, has nothing on which to stay itself before it passes on to the differences.

The dog is at times a noble creature, but more often a cur, or item of the rabble, worrying his betters, or gnawing in aimless rage the stone cast after him. This last image is used in contumely for Spenser's most grovelling personage, the hag Slander, who goes on reviling in solitude from pure force of virulent habit (iv. 8. 36). Atin gnashes at Guyon like a shepherd's cur (ii. 6. 39), and another mean beast of the same kind attacks the Squire (vi. 5. 19), trusting to his stronger companions to guard him. Of other figures drawn from the animal world, some few are striking. A prince sailing over seas to another kingdom is like a 'fell swift otter' (iii. 3. 33), who swims across the water. And no book-image comes between the poet and his own remembrance, when Guyon and Arthur (ii. 9. 16) rout their enemies as the north wind blows away the gnats in the Bog of Allan, and

> Their murmuring small trompetts sownden wide,
> Whiles in the air their clustring army flies,
> That as a cloud doth seeme to dim the skies.

Flowers, which are strewn freely enough in *Prothalamion* and the *Calendar*, Spenser does not watch intently, but seems to choose for the melody of their names. The withering of blossoms under heat, and their revival under rain, is a figure useful enough in a poem full of imprisoned and rescued damsels. There are a few images of grace and beauty like that famous one which Marlowe (in *Tamburlaine*, l. 4096) may have taken (almost verbally) from the unpublished *Faerie Queene* (i. 7. 32), and which he uses to prouder purpose. The crest of Arthur's helmet is

> Like to an almond tree ymounted high
> On top of green Selinis all alone
> With blossoms brave bedecked daintily,
> Whose tender locks do tremble everyone
> At everie little breath that under heaven is blowne.

Tamburlaine, as 'emperor of the threefold world', wears a similar plume. And the virgins at the bridal of Una (i. 12. 6) dance forth as fresh as morning flowers which are not yet dry of dew.

Such are a few significant instances from the scores of parallels drawn by Spenser from the world below man. Very few, on the other hand, come from human life, and not many from literature or mythology. Britomart, finding Artegall captain to an Amazon, and failing to recognize him in his servile womanish dress, is like Penelope (v. 7. 39), who knew not the 'favour's likeliness' of Ulysses when she saw him scarred and old. But such passages, which only compare one story with another, and so miss the bright and concrete presentation of a true simile, come seldom. And images from social life are duly banished from the dream-world of the *Faerie Queene*. Once a confused hissing din of battle is said to be

> Such as the troubled Theatre oftentimes annoys.

On the other hand, one or two traits of Shakespearean delicacy are taken from images of maternal feeling; 'for other none such passion can contrive In perfect forme' (vi. 12. 21); and nothing can be said against them save that they far outvalue the faint and gracious tapestry-personages whom they are introduced to illustrate. We are not keenly moved when Britomart shows her satisfaction at hearing of the fame and worth of Artegall, of whom, though she has seen him only in a magic glass, she is enamoured.   For this idea is eclipsed and killed by the simile that follows (iii. 2. 11) :—

> The loving mother, that nine monethes did beare
> In the deare closett of her painefull syde
> Her tender babe, it seeing safe appeare,
> Doth not so much rejoyce as she rejoyced there.

But such things are rare, and most of Spenser's images fall into the classes that have been enumerated—similes of light mingled with darkness, of sea-tempest and rapine, of animal combat and the chase.   The subject is a fragment of another one, which is much larger and only half explored, the thought and imagination of Spenser— that intricate and shadowy forest, in which it is well to clear a single pathway.

RECENT SHAKESPEARE CRITICISM

I. SHAKESPEAREAN LORE, ITS THREE ASPECTS. PROBLEM OF 'VALUES'. II. DR. GEORG BRANDES. III. PROF. A. C. BRADLEY: THE TRAGIC WORLD IN SHAKESPEARE; THE RADICAL ANTINOMY; ALTERNATIVE VIEW. IV. PROF. J. C. COLLINS. V. PROF. W. RALEIGH ; SHAKESPEARE AND 'MORALITY'; SCHOLARSHIP: ITS VALUE.

I

THE Germans like to tell of the *Nachleben* of Shakespeare, or that strange after-life of his in the industry of others, upon which his shade is silent. He has begotten, not only his own writings, but a vast and patient professoriate of archaeologists, like those who search the buried tombs or palaces of Eastern emperors. His biographers have gathered the curt or trivial papyri that reveal a marriage date, the entry of a child's birth or burial, a legal process and its judgement, a series of sales and purchases, a bequest, an epitaph, the names of shadowy relations, a mutilated list of books. These things might pertain to any man ; they tell us little more than we knew about the poems and plays of Shakespeare. His theatrical history and successes have been explored, and aid us to fix the order of his plays. All such matter has been so fairly sifted and presented by Mr. Sidney Lee that the outer biography of Shakespeare is perhaps in a final state. It is unlikely that any fresh discoveries concerning his life will throw light either upon his poetry or his soul.

Apart from this, the study of Shakespeare is threefold. We may ask what his exact words were, and how to construe them; that is the question of the *letter*; the affair of textual editing, of linguistics, and of the Shakespeare canon. Or we may ask whence his stories came, and how he used them, and how he seemed to his contemporaries and compares with them, and how he stands to the thought and art of his age, and where his temper and morality differ from that of the greater modern spirits; that is the question of *history*, and the affair of exegesis. Or, thirdly, we may ask what we think of Shakespeare and find in him, and what, after all, he is to us; that is the question of *values*, and is the affair of pure criticism. These distinctions are not rigid; the provinces overlap and are federate. In each of them Shakespeare has had an immense ' after-life '; such are the unforeseen forms that his glory has taken.

I am here most concerned with values, and do not pretend to estimate the present state of Shakespearean erudition, the slow improvement of the text, the unprogressive debates over the doubtful plays, like *Arden of Feversham*, or that rapidly advancing study of ' early modern English ' on a scientific basis, which is shown in works like that on Shakespeare's grammar by Dr. Franz of Tübingen,[94] in the revisions of Schmidt's great and exhaustive lexicon, and in Dr. Littledale's new edition of Dyce's old glossary. There is still much to be done, though much is doing, in the study of the English language from More to Milton. In comparison with the English of earlier and later times, it has been badly neglected. Nor can I touch on the field of prosody, rigidly studied in England and Germany by scholars like Dr. Furnivall and Dr. Goswin König, except to say that the artistic and musical side of this study has not kept pace with the scientific. Indeed, the various industries typified in the transactions of the German *Shakespeare-Jahrbuch* would demand a separate article, if not a separate German to read and review them. From the index of learned publications furnished by the Yearbook arises loudly the hum of the vast dissertation-factory that has been built above the poet's bones. The items in the index for one year number over six hundred. Many of the works entered are merely of the fungous kind, like those on the Baconian theory; others contribute to the understanding of ' Elizabethan ' literature.

But the next thing needed is a synthesis of this huge mass of illustration and apparatus. For the cold-storage of facts and parallels is of no use unless it helps us to perform better what for Englishmen surely is the chief critical task of our time, namely, to enter into the mind of the English Renaissance. It is our chief task, and there is also much in our own time that should make it easier to accomplish. For at the Renaissance awoke both the movement of poetry and the movement of thought and science. That is what we mean by the word Renaissance. The eighteenth century did not care enough about poetry; and the early nineteenth century did not care enough, in England, about thought and science. Now, once more, these two master-interests of humanity are quickened in unison. Thought and science are active ; and though we do not produce much poetry of value, we are trying to understand poetry as we have never tried before. Thus we are in a better mood than ever yet for understanding Shakespeare and his companions. There are definite intellectual impulses now at play which seem to bring the Renaissance back. The wish to see and render beauty, disinterestedly and for its own sake, is alive as in the day of Marlowe. The sense of unexplored mystery in the world of nature and invention is alive also ; and the triumph of Copernicus hardly stirs the fancy more than the discovery of the new kinds of ray. As when Montaigne and Bruno wrote, there is a desire to revise the whole of current ethics ; and this desire penetrates into art. The Imperial feeling, or the passion to further organize and enlarge our borders, now touches, for good or ill, the national fancy as it has never done since the day of Ralegh. Old conceptions of personal excellence are fitfully revived. The ideal of the courtier, that brilliant, many-faceted, effective personage, for whom art and letters were but one accomplishment the more, like riding or making love,—this ideal, that was strong in Sidney, and also in Hamlet, has been refurbished by the vocal if transient and pseudo-virile school of critics, of whom the late Mr. Henley, though a true poet, was a leader. Surely we have now an unrivalled chance to enter into the mind of the Renaissance.

We know something of the life around Shakespeare. A picture of the time has been pieced together by historians [95] : of its wars, its legislation, its *dramatis personae* ; of its manners, its ruling ideas, its moral sentiments, and its favoured books. We also know much of the external life of Shakespeare. Then, we have his mind revealed in plastic form throughout the dramas, and in confessional utterance throughout the sonnets. The problem is to choose out of the general history and out of Shakespeare's biography those elements that may serve to interpret his mind, and to discard carefully those which do not. The task of historical divination is to draw such lines between the life around him, his own life, and his works, as may aid us, in some modest measure and with the least of hazard, to live over again his life as an artist.

II

No one has been more resolute on this large adventure, and on the whole no one has found better fortune, than Dr. Georg Brandes, whose work, *William Shakespeare*,[96] began to appear in Danish twelve years ago, and is now in an excellent English version. The method of Brandes is the modern one, undreamed of a century ago. It is historical and psychological. To this method the secretive and manifold Shakespeare throws down a silent challenge, and Brandes takes up that challenge. He has made his mark already as a discoverer and explorer of other minds. He has disclosed, in their national or racial importance, the chief Dano-Norwegian writers, Holberg, Ibsen, Jacobsen. He has written well on the two figures in English history, Byron and Disraeli, who remind us most of Shakespeare's characters. He has studied the history of Romanticism ; and the English volume of his *Main Currents of Nineteenth Century Literature* has been translated. In that work Brandes is too much biased by modern liberal conceptions, and too indifferent to style and art, to be a satisfactory critic of poetry, though his criticism of the ideas pervading poetry is excellent. His book on Shakespeare is more scientific and impartial ; he expresses the diffidence of a foreigner on matters of style, but he has become sensitive to greatness and truth of poetical form in another tongue. The cosmopolitan turn of his brain, the sanguine pulse of his Jewish blood, help him to understand the spring-tides of mental life in the sixteenth century. The Jewish optimism, too, that survives his keen apprehension of suffering and tragedy is a credential in approaching

Shakespeare. Brandes, therefore, has done something to interpret Shakespeare; and all his other writings may fairly be called a discipline for this his largest task.

Brandes is so full of life that he can afford his faults, some of which are serious. They affect not only detail, but method too. He is, indeed, not primed with a one-sided doctrine, like the gifted Latin note-taker, Taine. He does not theorize about the English nature and ignore most of the phenomena on the pretence of being scientific. But Brandes's conception of the *milieu* or environment that actually shapes poetry is sometimes misty, lax, and untrue. He writes whole chapters on political or social matters that cannot be shown to have affected Shakespeare at all. Falstaff loved sack; so there must be a whole page on the many fermented drinks of the Elizabethans. The character of James I is analysed at length, because Shakespeare is (most unwarrantably) guessed to have alluded to his dislike of crowds in *Measure for Measure*, and to his learning and other qualities in *The Tempest*. The whole history of Essex and Southampton is told because Southampton may have formed a personal link between Shakespeare and Essex. The coincidence between the misfortunes of Essex and the change of the poet's interest from comedy and history to conspiracies with a tragic ending, has always been noticed. But to hear the whole story only makes us see how fragile is any inference. It seems to be assumed that a poet is stirred by the political events of his day in the same proportion as the historian who, centuries later, sees their significance.

This kind of error leads Brandes into the offence of rash and dogmatic reconstruction. He has read widely, but he sometimes fails in scholarship, or tries, by means of baseless hypothesis, to pierce too far. Two instances may be taken out of a number. Ever since an article written by Halpin [97] in 1842, it has been known that Oberon's speech about the 'fair vestal throned in the west' contains some allusions to Lyly's *Endimion* that are too close to be accidental. The 'little western flower' on which the bolt of Cupid fell is very like Lyly's Floscula, and the parallel between his Tellus and Luna and Shakespeare's 'cold moon and the earth' establishes the connexion between the two plays. Now the names in *Endimion* mask real persons of the time ; and Halpin, modestly enough, put forward his theory that 'Floscula' probably signifies Lady Essex, the widow of Sir Philip Sidney. The learned editor of Lyly, Mr. Warwick Bond, is not disinclined to this view, though his cast for the masque differs at many points from Halpin's. The whole ground is most treacherous, and Brandes sinks into it. He quotes no scholar since Halpin ; he assumes that the 'western flower' is *certainly* Lady Essex ; he thence infers that *Midsummer Night's Dream* was written in the year 1590, 'after the private marriage of Essex with the widow of Sir Philip Sidney.' He does not see that such reasons are slender for dislocating the whole chronology of Shakespeare's early plays. Hardly any other writer believes that the *Dream* was written sooner than 1594 or 1595. Were Brandes right, either the *Dream* would come before plays of the type of the *Two Gentlemen*, or else the whole dramatic *Lehrjahre* of the poet must be shifted some four years back.

Another instance of Brandes's haste is found in the chapter on *Troilus and Cressida*. He holds, like many others, that Chapman was the 'rival poet' of Shakespeare's Sonnets. Brandes sees even less than Dryden saw in the poetry of Chapman, and remarks with surprise that Mr. Swinburne 'loves' Chapman ; although, if his theory be true, Shakespeare referred to the 'proud, full sail' of Chapman's 'great verse'. That, however, is an affair of taste. Shakespeare treats the Greek heroes with a strange contempt in parts of *Troilus and Cressida*, as every one has noticed ; and why ? Because, says Brandes, he did not like either Chapman or the style of his *Homer*.

In all probability it was the grief Shakespeare felt at seeing Chapman selected by Pembroke, added to the ill-humour caused by the elder poet's arrogance and clumsy pedantry, which goaded him into wanton opposition to the inevitable enthusiasm for the Homeric world and its heroes, and so he gave his bitter mood full play. (Eng. Tr. p. 514.)

This is a house of cards ; it rests on the idea that Shakespeare would throw mud at Achilles because he was jealous of Chapman, from whose work he was actually borrowing. In such passages Brandes is acuter at seeing the problem than at solving it. But his book has a quality of greatness and insight that may lead more than one generation to return to it. He has the freest kind of German vision, comprehensive and pertinacious, without any peddling or dry-baked pedantry, and without the sentimental roar into which the German voice often lapses. He has tried to measure himself against the whole problem ; he has wrestled as stubbornly as his countryman Jacob for a blessing. His lines are broad ; his work is fresco rather than miniature, and it is all the better for that. His opening takes us at once into the wide and fresh air of the Renaissance, and in that air we move throughout the book, with its enduring lights above our heads. He links the English poet with Michelangelo his immediate forerunner and Cervantes his contemporary.

Michelangelo has depicted mighty and suffering

demigods in solitary grandeur. No Italian has rivalled him in sombre lyrism or tragic sublimity. The finest creations of Cervantes stand as monuments of a humour so exalted that it marks an epoch in the literature of the world. No Spaniard has rivalled him in type-creating comic force. Shakespeare stands co-equal with Michelangelo in pathos, and with Cervantes in humour. This of itself gives us a certain standard for measuring the height and range of his powers (p. 1).

Brandes often displays this power of seeing Shakespeare in something like true focus amongst those who are his only mental companions in his own century. Here, so far from being given to hasty constructions, he is judicial. Following the saner line of inquiry, and rejecting fantasies,[98] he shows how Shakespeare's relation to Giordano Bruno is almost one of mutual exclusiveness. He holds aloof from the fanatics who come to Shakespeare resolved to read Montaigne into him right and left, but he does justice to the real and strange coincidence of temper between the two. He would have pressed closer into this matter had he been able to read the recent investigation of Mr. Churton Collins,[99] who gives good reason for believing that the changes in the second quarto of *Hamlet* are not unaffected by the recent appearance of Florio's translation. But everywhere Brandes draws, from a large and vital reading, parallels that are full of light. The quotation of Spinoza's definition of jealousy [100] in the *Ethics* (iii. 35), as an exact description of Othello's imaginings before he falls in his trance, is an instance (p. 446). Yet his distinction between jealousy proper and the affection of Othello, which is less jealousy than 'credulity poisoned by malignity', corrects anything in such a quotation that might mislead. He also expounds well the true impression left by *Othello*—the impression which makes us wish to shake ourselves free from its overpowering force, and to turn to Shakespeare himself for the antidote.

A great work *Othello* undoubtedly is, but it is a monograph. It lacks the breadth which Shakespeare's plays as a rule possess. It is a sharply limited study of a single and very special form of passion, the growth of suspicion in the mind of a lover with African blood and temperament—a great example of the power of wickedness over unsuspecting nobility. Taken all in all, this is a restricted subject, which becomes monumental only by the grandeur of its treatment (p. 449).

On the whole Brandes shows less sureness of line in his studies of history and environment than in his psychological scrutiny of Shakespeare and Shakespeare's personages. He can speak freshly about the great enigmatic characters, Hamlet, Iago, Macbeth, though he does not press so closely into their mazes as Professor Bradley. On Hamlet he discourses from the standpoint of a fellow Dane. Hamlet, he says to his countrymen, is

of all Danish men, the only one who can be called famous on the largest scale; the only one with whom the thoughts of men are for ever busied in Europe, America, Australia, aye, even in Asia and Africa, wherever European culture has made its way; and this one never existed, at any rate in the form in which he has become known to the world.

And why is this? The critic himself betrays the unique power of Hamlet, amongst all creatures of fiction, to call out a personal sympathy, a sympathy which is really self-pity and self-scrutiny.

We love thee like a brother. Thy melancholy is ours, thy wrath is ours, thy contemptuous wit avenges us on those who fill the earth with empty noise and are its masters. We know the depth of thy suffering when wrong and hypocrisy triumph, and oh! thy still deeper suffering on feeling that that nerve in thee is severed,

which should lead from thought to victorious action. . . .
The breath from open graves has set us, too, dreaming,
with a skull in our hands.

The history of criticism from Hazlitt onwards shows this
power of Hamlet to mirror all angry and noble souls to
themselves whenever they are filled with that self-doubt
which is the tragic reflex and consequence of their disgust
with the world about them.   Hamlet, behind it all, keeps
his secret still, and so Shakespeare may have desired ; he
has all 'the untranspicuousness and complexity of a real
soul'.   There is not only obscurity of presentment, but
the presentment of obscurity.

Brandes is strong, like Sainte-Beuve, in portraying
secondary characters, and this is the best trial of a critic's
elasticity.   Emilia is

good-hearted, honest, and not exactly light, but still
sufficiently the daughter of Eve to be unable to understand Desdemona's naïve and innocent chastity.

The description of Friar Laurence, one of the poet's
most delightful embodiments of reason, is perfect.

Shakespeare knows and understands passionlessness ;
but he always places it on the second plane. . . . Friar
Laurence is full of goodness and natural piety, a
monk such as Spinoza or Goethe would have loved, an
undogmatic sage, with the astuteness and benevolent
Jesuitism of an old confessor, brought up on the milk
and bread of philosophy, not on the fiery liquors of
religious fanaticism (p. 28).

The man who wrote that can never be put aside as
a critic who is at root a politician blinded with liberal
formulas.   His words have a true liberating power, and
leave us quit of formulas.   He has learnt one of the best
things that Shakespeare has to teach, namely, to respect
all natural healthy types of character and calling, even
when our beliefs cannot be the same as theirs.   This

kind of respect comes easily to those who accept society as it is, but it comes too easily to do them credit.   When a reforming and unquiet spirit attains to it, he has made a conquest.   Brandes can also word the particular mood or *Stimmung* that lies behind a work of art, and this can only be felt, especially in drama, by a kind of antenna-sense, unknown to the criticism of rule and canon.   The errors risked by the intuitive critic tell us more than the truths of the mechanical critic.   What could be more happily touched than the divinations of the frame of mind in which Shakespeare wrote at the ages of about thirty and thirty-five?

No less sensitive and devoted to music than the duke in *Twelfth Night* or Lorenzo in *The Merchant of Venice* must their creator himself have been in the short and happy interval in which, as yet unmastered by the melancholy latent in his as in all deep natures, he felt his talent strengthening and unfolding, his life every day growing fuller and more significant, his inmost soul quickening with creative impulse and instinct with harmony. . . . In the Republican Calendar one of the months is named Floréal.   There is such a flower-month in almost every human life ; and this is Shakespeare's. . . . In spite of his latent melancholy he is now highly favoured and happy, this young man of thirty-five ; the sun of his career is in the sign of the Lion ; he feels himself strong enough to sport with the powers of life, and he now writes nothing but comedies (pp. 171, 213, 217).

The leading gift of Brandes is doubtless the clearness of his moral and human judgements.   In his *Shakespeare* he gets at these judgements, not through his social and political doctrine, nor through abstract philosophy, but through the richness of his artistic perceptions ; and this is the only safe path for a literary critic.   He does not see Shakespeare through the warping chromatic glasses

of liberalism, or of Hegel's philosophy ; yet he does not
fall into the vulgar error of making him an almost pure
feudalist like Spenser.   He sees the poet's morality in its
real and only legitimate light, as a series of 'motives' or
themes, recurring and intertwisted and modulating one
another, and never reduced by the poet himself into the
code or canon to which our false instinct is tempted to
reduce them.   He merely presents ; he never argues, and
so cannot be refuted.   Hence an impregnable grace and
elevation, some of which passes into Brandes's criticisms.
He says of *The Winter's Tale* :—

Looked at from a purely abstract point of view, as
though it were a musical composition, the play might be
considered in the light of a soul's history. Beginning
with powerful emotions, suspense and dread ; with terrible
mistakes entailing deserved and undeserved suffering, it
leads to a despair which in turn gradually yields to
forgetfulness and levity ; but not lastingly.   Once alone
with its helpless grief and hopeless repentance, the heart
still finds in its inmost sanctuary the memory which,
death-doomed and petrified, has yet been faithfully
guarded and cherished unscathed, until, ransomed by
tears, it consents to live once more. The play has its
meaning and moral just as a symphony may have, neither
more nor less.   It would be absurd to seek for a psychological reason for Hermione's prolonged concealment.
She reappears at the end because her presence is required,
as the final chord is needed in music or the completing
arabesque in a drawing (p. 639).

III

What I have written earlier shows how little I incline
to paying Dr. Brandes mere compliment ; indeed I am
rather thinking (as he would doubtless prefer) of the
readers he has yet to find than of himself. But in his case
we have passed over from the field of historical recon-

struction and interpretation into that of pure criticism. It is right to notice now a signal effort made by an English writer, in whom the historical sense is fainter, and the religious and hortatory instinct is strong, to appreciate the four tragedies into which Shakespeare flung his utmost powers—flung them sometimes with a serene and royal classicality of form, but often with a vehemence, a strain, an Etna-like convulsiveness of language, of which we forget the formal imperfections, because it must be the reflex of some for ever unknown and powerful agitation in himself. The value of Professor Bradley's book on *Shakespearean Tragedy* is this, that it revives the strictly philosophical criticism of Shakespeare, which has lapsed in this country since the time of Coleridge, and seemed to be almost dead. Coleridge was first of all a creator ; but, even while his imaginative powers were at work, or he was looking back on the powers he had spoiled with a sadness that could revive the sense of them but not their energy, he had within him a second principle, a watching familiar that told him the path his mind had taken ; and this was the philosophic, analytic principle that drove him, as the pure artist is never driven, to consider the artistic process, not from the side of its effectiveness for beauty, but from that of its ground in reason and its psychological impulse. The same power made him a critic—as great in this field as the world has known—of the poetry of others, the poetry of Shakespeare, of Wordsworth. This co-equal warmth of the philosophic and artistic processes in Coleridge, interpenetrating and illuminating each other, is unequalled ; it is not greater even in Goethe. For Coleridge applied his judging intellect not only to the thought and stuff of poetry, like Goethe and most of the Germans, but also to style, expression, and music.

Since Coleridge, most English critics have fought shy of philosophy. Some have followed Lamb and Hazlitt, studying the poet's humanity and careless of the fruits of learning. Such was Walter Bagehot, who for relish and acumen united was in the direct line of Hazlitt, and whose one essay puffs away whole tomes of pedantry : ' *Via*, goodman Dull ! ' The great difference between these men and their successors lies in the presence of a new erudition and a new method, which minister to a new conception of Shakespeare ; the conception, namely, that he changed and grew, instead of being *cast* once for all ; that his moods and interests varied, that his writings fall into groups and phases. These ' disks of light and interspaces of gloom ' in his career have become more definite, thanks to the new erudition and method ; ot which there are many founders, and who shall enumerate them ?   They have made Shakespeare seem different ; we can follow his track less blindly.   In England alone they are many : Dr. Furnivall, the senior, the youngest-hearted, brought so close to the poet by his fire and his simplicity ; Mr. Swinburne, sharp-judging under a surface of foam and violence, whose writing is always that of a fellow-poet ; and the professors and editors without number, such as Mr. Dowden, who has none of the heavy-footedness of the pundits, and whose best pages are so full of light, even if modern sentiment is apt to come between him and Shakespeare ; and Dr. Herford, whose mastery of Shakespearean[101] lore fortifies and does not chill his power to interpret. ' All these and more came flocking ': the work of each of them might claim an article, but here I have most to do with the philosophical judgement passed on the poet by those who have lately written on him.   With this Mr. Bradley has concerned himself more deeply than the rest.   Two others,

Professor Churton Collins and Professor Walter Raleigh, who touch here and there on the same problems, will claim attention.

Mr. Bradley, giving a whole book to the four major tragedies, may well feel that his long delay before printing any original work of length has been rewarded. If he moves most easily and freshly in the abstract region, he writes with a strength of human feeling not always seen in metaphysicians. His manner is a curious mixture of preaching at high pressure with a nervous, guarded, Oxford accuracy of analysis. His style, if a little what artists called ' tight ', has the rare gift of being entirely lucid in the expression of subtleties. But the sense of mental ease and fundamentally tranquil power which we receive from the most highly wrought of the tragedies (perhaps excepting *Othello*) disappears when we read the close and searching expositions of the critic. The tension there is of another kind, and sometimes destroys the pleasure proper to tragedy. This, however, does not affect the substance of his comment. His book strikes one, for good more than for ill, as that of a man who has gone his own way, not troubling much about other writers, caring more for the soul, ethics, and characters in a play than for its historic setting or its style, and not minding if he makes rediscoveries. Hence the result is his own. He offers a striking theory of tragedy considered on its moral side, a theory which springs out of Hegel's and then parts company with it and thus brings the whole problem a step forward. It runs somewhat as follows, though for the metaphors and parables used Mr. Bradley is not responsible.

The foremost person or hero in these tragedies of Shakespeare's prime is a man eminent both in nature and in public rank. He errs, suffers, hurts others, and at

last has to die.   It was his own action, of his own
choosing, that started the fatal train of events. He is
immeshed in just the one situation, and meets just the
persons, to touch the point of danger in his nature.
Hegel says in his *Aesthetik* that Shakespeare's subject
is often the rise and growth in a great soul of a passion
that leads it into a self-destructive conflict with circumstance. This outer conflict is also mirrored in the strife
within his own soul of blood and judgement, ambition
and loyalty.   Sometimes, adds Hegel, Shakespeare
exhibits almost perfectly firm and consequent natures
like Coriolanus, who, either by virtue of their firmness,
or through forgetting the spot of fatal tenderness in
themselves, fail of their end and perish.   Hegel's theory
is the most suggestive contribution since Aristotle to the
metaphysic of the drama, but in various ways it is very
one-sided ; for Hegel's portentous optimism leads him
to underestimate the whole element of apparent injustice,
unreason, and immoral-seeming fate in Shakespeare's
tragic world.   Mr. Bradley's theory modifies that of
Hegel [102] by freely admitting the presence of this element.
In any case it is clear that Shakespeare does not found
a tragedy merely on intrigue and incident, nor yet on
mere psychology without incident.   Nor does he suffer
the fatality to spring from causes that lie wholly outside
our voluntary choice.   Among such causes are pure
madness and other abnormal states, and supernatural
compulsion.   Accident, says Mr. Bradley discerningly,
only appears, if at all, very late in the series of tragic
events, when our sense of cause and effect can no longer
be shaken.   And we may add that accident is deftly
concealed or passed lightly over when it comes, so that
in the theatre we scarcely notice it.   If, then, such
is the course of tragedy, what is the impression made

by the tragic world upon a philosophical and sensitive witness?

Mr. Bradley tracks down this impression to the sense of a contradiction in things, or 'antinomy'. We are left with two sets of feelings that cannot be expelled, or separated, or reconciled. The Christian doctrines, in whatever measure Shakespeare may have accepted them, were not before his mind in the sense of affording any solution of this 'antinomy'. One side of it leads to disheartenment. We are filled for part of the time with the sense of waste, of injustice, or rather of blind chance, at any rate of unreason, in the world represented. It is a scene of great souls cruelly overtaxed in their weakness, of large minds whose plans run counter to their best hopes, and of guile at least half-triumphant. Pessimism, a philosophy not formulated in Shakespeare's day, would say that such a world had better not have been, or that it has a necessary overplus of pain and unreason. Yet this is not the actual impression left on us by the noble close of *Hamlet*; and so the other face of the contradiction is slowly turned toward us. Here we mysteriously feel that there is, after all, some kind of pacification, some cancelling of bonds, some final settlement, even if it be not made in terms of the justice that we know. We are left in 'calm of mind, all passion spent'. And this feeling is incompatible with a mere sense of waste and chaos. Mr. Bradley then turns from the psychological to the external or objective statement of the problem and asks: What, then, is the presiding power in such a tragic universe?

The contradiction only defines itself the more. The presence of moral law somewhere, of orderly cause and effect, of Nemesis, is irremovable. We can never get rid of that. The tragic trouble springs from the hero's voluntary act ; Brutus has to pay for blindness and Macbeth for guilt. People are punished, not merely sacrificed—often overpunished, but still punished—by some principle in the nature of things. The bad are always punished in Shakespeare's tragedies. The merely faulty are punished. The 'innocent who belong to the guilty' (as Dr. Furnivall puts it) are punished because they do belong to the guilty. Such a world is not one of mere disorder. On the other hand, the conception of some power working, if not blindly, yet regardless of individual desert, is equally unavoidable as we read on. It is no crude form of predestination ; for Shakespeare's view, on the whole, is Helena's, that *the fated sky gives us free scope*. No ; the tragic fate suggests a great impersonal system of some kind, cutting across our aims and hopes, working without reference to them, and grinding them up in its relentless march. We cannot get rid of this idea any more than we can get rid of the idea, which conflicts with it, of law and morality in the tragic world. Here, then, are the two aspects of the contradiction.

The most original part of the theory now follows. Where, in such a scene, is there any clear place for the conceptions of good and evil, for what we now term 'values'? Drama does not profess to solve the riddle, but asks it in the most pointed way. Mr. Bradley works in metaphors, as we all must do ; we will quote his own, and may then suggest an alternative metaphor. He says that evil, such as that embodied in Iago and Goneril, produces a convulsion in the society it invades ; it acts as a poison, and therefore there must be a healthy body, a living body, to poison. You cannot poison a corpse or a stone. There must, then, be some impulse or principle that we call *good* which animates the condition of normal health. Evil is that which produces a violent reaction and a desire to cast it out in the healthy body. But we have not even now arrived at the essential point of tragedy. There is nothing necessarily tragic in the mere conflict of good and evil and the victory of evil. Mr. Bradley does not put the matter in so startling a way, but it seems to follow from his theory, and I believe it to be true. Tragedy only comes in, or is only complete, when the struggle to cast out evil involves evil of a fresh order; when the faulty hero of mighty make cannot be purged of his fault without being overpunished and perishing; nay, without wrecking others, the good and the evil, together. Tragedy culminates, not when Goneril is triumphant, or when Lear is vexed, but when the contact of Lear's weakness and Goneril's wickedness generates the destruction of Cordelia. The good principle, or Ormuzd, cannot defeat the bad, or Ahriman, without ' self-torture and self-waste '. Thus a Shake-spearean tragedy ends with a faint, weary, and feature-less convalescence of the tragic world, with a few secondary figures standing round a heap of bodies. Life will go on, but this play is over. The houses strike up a shamefaced peace, but this is nothing to Romeo and Juliet, and little more to us. At the end of *Lear* the earth has purged itself of several reptiles at a portentous cost. It is like a body that almost dies, and actually forfeits all grace and beauty for awhile, in the effort to cast off a poison. We are thus faced by the contra-diction in an acuter form than ever. If the world is not in principle good, why should it try to save itself by expelling evil? But if it is good, why should it have evil? Above all, why should the effort to be rid of evil bring in more evil still as the condition of success? On this problem the drama, so far from solving it, puts a finer edge. And yet the result is somehow calming

H

and elevating. The mystery without is thus reflected in the mystery of our feelings towards it.

I have been less than just to some of Mr. Bradley's distinctions, and have used my own words. His theory is a thoroughgoing and original effort to re-state the difficulty of evil in the world as represented in four tragedies. He virtually asks how Shakespeare would have put the riddle of life had his mind been methodical and not artistic. One obvious comment is that life is larger than the stage. Many situations which the philosopher must face, the dramatist may never face. Some disasters are not tragic at all, such as mere physical accidents. Villains, again, like Bunyan's Mr. Badman, prosperous on earth to the last; and good men, too unlike ourselves, who are brought low without any fault; are not for the drama, or at least must not be in its forefront. Yet the theologian or philosopher must place them in his system somewhere. And, as Mr. Bradley carefully implies, even within the drama itself tragedy is not everything; for the side of life shown in philosophic comedy and romantic play has also to be counted with. Further, even within the sphere of tragedy, it is wrong to lay too much stress upon the mere upshot; for this is largely dictated, not by ethical theory at all, but by the amount of imaginary pain that the average spectator will tolerate. For the fate of Desdemona he must be indemnified, if only a little, by that of Iago, and for the fall of Hamlet by that of Claudius. These bad men might very well, in the real world, escape and prosper, as the philosopher must remember. In Shakespeare's plays they may not. This is only to the praise of Shakespeare. He felt, being a theatrical artist, just how far he might take his hearers, who were not philosophers. In real life, again, comedy often has a death in it, but not so upon the stage. We must not therefore slip into thinking that the themes of the highest tragic art exhaust our types of evil in the world. Tragedy, by its nature, only mirrors a bit of the world. In order to judge the world we must also reckon in the other part, which tragedy cannot mirror. And this part makes a vast difference.

Mr. Bradley's exposition therefore attends at this point somewhat exclusively to the administrative side, so to call it, of tragedy. He is, so far as we understand him, the first to grant that the poet is equally, or more, concerned with character; not only with what men do and deserve and suffer, deservedly or otherwise, but with what, through these experiences, they are. There are complex natures pictured in the plays, of whom Hamlet is the chief; but, with his eye on the audience, Shakespeare usually tells it plainly where its sympathies, personal as distinct from dramatic, are to lie. There is no doubt that Lear is, on the whole, a healthy member of the world despite his error, and Macbeth a poisonous intruder despite his grandeur. There are indeed cases where the dramatic sympathy is so great that it almost carries the favour of the spectator with it. In *Macbeth* we begin to feel that his enemies are on the other side; and we find it hard to feel the due pity for Duncan and Banquo, because their slayer is more interesting. Shakespeare has to burden Macbeth with the stupid and pointless murder of Macduff's family, lest Macduff should, like Richmond in *Richard III*, be a dull and perfunctory justicer.

If we are to seek an ethical point of view in these tragedies, they cry with a thousand voices, that it matters (as Mr. Bradley well says of Cordelia) what we are, and that it does not matter what happens to us. Sometimes, although good, men triumph; sometimes their error is punished too much, sometimes too little; sometimes their end seems to be a proof of moral order, sometimes of blind chance or of impersonal fate. And, to speak in myth, the tragedies might well tempt us to separate the creative from the executive powers of the universe. It is as though the labour of making men and women had fallen to a band of supernatural artists of varying skill and bent. Some of them mould creatures that are almost perfect, others mould creatures exquisitely and immutably fitted for hateful ends. The average products, however, of the workshop are the soft instruments of circumstance, and what they will be at the last is only clear after they have clashed blindly together. But the web of actual happenings in which they are trapped might seem the work of a wholly different set of powers, who administer and do not create at all. These are rarely good fairies; sometimes they are blind furies, oftener half-intelligent fates. Or, if we are to figure them as a single executive power, it would resemble in many ways King Lear—a blind judge with a raw, angry sense of discipline and justice, who can hear the voices of men but cannot see to aim his bolts aright. These often glance on the innocent, even if they are sent in the right direction; and they are sure to scatter on good and evil alike, like bombs, rather than to pierce one victim only, like arrows. Earthly justice resembles the faltering efforts of this blind and petulant but listening Minos. To suppose there is some ulterior and sovereign reason behind his chair is only a pretence of the human heart that cannot bear the truth. Such a myth as this, it may be granted, unduly separates character from the web of circumstance that elicits it. It is also too polytheistic to satisfy our desire for a single clear solution. But Mr. Bradley himself ends in a dualism which only transfers the problem from the hands of the poet to those of the

philosopher. Perhaps the philosopher may himself come
to think that the poet's statement of the problem is
worth more than his own. Perhaps, owing to the very
make of our minds, the question of the worth of life, as
life is shown in tragedy, is as illegitimate as that of the
infinity of space according to Kant—a question that we
must ask, and may not answer, and which, therefore, is
out of the sphere of possible knowledge. The artist is
the best person to intimate its existence.

I pass by Mr. Bradley's chapter on the structure of the
plays, which confesses some debt to that too little known
if scholastic book, Gustav Freytag's *Technik des Dramas*.
It is a good example of his introspective method, as he
sits in the boxes, with a philosophic finger on his own
pulse, watching the ebb and flow of his sympathies. Most
of his book is given to interpreting the four great
tragedies. With all his metaphysical turn, Mr. Bradley
does not ride away from the text or become too abstract
in treatment ; he even grapples the text with too much
rigour. His spirit is scientific, it is that of a minute
theologian who is also, what many theologians are not,
deeply religious. Even when we think that he is wrong,
or that his view is less new than he supposes, it is clear
that he has come to Shakespeare with fresh eyes, and
that the work has formed part of his life. Such a man,
the Germans would say, has *erlebt* or lived through the
tragedies of Shakespeare. His close and serried exposition is varied with passages of eloquent lay preaching.
Intensity is the mark of his style, which yet is light in
movement and rhythm, though the intensity is, if we
may use the word, at times overwound. A happy
instance of Mr. Bradley's exact method is his account
of the atmosphere of *Macbeth*, which is a sanguinary
darkness shot with lightnings.

The atmosphere of *Macbeth*, however, is not that of unrelieved blackness. On the contrary, as compared with *King Lear* and its cold dim gloom, *Macbeth* leaves a decided impression of colour; it is really the impression of a black night broken by flashes of light and colour, sometimes vivid and even glaring. They are the lights and colours of the thunderstorm in the first scene; of the dagger hanging before Macbeth's eyes and glittering alone in the midnight air; of the torch borne by the servant when he and his lord come upon Banquo crossing the castle-court to his room; of the torch, again, which Fleance carried to light his father to death, and which was dashed out by one of the murderers; of the torches that flared in the hall on the face of the Ghost and the blanched cheeks of Macbeth; of the flames beneath the boiling caldron from which the apparitions in the cavern rose; of the taper which showed to the Doctor and the Gentlewoman the wasted face and blank eyes of Lady Macbeth. And, above all, the colour is the colour of blood (pp. 334–5).

The enumeration of the contemptuous metaphors drawn from animal life that abound in *Lear* is of the same quality. The play of these dramas upon the nerves and senses of the imaginative reader, as well as their play upon his heart and intelligence, is well kept in view. And as we have treated Mr. Bradley so much as a philosopher, let us quote a passage that shows how little he drags in metaphysics where they have no place. He is not seduced, as Milton's demons might have been, by the question whether the foreknowledge of the witches interferes with the moral 'freedom' of Macbeth.

Macbeth was not written for students of metaphysics or theology, but for people at large; and, however it may be with prophecies of actions, prophecies of mere events do not suggest to people at large any sort of difficulty about responsibility. Many people, perhaps most, habitually think of their 'future' as something fixed, but of themselves as 'free'. The Witches nowadays take a room in Bond Street and charge a guinea; and when the victim enters they hail him the possessor of 1000*l.* a year, or prophesy to him of journeys, wives and children. But though he is struck dumb by their prescience, it does not occur to him that he is going to lose his glorious 'freedom'—not though journeys and marriages imply much more agency on his part than anything foretold to Macbeth. The whole difficulty is undramatic; and I may add that Shakespeare nowhere shows, like Chaucer, any interest in problems concerning foreknowledge, pre-destination, and freedom. . . . The words of the Witches are fatal to the hero only because there is in him some-thing which leaps into light at the sound of them; but they are at the same time the witness of forces which never cease to work in the world around him, and, on the instant of his surrender to them, entangle him inextricably in the web of fate (pp. 346, 349).

This is a good instance of philosophy saving us from herself. But the witches have yet another dramatic purpose; they give a lead to the audience. Though they do not advise Macbeth, they show what is coming; and this result is remembered all through Macbeth's struggle. Were it otherwise, their words would be grotesque. Somehow and at some time—and it is very soon clear how and when—Macbeth, the greatest man in Scotland, will get the crown and show himself also the worst. We feel at once that Macbeth is free, in the common sense of the term, but we do not doubt how he will use his freedom. If goodness ever threatened to be too strong in Macbeth, the interest would quickly slacken.

Sometimes Mr. Bradley has wrung the text too hard. He manages to read a deep moral lesson into the story of Banquo, who is made out to be a kind of accomplice after the fact in Duncan's murder, so that 'his punishment comes swiftly, much more swiftly than Macbeth's, and saves him from any farther fall '. But in reality there is only one speech of Banquo at all to the purpose :—

> Thou hast it now, King, Cawdor, Glamis, all,
> As the weird women promised. . . .

And few will say that Shakespeare bears as hard as Mr. Bradley upon Banquo. Not knowing, but only suspecting the murder (for the witches had foretold no murder, only kingship), Banquo merely says, ' Perhaps their prophecy about my race will be true also.' What is he to do, and what wrong has he done? He had to acquiesce in the authority of his friend, about whom he only had certain misgivings? ' Doubtless,' says Mr. Bradley, ' he was present at Scone to see the new king invested.' Doubtless! And Banquo is to be punished for this ' doubtless '! If we once go behind what Shakespeare tells us concerning his creatures, it would doubtless often be a hanging matter. This odd habit of treating them as if they were real, and guessing what would in that case be likely, is a tribute to the poet's illusive gift, and few other writers have received it, though we sometimes hear in the pulpit edifying fancy lives of Judas Iscariot from his childhood upwards. Even if Banquo is not wholly heroic, he is an innocent victim. Macbeth distrusts his ' royalty of nature ', and puts him out of the way.

Mr. Bradley is at his best in describing Hamlet's melancholy, which he propounds, with sympathy and ingenuity, as the key to the character. He modifies in important points the ' Schlegel-Coleridge theory ', according to which Hamlet suffered from a combination of over-thinking and palsied will. Melancholy, in Burton's sense, well covers that seventh sin of the Church, ' accidia,' or listless desperation, which so buried the sinners in Dante's mire that their breath only bubbled to the surface.

It is true, as Hegel says, that ' Death is from the first in the background of Hamlet's mind ; the sandbank of the finite is not enough for him '. But Hamlet, it might be safer to say, is rather touched than constituted by this mood ; he is touched by it only at intervals, and chiefly in the fourth act, when he feels himself the prey of ' bestial oblivion '. We can hardly impute this frame of mind to him through all the play; we must remember that he is in a state of sick revulsion after killing Polonius and indecently blustering at Gertrude. One would also like to quote Mr. Bradley's analysis of Hamlet's tricks of thought and phrase, his inquiry into Hamlet's bearing to Ophelia (which ends in a well-warranted suspense of judgement), and his opinion that the play of Gonzago is unintentional bombast. This last conclusion may be too harsh. To quote separate scraps of rant from other plays of Shakespeare is not enough. It may be that here he consciously used a style of mingled bombast and power that was still within playgoers' memory and perhaps had once been his own style also; archaising thus, perceptibly, in order to distinguish the diction of the strollers from that of the main play.

Here and there Mr. Bradley may have forced the sense of *Hamlet*. He thinks, with some other critics, that the Queen was unfaithful to her husband while he was alive ; because the Ghost speaks first of Claudius as ' winning her will by gifts', and next of the murder. The Ghost and Hamlet also call the offence incest. But the term would apply, in the sentiment of the time, to marriage with a dead husband's brother. And the Ghost is speaking of events, not in the order of time, but in the order of his indignant emotions. Her lapse was bad enough. The notion of her previous adultery is needless to the dramatic idea, and is not in the old tale. In any case it is a point that Shakespeare leaves in twilight, and here, if ever, it is safer to respect his reserve if we wish to understand him.   Mr. Bradley also thinks that Hamlet's action in sparing Claudius while he prays is merely a piece of self-deception to excuse his own delay.   Tragic self-deception of such a kind is hard to exhibit, though Shakespeare probably does exhibit it in the case of Iago.   But the dramatist would thus place himself in the curious position of providing one meaning for the audience, who certainly think Hamlet in earnest, and for the initiated a further meaning, which is not only a subtler one, but exactly opposite to the public meaning.   Mr. Bradley, by one of his odd refinements, grants that the hatred of Hamlet is genuine, but still refuses to accept it as the cause of his forbearance because we can see that 'his reluctance to act is due to other causes'.   But the cause alleged, namely, the desire to kill the king at some sinful moment that would damn him straightway, is a highly adequate cause.   Hamlet's wish not to 'meet his dearest foe in heaven', but to send him to hell, is quite in keeping with that barbaric, saga-like side of his nature which Goethe ignored.   It is not many steps farther to Sir Thomas Browne's Italian, 'who, having been provoked by a person he met, put a poniard to his heart, and threatened to kill him if he would not blaspheme God ; and the stranger doing so, the Italian killed him at once, that he might be damned having no time to repent.' There are worse touches than this in human nature.

   To say that a critic can speak with some adequacy of *King Lear* is to say much.   The most firmly and masculinely written of Mr. Bradley's chapters are those on *Macbeth* ; those on *Lear* best show all his gifts.   It is surely right to say that *Lear* is not only too huge a work for the stage, but is not Shakespeare's 'best play'.   There are incongruities in the detail, breaks in the line, clots in the colour, cloudiness in the grouping. It could not be otherwise in this gigantic design, which a wild fancy might dream of as frescoed large within the dome of the lowering sky itself. And it is on *Lear* that the philosophic theory of the critic is most fully tested. He shows how the personages fall, more clearly than elsewhere, into two camps or groups, good and evil severally :—

Almost as if Shakespeare, like Empedocles, were regarding Love and Hate as the two ultimate forces of the universe. . . . While it would be going too far to suggest that he was employing conscious symbolism or allegory in *King Lear*, it does appear to disclose a mode of imagination not so very far removed from the mode with which, we must remember, Shakespeare was perfectly familiar in Morality plays and in the *Faery Queen* (pp. 263, 265).

Here, as elsewhere, Mr. Bradley shows less heed for poetry, in the sense of transporting language and of metrical music, than for character and structure and philosophy. To the last of these, his master-interest, he returns with the question, why does Cordelia die ? His discussion of this problem is a good example of the high, humane, and intensely pitched writing of Mr. Bradley at its best ; and so is what follows :—

The whole story beats this indictment of prosperity into the brain. Lear's great speeches in his madness proclaim it like the curses of Timon on life and man. But here, as in *Timon*, the poor and humble are, almost without exception, sound and sweet at heart, faithful and pitiful. And here adversity, to the blessed in spirit, is blessed. It wins fragrance from the crushed flower. It melts in aged hearts sympathies which prosperity had frozen. It purges the soul's sight by blinding that of the eyes. Throughout that stupendous Third Act the good are seen growing better through suffering, and the bad

worse through success. The warm castle is a room in
hell, the storm-swept heath a sanctuary. The judgement of this world is a lie ; its goods, which we covet,
corrupt us ; its ills, which break our bodies, set our
souls free ;

> Our means secure us, and our mere defects
> Prove our commodities.

Let us renounce the world, hate it, and lose it gladly.
The only real thing in it is the soul, with its courage,
patience, devotion. And nothing outward can touch
that (pp. 326–7).

IV

Professor Churton Collins, a follower of Macaulay in
style, and a follower—strange combination !—of Matthew
Arnold in some of his poetic theories, excels, by virtue
of much learning, in comparisons and analogies, though
perhaps less in his discriminations. His style is fierce,
blunt, and rhetorical, but accurate and lucid, and when
he can forget the iniquities of his brother-critics his true
passion for poetry and letters finds free play. His notion
of literature is only too simple. He tends, unless I
misread him, to find, like Arnold, the essence of religion
in poetry, and religion in the essence of poetry. It is
a noble dream ; but the historical sense of mankind will
always distinguish religion from poetry. Those critics
are tempted to confound the two things, who find
morality at the heart of both. But, even so, the question
would remain whether it is the same morality. We
may doubt whether either the saints or the poets would
admit it. For one thing, the *expression* of morality differs
in religion and in poetry, and the expression is vital.
It is only in one kind of poet, like Dante, that the
expression for the two things coincides. Religion and
poetry, further, are different ways, not only of expressing, but of conceiving the spiritual world, though here

and there the ground is common. The difference is at its widest when we confront a tragedy of Shakespeare with a treatise by one of the great mystics, St. John of the Cross or Molinos. It is the whole difference between reading the world and making the soul. Still, we are always impelled to draw some rational lines of connexion between religion and poetry, since both are permanently rooted in humanity.

And in order to press closer to the problem, we must first find the connexion between high poetry and the ethics which it implies and which form part of its *mòtif*. This is attempted by Mr. Collins in his essay on ' Sophocles and Shakespeare '.[103] His parallel rests on the supposition that both tragedians do not merely imply or suggest morality, but that they are ' essentially didactic ', and that therefore they held doctrines for which we can use strict philosophic language. ' Both began, not indeed by being pessimistic, but as bordering on pessimism ; both ended in being absolute optimists.' The nature of poetical creation, which is not necessarily the clothing of a moral theorem in ornament, should make us cautious in such imputations. Anyhow, the creator of Caliban ended only in a modified optimism. And we have seen that the feeling of moral law is only one of the feelings that Shakespeare leaves ; and this feeling he leaves somewhat fitfully, though he does leave it. Like the world, he also leaves the feeling of injustice, of caprice, of some law or fate or chance which is not moral at all ; and the business of criticism is to follow his footsteps and interpret his varying mood. In fact, one side of this impression could not be better phrased than by Mr. Collins himself, when he speaks of the ' suffering, which, befalling the guiltless, cannot be penal, and, as it involves their extinction, cannot be purgative '. And he further speaks of the law that ‘if the innocent be associated with the guilty, both perish together’. But that is a moral law only in a desperate sense ; it reflects poorly upon the equity of the ruling powers. Once more, we have here a contradiction and discord deep in things, which Shakespeare sometimes drives home to us, sometimes softens and obscures by the harmony of his art.

V

Professor Walter Raleigh, in a book of dashing and generous, if sometimes impatient eloquence, stands at extremes with Mr. Churton Collins, and has confined himself to the other side of the contradiction. In his *William Shakespeare* [104] we hear that ‘There is no moral lesson to be read, except accidentally, in any of Shakespeare’s tragedies ’ (p. 197) ; including, it is to be supposed, *Macbeth*. In proof, he says that Shakespeare (with whom he seems here to sympathize) set small store by creeds and abstract ideas, or by their power to help men at a tragic crisis.

Doctrine, theory, metaphysic, morals—how should these help a man at the last encounter! Men forge themselves these weapons, and glory in them, only to find them an encumbrance in the hour of need.

Millions of Christians and Mohammedans, not to speak of Stoics like Brutus and Cassius, have died with their formularies on their lips ; and the historic creeds, pagan and other, could not have lived a generation if they failed to help men at the last encounter. Mr. Raleigh goes on to say that ‘Shakespeare’s many allusions to philosophy and reason show how little he trusted them ’, and quotes the line that no philosopher ‘could endure the toothache patiently’. He might have added Romeo’s cry, ‘Unless philosophy can make a Juliet——.’ It may be going too

fast to pin Shakespeare to these casual and dramatic
utterances, or to the simple philosophy of the shepherd
Corin, who knew that 'the more one sickens, the worse
at ease he is', or even to the word of Lear, 'They told
me I was everything; 'tis a lie, I am not ague-proof.'
Each of these passages has a different bearing : the poet
is seeing and playing with delightful humour round the
creed of Corin, beyond which lies the whole world of
tragedy and romance ; and Lear had been fed, not on
metaphysics, but, as Mr. Raleigh says, on 'flatteries
and deceits'.

It is therefore vain to seek in the plays for a philosophy
or doctrine which may be extracted or set forth in brief.
. . . All doctrines and theories concerning the place of
man in the universe, and the origin of evil, are a poor
and partial business compared with the dazzling vision
of the pitiful estate of humanity which is revealed by
tragedy.

No doubt Shakespeare, being an artist and showman,
is not concerned to formulate, and our only safe clue to
his personal attitude is found in the Sonnets, in which
there is much passionate moral utterance, and which,
though they are not plays, rest on a tragical situation
that is dramatic in all but form. However this be, it is
plain that *we*, being sometimes moral beings, and in
possession of our reason, and inclined to watch life carefully, and finding in Shakespeare's plays a profound
picture of part of life, are irresistibly led to ask what
light he throws on the heroic way of taking life, on the
manner in which we are to love and judge those who
seem to fail in life, and on the spiritual laws of life that
may thence be inferred. And in this sense we may be
tempted to say that doctrine and metaphysic tell us less
than those dramatic pictures. Yet even here we must
take care; for there are philosophic doctrines like the

Buddhist which tell us of the misery of personal existence and of the salvation won by escape from desire; and these, among the deeper of human experiences, are none the less so for being doctrine. Not that Mr. Raleigh is to be taxed with denying this; but when he goes on to exemplify the impotence of doctrine and 'morality' from the foolish old convention of 'poetic justice', and from the dislike of Dr. Johnson for the bad ending of *King Lear*, he limits the term 'morality' to a sense that is not worth saving. In such a narrow sense it is true enough that 'there is no moral lesson to be read, except accidentally, in any of Shakespeare's tragedies'. But it soon appears, as we should divine, that something much larger is intended.

They deal with greater things than man; with powers and passions, elemental forces, and dark abysses of suffering; with the central fire, which breaks through the thin crust of civilization, and makes a splendour in the sky above the blackness of ruined homes. Because he is a poet, and has a true imagination. Shakespeare knows how precarious is man's tenure of the soil, how deceitful are his quiet orderly habits and his prosaic speech. At any moment, by the operation of chance, or fate, these things may be broken up, and the world given over once more to the forces that struggled in chaos.

This is true, and it is finely said; it has the cadence and the language that make Mr. Raleigh not only a critic but a writer, whose words give physical pleasure. But what is it to the argument? If we see nothing 'moral' in the play of elemental passions and forces among human beings, we are not making the word 'moral' big enough. Filial piety or cruelty, justice and injustice, gratitude and petrifaction, loyalty and love and lust, these are the *passions* and the *elements* that animate the world of *Lear*. They are moral ingredients; for to think of them

is the very cure for the unthinking, relative, and pro-
visional 'morality'—half of which is obsolete tribal
custom—of the undisturbed vulgar life.   Other passages
in Mr. Raleigh's book, which are less perplexing, suggest
that his reading of the tragedies is, after all, not very
different.   Of *Othello* he writes :—

There is a strange sense of triumph even in this
appalling close. . . . He points to no conclusion, unless
it be this, that the greatest and loveliest virtues, surpass-
ing the common measure, are not to be had for nothing.
They must suffer for their greatness.   In life, they suffer
silently, without fame.   In Shakespeare's art they are
made known to us, and wear their crown.   Desdemona
and Othello are both made perfect in the act of death,
so that the idea of murder is lost and forgotten in the
sense of sacrifice (p. 208).

Here is morality : it is true that it is not of the vulgar
kind.   Worked out, it would seem to come to a kind of
dualism.   There is a deep relentless element of indifference, if not of evil, in the arrangements of the earth,
and it often destroys the good by reason of their unusual
goodness.   But the victory is still theirs.   This is clearer
when we remember that we would prefer to be in their
place—and, what is harder to say, we would prefer that
those we love should be in their place—even at the price
they pay, rather than in the place of the meaner kind
who slip through the meshes.   Or we know that we
should prefer this if we had the courage.   We are back
again with the view, somewhat differently put, of
Mr. Bradley ; with that schism in the tragic world, and
with those clashing impressions of moral law, blind
chance, and regardless Fate, that the great poet leaves.
   What Mr. Raleigh means by the 'subtle and profound'
morality of the poet may be seen by his pages on
Measure for Measure, which are among his best written,

although they end in a certain obscurity. Some of his
criticisms are acute and necessary. We cannot turn the
play into a simple contrast between Isabella and her
surroundings without violating and forgetting the poet's
intention.

We are commonly presented with a picture of Vienna
as a black pit of seething wickedness; and against this
background there rises the dazzling, white, and saintly
figure of Isabella. The picture makes a good enough
Christmas card, but is not Shakespeare (p. 166).

The critics who draw such a picture have doubtless left
out all the *nuances*. Their morality, we further hear, is
merely one of condemnations and avoidances; they are
blind to Shakespeare's 'sympathy', which extends to the
bawds, criminals, and fribbles, and they are also blind
to his thought and criticism, which glances against the
virtuous Duke, and even, perhaps delicately, against
Isabella herself. And Mr. Raleigh, in what he deems the
spirit of the poet, has a gentle phrase of tolerance for
each of the blackguards in the play—except that he might
not admit so hard a word.

The world of Vienna, as Shakespeare paints it, is not
a black world; it is a weak world, full of vanities and
stupidities, regardful of custom, fond of pleasure, idle,
and abundantly human. No one need go far to find it.

This is perhaps extreme. After all, if not a black it is
a tolerably beastly world, on the mildest interpretation;
and that is why we need not go far to find it. Moreover,
the thought of Shakespeare, if it is to be gleaned, as
Mr. Raleigh well shows, from the *whole* of the utterances
in the play, includes an abundance of stern censure. The
Duke's words to Pompey must be reckoned in, as well as
the rollicking ironic comment, noted by Mr. Dowden long
ago, of Lucio at the cost of the 'old fantastical duke of

dark corners'. No single character is a chorus, telling us all that we ought to feel.   This is a just enough remark : and yet the poet seems to point, not to confounding the faults of the senses in a sort of general sunshiny indulgence, but in correcting the common, and even the legal, estimate of their relative heinousness.   That he does, by choice, through the mouth of humorists and irresponsibles ; but he does it.   His initial difficulty lay in the story itself, in the monstrous and absurd regulation by which fornication is punished with death.   This is one of the suppositions, like the pound of flesh and Lear's division of the king-dom, that are a mere means of launching the play.   But here the supposition is always getting in the way of our sympathies.   Isabel has almost to apologize, on the strength of her sisterly love, for pleading against Claudio's death.   But no one, however ascetic, could sanely admit the justice of such a law.   And yet, by his hypothesis, Shakespeare can never allow Isabel to go to the root of the matter.   Any hints of protest are left to Lucio.   All this interferes now and then with the sublimity of the play.   It interferes even more than the cheerful scrambled-up ending, which Mr. Bradley calls a 'scandalous busi-ness', and in which, in so far as touches the fate of Isabel, Mr. Raleigh manages to see a dramatic intention ; the holy 'sister' being redeemed, after all, for earthly uses. As Shakespeare says nothing about that point, we may think what we like.

In this play there is thus no single character through whose eyes we can see the questions at issue as Shake-speare saw them.   His own thought is interwoven in every part of it ; his care is to maintain the balance, and to show us every side.   He stands between the gallants of the playhouse and the puritans of the city ; speaking of charity and mercy to these ; to those asserting the reality of virtue in the direst straits, when charity and mercy seem to be at league against it. Even virtue, answering to a sudden challenge, alarmed, and glowing with indignation, though it is a beautiful thing, is not the exponent of his ultimate judgement. His attitude is critical and ironical, expressed in reminders, and questions, and comparisons. . . . This wonderful sympathy . . . is the secret of Shakespeare's greatness (p. 173).

This passage makes one thoughtful. The 'subtle and profound morality' of the poet was the original quest; it turns out to consist in his 'sympathy', and this again consists in his refusal to identify himself with any one of his creatures. This, then, is what 'morality' comes down to, if we look at Shakespeare. Presumably it is also what it comes down to, if we look at life itself.

Certainly such a view saves some trouble. Nobody is damnable, if we only stare hard enough; for does not the great poet's sympathy shine on all like the sun? Nor is any one quite perfect; the man in the street can always pick a hole. The more we read Shakespeare, the more we are to suspend judgement, and perhaps also to qualify admiration. Now was this really his temper and intention? We can only tell by studying his art, and, since he is a dramatist, the only point in his art that throws light on such a problem is his *emphasis*. What are the scenes, what the speeches, on which he puts forth his full power? It is true that we must not forget the cross-lights, ironies, qualifications that come elsewhere. But neither must we forget the large masses of light and shade. His 'sympathy', in the true sense of the word, must be more than the mere humorous and tolerant understanding, some share of which goes to every pimp and cut-throat. His sympathy is not such as to forget what they really are, or what Isabel is. It may be therefore wrong to say that his last word is critical and ironical. Who can doubt that even though Isabella has a touch of the ascetic bias, of estrangement from human frailty, Shakespeare means that she is entirely, when it comes to the crisis, in the right? Any other answer than hers either to Angelo or to Claudio would be intolerable, and yet an ordinary woman would have given another answer. Nay, by another woman, we may say, another answer might have pardonably been given. But her answer is right for *her*, right under all the circumstances: it is sublime, and not the less so for being inevitable. Nothing can alter this. As for Angelo, Mr. Raleigh, remarking that the poet ' condemns no one, high or low ', adds that he is ' considerably, even mildly treated', and analyses his nature keenly :—

His hypocrisy is self-deception, not cold and calculated wickedness. Like many another man, he has a lofty, fanciful idea of himself, and his public acts belong to this imaginary person. At a crisis, the real man surprises the play-actor, and pushes him aside. Angelo had underestimated the possibilities of temptation.

True, again, as far as it goes; but the fallacy seems to be that dramatic analysis excludes approval or condemnation. Angelo, after all, had tried to buy off his own law, which to him was justice, by the prostitution of a saint. The poet is not angry with him after the manner of a dramatic satirist whose anger mars his art (which may be only what Mr. Raleigh means); but Angelo's intended crime is of the essence of the situation, and there is no getting out of its enormity. The lash of Isabella's retorts would otherwise fall idly. It is impossible to think of Shakespeare simply as an amiable and profound student of psychology. Being a complete man, he was also, at the right moment, as stern as Dante, as well as more widely sympathetic, so that he can strike the chord of outraged shame and justified wrath as no man has ever struck it. To leave this out is to enervate Shakespeare, or to confuse him with minds of a lighter type. We are content to adopt something of Mr. Raleigh's conclusion, though it does not accord with the idea that the poet is chiefly critical and ironical.

Many men make acquaintance with Christian morality as a branch of codified law, and dutifully adopt it as a guide to action, without the conviction and insight that are the fruit of experience. A few, like Shakespeare, discover it for themselves, as it was first discovered, by an anguish of thought and sympathy ; so that their words are a revelation, and the gospel is born anew.

It might be argued that Shakespeare's morality is more searching and profound than Christian morality, or at least raises many an issue which it tasks Christian morality, as usually read, to meet ; but to pursue such a contrast would be to quit Shakespeare.

It will be clear that Mr. Raleigh's book, which has been flattered and reviled by the press in a way that does little honour to our English criticism, contains precious metal. There is alloy. There are signs of a light, inexpensive, and not always covert scorn for the scholarship without which the author could not have written one page in security. This disappears when he comes to speak of the higher things of poetry, and therefore it can be only a superficial attribute. On the search for the literary sources of Shakespeare he writes :—

The slow-footed and painstaking pursuit of him by the critics through ways that he trod so carelessly and lightly would furnish a happy theme for his own wit and irony. The world lay open to him, and he had small patience with the tedious processes of minute culture (p. 63).

A little later the labours of these critics are freely drawn upon. Later still (p. 109) the difficulties of the Shakespearean text and canon are stated, with the comment :—

The results attained by the most laborious scholars command no general assent, and depend, for the most part, on a chain of ingenious hypotheses.

This is too indiscriminate. There are still many open questions, like those which arise from *Titus Andronicus* and *The Two Noble Kinsmen*. But many of the results of laborious scholars do command general assent. They have established, what was unknown in the time of Coleridge, an approximate order and grouping of the plays; they have made patient way towards a solution of the puzzles that overhang the texts of *Hamlet*, *Richard III*, and *King Lear*; they have settled, with the exception of some doubtful scenes, which parts of *Pericles* are due to Shakespeare. Crazy sand-spinners are fair game, but the first need of criticism is to separate them from the sound and acute reasoners, who have laid siege, not without success, to the central problems. Mr. Raleigh offers them little acknowledgement, though he joins their ranks, and proceeds to some hypothetical, often acute, reasoning of his own upon the original of *The Taming of the Shrew* and the possible relationship between *Timon of Athens* and *King Lear*.

Another passage might cause misconception. The words may have a wide audience, and nothing could better please the general public, or the shirker. They are too much in the strain of '*Via*, goodman Dull!'

The rapid, alert reading of one of the great plays brings us nearer to the heart of Shakespeare than all the faithful laudable business of the antiquary and the commentator (p. 7).

In one sense it is self-evident. We all know that the humanity and poetry of Shakespeare are the chief thing.

If that were all, no one would write down such a commonplace.   But when we see how little cordial praise
is paid to the antiquary and commentator throughout this book, we suspect an intention to sneer at them.
It will not do.   Many of them have felt the poetry of
Shakespeare.   Theobald read the poet's text 'alertly',
though perhaps not ' rapidly ', and his emendations have
the stamp of genius, if they are sometimes better than
the truth.   They would not be stigmatized as 'laudable'.
Moreover, the antiquaries and commentators are as mixed
a company as any that inhabits a play of Shakespeare.
They number forgers and pedants, lunatics and Bacon-
ians, pulpiteers and Ulricis and Rymers.   Among them
also are Delius and Malone, and some living men who
deserve well.   They are modest men and benefactors in
their time, and it is a poor thing to step carelessly among
their prostrate forms, especially when we cannot do our
work without their help.   *Ça porte malheur !*   To end here
would be unjust to a book of mark.   It is not everywhere
alike ; but many a page has the resonance that comes
only from long-hoarded thought and feeling ; and there
is also a rare intellectual precision in handling intangible
matters.   There is great freshness of reading and illustration.   The lights thrown on Gadshill robberies from the
pages of Harrison, on Falstaff's wit from Wilson's *Art of
Rhetoric*, or on Dogberry from Burghley's letter to
Walsingham (pp. 47–52), are all felicitous.   Some of the
artistic criticism is excellent.

The poems are as delicate as ivory, and as bright as
burnished silver.   They deal with disappointment, crime,
passion, and tragedy, yet are destitute of feeling for the
human situation, and are, in effect, painless.   The pain-
lessness, which made Hazlitt compare them to a couple
of ice-houses, is due not to insensibility in the poet, but
to his preoccupation with his art.   He handles life from

a distance, at two removes, and all the emotions awakened by the poems are emotions felt in the presence of art, not suggested by life (p. 81).

By art is here meant technique in the narrow sense: nothing could be more exact, and no critic has so well put his finger on the source of the discomfort which the *Poems* of Shakespeare inspire in every reader. In another passage a vulgar superstition is brushed away:—

The boys were no doubt very highly trained, and amenable to instruction; so that the parts of Rosalind and Desdemona may well have been rendered with a clarity and simplicity which served as a transparent medium for the author's wit and pathos (p. 120).

It is hard to subscribe to Mr. Raleigh's or to Lamb's dissatisfaction with the modern theatre; but the vindication of the boy-actors is a courageous heresy, to be welcomed however much it may shock the professional actors. One more sentence may be quoted, which makes short work of much of futile speculation.

If Cordelia had been perfectly tender and tactful, there would have been no play. The situation would have been saved, and the dramatist who was in attendance to celebrate the sequel of the situation might have packed up his pipes and gone home. This is not to say that the character of Cordelia is drawn carelessly or inconsistently. But it is a character invented for the situation, so that to argue from the character to the plot is to invert the true order of things in the artist's mind (p. 135).

Mr. Raleigh has the true eighteenth-century objection to cobwebs, and gives us plenty of these refreshing remarks. He has also the gentler and finer strain that was first heard in the contemporaries of Coleridge. Thus Mr. Raleigh is, doubly, in the true line of English critical tradition.

THE MEANING OF LITERARY HISTORY

I

STRONGLY rooted, and growing in power to quicken and to liberate, is the conviction that literature, being an art, must belong to the world and disown the quarrels of the nations.   The hope is that Europe and America shall one day be a league of intellectual commonwealths, wherein each draws from the others all the thoughts and all the forms of beauty that it can without loss of independence.   Now that this federal hope has been once conceived, it can hardly prove a mere vision of the night. There is none higher to supersede it; it must always live, for it can never be exhausted by fulfilment; and there have been signs for three centuries that it is not idle.   Indeed, like all vital ideas, it was acted on long

before it came to consciousness.   It has received a blind
tribute whenever any literature, like the Roman, accepted
a foreign influence.   To the German mind we owe its
plainest proclamation, and it is found, as we might
expect, in a noble form in Goethe.   In a note written in
1828 on the *Edinburgh Review* and the *Foreign Quarterly Review*, Goethe lays down the higher aim of all
such journals.

As they win, step by step, a larger public, they will
contribute in a most effectual way to what we hope for—
an universal world-literature.   We only repeat, there
can be no question of the nations thinking in accord.
But they must simply become aware of and comprehend
one another ; and, if they cannot attain to mutual love,
they must at least learn to bear with one another.

Goethe owed something here to pioneers like Herder.
The same voice is heard afterwards in the sentence of
Matthew Arnold :—

The criticism which alone can much help us for the
future is a criticism which regards Europe as being, for
intellectual and spiritual purposes, one great confedera-
tion, bound to a joint action and working to a common
result.

In this direction Goethe worked more effectively than
any other man.   By his creations and his fame, by his
universal and exotic sympathies, by his translations, by
his dismissal of politics and of the illusions, counter to
his ideal, that politics generate, and by his transference
to art of the international spirit of science, he heralds the
new conception of literature, to which he left Europe
readier to listen.   'Great talents,' he says, 'are the finest
peacemakers.'   In philosophy and science and religion,
and in fine art, the national barriers are weakened also.

But in literature the conditions are peculiar, and one way to study them is to notice the sundry ways in which literary history has been written; for every page of the historian must show how far he is alive to the federal idea. Let us see how far this is the case in England.

But we must first remember that the notion of a free exchange for thought and knowledge, and even for poetry and letters, is an old one. There was once a suzerain language, Latin, and the others were pretenders. The rise of the modern states and their languages broke up, at the beginning of the Middle Age, the traditional primacy of Latin as the medium of verse and eloquence and piety. The Renaissance, while it gave a fresh and artificial lease to Latin for the time, ended by stimulating the vernaculars through the disclosure of the ancient art, thought, and life. To some of these the Reformation gave new rank as languages of ritual and hymnody, and as the only bearable vesture for the Bible. And yet, far into the seventeenth century, Latin was still chosen by some of the strongest minds in the world, from Grotius and Bacon to Spinoza and Newton, as the natural voice of scientific truth, and as commanding an elect audience. By the time of Leibniz, who died in 1716, we can apply to Latin the words that Hobbes used of the Papacy : it is ' the ghost of the deceased Roman empire, sitting crowned upon the grave thereof '. The books of Leibniz are in three languages. Latin is there, but French is paramount, and abstract German is proving its infant muscles. Far as French was to spread, it could never succeed to the throne of Latin. It was so constantly checked by English that the swift growth of German was hardly needed to overthrow for ever, except in crazy minds, the notion of a universal literary tongue. The federal idea has long had to do without any crutches of that sort, and all the same it has spread irresistibly. In asking how far it can ever be applied to literature, as distinct from science, we have to face one obvious hindrance that lies in the nature of things, and to see how far that hindrance is fatal, or must be overcome before we can ever safely think of Europe and America as a possible republic of letters.

Knowledge is international or nothing; its matter does not alter with the language in which it is carried. Science, or the body and method of knowledge, is impersonal and above race; it cares nothing for the identity or character of its servants, save as sources of error; their contributions all go to the common fund. Thus science, being federal, unites and confounds, while art, being personal, sunders and identifies. The aim and power of art is to realize, in unique unchanging form, the spirit of the individual. Nothing but art saves his identity; for the children he leaves, the polity he forms, and all the other works of his hands, change when he is gone, only what has received form retaining permanence. Also the aim of art (in contrast with science) is to give pleasure through beauty. And the beauty realized by each artist, nay, the beauty of each of his works, must be unique, and the corresponding pleasure unique. Form is thus the last and only abiding home of personality, and is the source of a series of pleasures, each unique. Art lives by form, while works of science possess form only by luck. Besides this difference between art and science, there is a palpable barrier, in the case of literature, though not in that of music or the fine arts, against assuring a full mutual comprehension between men of different languages. For behind the scientific reason that is common to all nations there lie the associations of each language, on which its masters play, as on the heartstrings of their countrymen. The inner cell of the poet's mind is not hung with charts or diagrams of doctrine that are equally true or false in every idiom. It is peopled with wandering tunes that seek their appointed thought, and lonely phrases that seek a completing cadence, until at last, from some chance union that eludes all our psychology, the immortal word is born. And this cannot be transferred to another tongue. The sound and *aura* of the word are lost in translation, and in them the very substance of the thought has come to inhere. The practices of writing and printing make us forget that style lives in the ear and not in the eye. In presence of a work of art in verse or prose, its true lover ' knows not the body from the soul ', or the rhythm from the message. Now and then a version made by a congenial soul of another race moves us like the original. Better than Poe's countrymen, Baudelaire felt the essence of Poe's work, and his French reproduces the same emotional effect. Shelley's verses from the *Cyclops* and the *Faust* are renowned exceptions to the fate of translated poetry. So hard is it for literature to change its dress or be cosmopolitan. But all the more must it strive to be so, in this or other ways. It must join with education and science, the forces that unite, and not with those that serve for estrangement, such as racial distrust and war ; or civilization wastes a chance.

At this point history offers us a certain comfort. The artist, in the past, has ever been an explorer who returned the richer for his raid on foreign countries. Written large on the face of history is the wide interplay of poetry and art between the literary nations. It is a process whose laws we but dimly know ; we can only see it in the event. We find, for instance, that close neighbourhood is not always a stimulus, in art any more

than in love. The Rhine has been a greater spiritual
barrier, for a hundred years, than the Channel. In
Molière's time the Scandinavian North owed more to
France than to Germany, which fences it southward on
the map. And the problem is made harder by the
number of forces that affect literature whilst lying outside it. Some of these are tangible—wars, and perse-
cutions, and emigrations, and the course of trade, all of
which have carried letters abroad in their train. Thus,
to take stray instances, France taught us at the Restora-
tion what our whole history had led us to disregard, the
need for lucidity, composition, and a working prose.
Long after, the Holy Alliance provoked the nobler part
of Byron to expression, and thus spread his influence.
To-day, the stage skill of Ibsen, an exile and traveller,
has grafted a strain of alien sentiment on the drama of
the German and the Latin countries. In a thousand
ways art, like all things of the spirit, is determined by
causes beyond itself that lie deep in general history.
But the historian of art, while keeping these causes in
sight, has more to do with their results within art itself,
with the impact of mind on mind and the interfusion
of alien forms and styles.

Nearly all the Western literatures of modern times
have affected each other more or less. The general
destiny of some countries, like Italy and France, has
been to radiate and kindle power abroad; the strength
of others, like Germany and England, has been to use
what is thus bestowed and blend it with their native
stocks. We find the hunger to appropriate from Italy
active at every phase of our English Renaissance. And
it is different at the beginning and the end of the
chapter. Wyatt, finding the battered forms and metres
of English too weak for the new energies of poetry,

leaned on the schools of Italy—on the porcelain sonnet of the Petrarchans or the middle style of Alamanni's *terza rima.* Drummond, when the inspiration of the time was chilled, went to similar masters to study and introduce foreign finish. Different is the careless borrowing of Shakespeare the prodigal, who while he took many tales from the Italians, paid such usury, in creating Romeo or Iago from light materials, as to overwhelm his creditors. Another chapter is that of the revulsions inspired by a foreign literature. The Puritan distrust of Italy arose for reasons not artistic; the rebellion of Lessing against the edicts of French tragedy meant that a young art was restive under an alien superstition.

II

The study, then, of these wind and ocean currents, apart from all political boundaries, is a main part of literary cartography. The leading forces to consider are three or four. Two of them arise from the impulse to travel for inspiration beyond the limits of the native language. A people wishing to pour a new life-blood into its art may either turn to other living nations, or may turn to antiquity : and this, again, may be studied either in itself or through the modern writing that it has moulded. In either case the federal ideal is served, and a chapter of 'comparative' literary history falls to be written—another page in the long story of the 'revival of learning'. But these two impulses, to seek abroad and to seek backward, are for ever crossed and checked by two contrary ones, that spring from the wells of national pride and power. For we may turn for renewal to the writings of our own far past. They have some of the strangeness of things foreign, and some of the

dearness of things familiar. The more the tongue
has altered, the more foreign they seem; but, until the
sense of race and history is dead, they still seem ours.
England has been worse off in this matter than other
countries. Old English literature has stood for next
to nothing to our modern poets, because Old English
has to be learnt almost as an alien tongue, although
when we begin it we soon see it is not alien. Despite
Beowulf, and the *Wanderer*, and the poem on Satan
that Junius may have read to Milton, and the translations of Tennyson and William Morris, Old English
has less to say to us than almost any literature of note
in the West—far less, for instance, than French or Italian.
Hence we are wrong, in our schemes of education,
to tie it up rigidly with the study of modern English
literature, at the expense of French or Italian literature,
which are more important. Despite all this, the
Germanic past still speaks to us and to our artists.
To see that, it is enough to read Mr. Swinburne's
tragedy, *Rosamund, Queen of the Lombards*, or the late
Miss Barmby's noble play, whose reputation must slowly
but surely grow, *Gísli Súrsson*, founded on the Icelandic
saga of Gísli. But these tales do not come from Old
English. In France and Italy, and in Iceland, the
continuity of language and tradition has been far
less broken during eight or nine centuries than in
England.

But these three impulses, which lead us severally to
foreign writings, or to our own past, or to the antique,
can after all be only secondary. This truth is often
forgotten by those who fill volumes with the history of
'sources'. Before it can stir, or assimilate what is not
of its own time and land, a nation must first be moved
within itself and must assert its own identity and power.

Rarely, on the other hand, does it create a fresh art without also drawing upon other times or countries. Few literatures, like the ancient Greek or the Norse, can be said to be wholly self-sown. It would be hard to name a single one that has flourished since the twelfth century which has not gone for part of its stimulus beyond its own immediate energies. There has hardly been a moment in which the antique, and the foreign, and the native ancient writings, have not all counted for something, and have not modified the pure initiating impulse. These forces work in varying proportion : together they make up the pattern of a literature. The occurrence of dead studio-work, like the German imitations of French romances in the seventeenth century, or the English imitations of Racine's tragedies, is a natural incident, and the historian has to notice these waste products, to which the artist never gives a thought.

III

The whole way of conceiving and writing literary history must be affected by these considerations. The best of the older critics were never historians. Dryden, Boileau, and Johnson judged half by rule and half by mother-wit. Even Lessing judged much by rule, though on deeper principles. The rich birthright of Lamb and Hazlitt did not include the historical sense, for it was hardly born as applied to literature. Coleridge could recall and re-word philosophically, better than any man that ever lived, the creative process of the poet, but his searchlight was turned upon the depths of an isolated work of art, or of the spirit that lay behind it, not upon the perspective of poetry, seen down a long period of time.

All these men have their message of scorn or reproach
for the learned who merely hunt for tendencies and are
deaf to the living word, in which alone a ' tendency ' can
really come to birth. The task of literary history fell,
in England, to men of more learning than genius; for
neither Gray nor Pope carried out their wish to write
a chronicle of English poetry, and Thomas Warton's
experiment (1774–81) was the earliest. He opened fresh
ground, he showed the wealth, and pleaded (in a way that
soon became needless) for the beauty, of old romance. But
his contribution was chiefly one of erudition, and so was
superseded; nor was Warton troubled with catholicity of
insight. The first history in English that covered both
verse and prose and was written spaciously and with due
knowledge was Hallam's *Introduction to the Literature of
Europe during the Fifteenth, Sixteenth, and Seventeenth
Centuries* (1837). In his preface are named the encyclo-
paedic Germans who had tried such tasks before. Hallam
divides his theme, not by nations, but according to the
kinds of literature—poetry, philosophy, and so forth—
each chapter treating of the history of a single branch
between certain dates. We certainly get from this order-
ing the sense of Europe as a great and productive society
of minds. But Hallam's real subject is not the monuments
of the art of writing, but the culture recorded in books.
By literature he means everything useful that is printed.
He admits almost every published thing that furthered
knowledge; and a numismatist is as good a quarry to
him as a poet. Thus the literature of knowledge and
that of power are confounded, and the systematic study
of the mutual debts of nations is but dimly recognized.
Yet his book is not dead, for it is learned, clear, and
honest; and his chilly ray of flat impartial daylight is
worth more than any sham-patriotic idolatries. All who

attempt a fragment of the same task are in Hallam's debt.

Hallam shows that a critical method which had already come into flower had failed to reach him. Sainte-Beuve, the greatest of literary historians, never wrote a history of letters ; for his *Tableau* (1828) of the sixteenth-century writing of France was done in youth, and the master-piece *Port-Royal* traces a spiritual movement and its apostles rather than a literature. Yet the *Causeries* revealed a new task for all future historians. Sainte-Beuve had erudition, science, method ; but his sensitive-ness, his judgement, kept pace with his science ; he accepted all writers, but surrendered to none, and his insight into the lesser minds that people literature has never been excelled. He left criticism in a state of disquiet by showing that its work is not to judge by pre-formed canons of artistic, and still less of ethical, excellence, and that it must never be content with the mere study of outward conditions, sources, and influences ; but must use these only to press on to the discovery of what each artist, inalienably, uniquely, brings—of that within him which determines *what* influences he shall accept. On this track Sainte-Beuve advanced in triumph ; and he has shown us his motive power as a critic in his remarks on a book that, with all its blindnesses, yet remains the most quick and real one ever written on the subject, Taine's *History of English Literature* (1863–4). Taine spoke as though he could deduce the artist and his work from a study of the *milieu* or personal, social, and racial environment. Sainte-Beuve pleads for the artist's freewill, which remains when all the conditions of his growth have been analysed. He says :—

However well the net is woven, something always remains outside and escapes ; it is what we call genius, personal talent. The learned critic lays his siege to attack this like an engineer. He trenches it about and hems it into a corner, under colour of surrounding it with all the outward conditions that may prove necessary. And these conditions really do serve personal originality ; they incite it, they tempt it forth, they place it in a position to act and react, more or less ; but they do not make it. This particle which Horace entitles divine (*divinae particulam aurae*), and which, in the primitive, natural sense of the term, really is such, has never yet surrendered to science, and abides unexplained. That is no reason for science to throw down her weapons and renounce her daring enterprise. The siege of Troy lasted ten years ; and there are problems which perhaps may last as long as human life itself.[105]

It is true that Taine often escapes the weakness of his theory. In his last section he turns to portraiture and pierces with justice, even with sympathy, into the spirit of Dickens and Carlyle ; the flashes of truth which animate his earlier volumes redouble here. And throughout he cast a new light upon the English nature. He began with a notion, partly true, that our race is barbaric, and ebullient, and heedless of form, and alien to art ; and, slurring the rest, he chose the writers who seemed to answer to this notion. His fault, serious in a man of science, was ignorance of our literature as a whole ; he wrote before the modern means of knowing it existed. But he tried his best to shake our superstitions about ourselves and our superstitions about Shakespeare and Milton. He wished (in vain) to eradicate our private belief that our great authors are in some mysterious way types from which all others are aberrations. Were he writing now, he would have a large new store of facts, and he might have deepened and cleared his theory of the *milieu* by discarding those accidents of dress or custom of which literature is the record not the product, and by reckoning into it the forces of mind and spirit, often of distant origin, which have been recounted here. A keen one-sided essay, interpreting our romantic poetry, with Byron for hero, in the light of the growth of liberal thought and artistic tendency, was made by Dr. Georg Brandes in 1875.[106]

The later nineteenth century will be remembered, not so much for any young creative power, as for the application of method and the allotment of labour to the study of all kinds of history. The roots of this movement lie far back in the record of classical scholarship, which long remained the type of minute and rigid inquiry, and passed its conceptions on to the historian. Bayle's *Dictionary* is the first landmark ; biography and exegesis, secular and otherwise, could never be quite uncritical after Bayle. But the transference of method to the treatment of the modern literatures is a much later step. It could only be taken when the conviction, long hindered by the Renaissance, was once assured, that the modern equally with the classic masters claim the rigour of the historian and scholar. After the work of Hallam and Sainte-Beuve, that truth was more clearly seen ; the question was how to apply it in practice. No one man's talent or pains can suffice ; there must be the co-operation of labour. And this can only be achieved by schools of learning, which, though they can at most permit genius, and often only annoy it, can at least break in talent. Such schools are most naturally formed in universities, which can train an army of students in method during pupilage and save them from the painful and wasteful forms of self-education. The fabric of historical knowledge, whether literary or political, can only be the work of such an army. At this point we see the value of the system of monographs that rules in Germany and in some other countries, including America. The monograph submitted for graduation teaches a little method, and may build up knowledge, though it is often at present founded on a sorry general culture, is full of rubbish and repetition, and ought not in most cases to be printed, as in Germany by ordinance it has to be. But the system is the foundation of national scholarship. For instance, Italian literary history has been revolutionized since the days of its *doyen*, Tiraboschi. It has of late been portioned out amongst a 'society of professors', each of whom writes on a single epoch. Their work is a great and well-shapen monument, of which every stone is a monograph, edition, collation, biography, or study of sources. The *Histoire littéraire de la France*, guided by M. Petit de Julleville, is another large and generous venture, where the labour is more divided, so that the variety of talent is greater and the total impression of unity is less.

In France and Italy, in Germany and the States, the international side of literature is studied to an extent that England does not realize or imitate. A recent bibliography, *La Littérature comparée*, by Herr Louis Betz, contains some three thousand titles of articles and monographs on the relationships between France and Germany, France and England, Germany and England, and so following, in almost every combination. Sorted out, these dissertations fall into three or four types. In one of them is examined the 'sources' of an artist's themes, or thoughts, or forms; an inquiry that may become mechanical and ignore the step by which borrowing becomes creation. Another traces the influence or repute of a writer, or of a school of writers, at home and abroad; and this fills an enormous chapter. A third traces the fortunes of a species of literature, such as the

sonnet or picaresque novel or critical treatise; and here
is implied a study of the general history of thought and
culture. Fourthly, and abutting on folklore, is the
study of a particular story, that of Hamlet or Pyramus,
in its birth and growth, as it wanders over the world
finding new vigour in every soil, until perhaps in the
end it dies to live in a masterpiece. Lastly, the literary
contact between two or more lands may be investigated
and deduced from a multitude of observations in the
other four departments. None of the younger scholars
of France, whose names are too many for mention here,
had a finer historic vision, or wrote what is of more
concern to ourselves, than the late M. Joseph Texte.
The 'comparative' study of letters—which is only a
disciplined effort to carry out the ideal of Goethe—
he pursued with somewhat exclusive zeal, but with delicacy of touch, and not at all in the external, indiscriminate style that is the danger of this kind of work. His
chief book traces the origins of the international feeling
itself. *Jean-Jacques Rousseau et les Origines du Cos-
mopolitisme littéraire* is a title which could not have been
imagined fifty years ago.

Knowledge of this kind, and the study of literary
history, is nowhere worse organized than in England.
Good work is done, as will presently be seen; but that
is in spite of our having no organization, and is largely
due to the classical basis of our training. Until the
Modern Language Review was founded lately, we had
no journal of the first rate, of more than the weekly
scale, given up to the scientific study of our language
and literature; Germany has long had *Anglia* and
Englische Studien.[135] We still have nothing like that
valuable annual, the *Revue d'Histoire littéraire*, which
draws on the best talent in France. We have no academic

school like that of Columbia University, which issues
a series of books—not little theses, but books—on various
aspects of Tudor literature. In these works there may
be some lack of tint; some oblivion of the truth that
criticism is at last a fine art like friendship, and requires
colour and personality; some sign that the scientific
training intimidates a little, and teaches self-suppression
in the wrong as well as in the right way; but there is
clear and strict method, fresh digging, sober statement,
and real progress. There are volumes published from
Columbia University on the Italian Platonism found in
our Elizabethan verse, by Mr. J. Smith Harrison; on
the literary critics of our Renaissance, by Mr. Spingarn;
and on the Elizabethan lyric, by Mr. Erskine. Each of
these would merit a careful review. But the point for
remark is that they are the fruit of a school. A handful
of smaller papers comes from other universities; from
that of Pennsylvania arrives a valuable study of Fulke
Greville, Lord Brooke, by Mr. Morris Croll. What have
we in England like this? Nothing: unless we count the
Dictionary of National Biography, whose aim is strictly
defined and excludes leisurely criticism.

The great syndicate-history of English literature,
which we have delayed so long to make, is now promised
from Cambridge. Whatever its fruits, let us be glad that
the mother-country has taken the initiative. On the
whole our scholars write better, and seem to keep closer
to the work of art they study, than the Americans, who
are prone to relapse, in protest against the glare of their
popular style, into a decent and whity-brown academic
diction. Englishmen usually are fresher; though they
have not been taught method, they have been reared on
the classics; and, after all, for the student of Milton and
Berkeley, Virgil and Plato are a rational schooling, while

the waste of youth upon a dissertation concerning the metre of Glapthorne or the debts of Lydgate to Boccaccio is an irrational schooling. We want a blended system if we are to train scholars and historians of modern letters; a knowledge of the classics as a foundation, a training in minute method, and the application of this knowledge, of this training, to the historian's task. Men of insuppressible bent have wrought well in spite of the chaos, but have often been coerced, as to the scale of their work, by the market rage for manuals. In books like Dr. Herford's *Age of Wordsworth* and Mr. Seccombe's *Age of Johnson*, there are the knowledge and tact that might have shaped an ample history.

IV

But our present text is better served by two other books, Dr. Courthope's *History of English Poetry*,[107] which is planned to extend to the death of Scott, and has reached the middle of the eighteenth century; and Professor Saintsbury's *Short History of English Literature*.

Dr. Courthope comes to our poetry in the temper of the historian. He considers not so much what is the unique character of each poet, of each masterpiece, or the unique pleasure that either yields, as the large historic forces, often lying outside art altogether, by which poetic art has been shapen. The determining causes of poetry, we have seen, lie partly in politics and society, partly in metaphysical or ethical theory, and partly within art itself. All these causes together form the true environment of poetry, the *milieu*, though the shallower usage of the term by the school of Taine is not in its favour. The *milieu*, in this larger sense, operates over tracts of space and time ; the sway of antique political ideas, of the thoughts of the Church, reaches far both backwards and forwards. This is also true of the artistic environment ; the *milieu* of the *Ode on a Grecian Urn* is not Hampstead but the workshop of the dead Greek designer ; that of Spenser's *Hymn to Beauty* is the cell of the Alexandrian or Italian mystic. The strength of Dr. Courthope lies in his effort to apply such ideas to the story of English poetry, and may be acknowledged all the more frankly that his execution can often be criticized. He wipes out the reproach that no Englishman has attempted a philosophical history of the subject.

In the preface to his first volume (1895) Dr. Courthope distinguishes his own method from that of Warton, who thought little about currents and forces, and also from a later method, which he seems to say was practised by Mr. Walter Pater, and which seeks ' to interpret the mysterious phenomena of the remote past by mere personal sympathy '. But Mr. Pater, though he did not choose to write in the form of a history, gave himself a hard schooling, and was far more at home than his critic in the streams of old poetic feeling and in the actual recesses of the Renaissance intellect. He read his own experience and problems, not into history, but in the light of history. In Mr. Pater's power to recapture and express the volatile essence of a dead author, like Montaigne, or Shakespeare, or Sir Thomas Browne, Mr. Courthope is deficient. Pater had more of that power than any writer since Coleridge, and his best criticism ranks as new creation by virtue of its inwardness and its profundity. Perhaps it was not his work fully to satisfy the historical sense, unless it be in his *Marius*. He certainly did not try, like Dr. Courthope, to see how poetry and letters are rooted in civilization

at large. But he never let go, as Dr. Courthope often
does, of the individual mind, the single work of art, for
he knew these to be the primary object of inquiry,
while the connexion of art with forces outside itself,
however important, is not the primary object of inquiry.
Dr. Courthope is the first Englishman in the field with
his own large experiment. Let us own the value and
the freshness of much that he has said, and try to trace
his path after him here and there.

He begins very far back. His picture of the Empire
and the Papacy and of mediaeval polity is a portico to
the history of all modern culture, not merely to that of
English poetry. His picture, in the second volume, of
the ideas of Luther, Macchiavelli, and their time is a
portico to the study of all the later Renaissance. Luther
and Macchiavelli touch our poetry, it is true, but they
touch our prose more, and of that Dr. Courthope is not
writing. The building, when we get inside it, is not in
the same style or on the same scale as the portico. But
let us not complain; it is good to come to our poetry
with the murmur of Renaissance thought, or of mediaeval
thought, in our ears, and no other historian has tried to
come to it that way. But Dr. Courthope does not begin
well. The 'poetry of the Anglo-Saxons' is coldly and
ungratefully hurried over, its deep affinities with the
Northern and other Germanic verse are not seen, and
for an antidote we turn to Mr. W. P. Ker's *Epic and
Romance*, that understanding essay on the old Germanic
genius. But Dr. Courthope's chapter on 'The Early
Renaissance' is a good example of his peculiar power.
He gives us a real setting for the appreciation of Langland and of Chaucer. They are seen not as unexplained
miracles, but as sons of their age and of England. Wider
natural sympathy might have saved the historian from

comparing Boccaccio, whose pot of basil is ever fresh, with Milton's Belial, and from lecturing Chaucer, whose *fabliaux* show his genius more than anything except his *Troilus and Cressida*, for 'illegitimate coarseness and materialism'. And the alliterative romances of that age might have been better honoured. A word is due to their always stately matter and their often lovely form, for their form links two ages of our verse together, while their matter links England with Europe.

These, then, are lapses; but it is more grateful to hear Dr. Courthope where he is on his own ground. The chapter already mentioned on the early Renaissance might be quoted at length in illustration. There he traces some of the sentiments that began in the fourteenth century to be transmitted from the ancient to the modern world; not only by Petrarch, whose work as a torch-bearer is well understood, but, as is less often perceived, by Dante, whose conception of civic duty and nobility is by no means strictly mediaeval, resting as it does on 'the antique image of Roman citizenship'. The useful essay on 'Chaucer and Petrarch', in the *Studj Petrarcheschi* of Signor Carlo Segrè, has come out since Dr. Courthope's chapter. But the account of the *Romance of the Rose* and its influence, and of the course of allegory at the close of the Middle Ages, show Dr. Courthope's hold on those remote causes and subtle uniformities without which our poetry is unintelligible.

Allegory as it was understood and used by Dante, the accepted method of interpreting nature and Scripture, derived from the Platonized theology of the fifth and sixth centuries, and methodized in the system of the schoolmen, first becomes a mechanical part of poetry, and then slowly falls into disuse, in proportion as the scholastic logic itself gives way before the new experimental tests applied to the interpretation of nature. Allegory, again, regarded as a literary form of expression, has its original source in the genius for abstraction peculiar to the Latin language, which encouraged the use of the figure of personification in poetry. In this sphere it enjoyed a longer life than in philosophy. . . . Lastly, the habit, common to the mediaeval poets, of inventing allegories, in which all these abstract personages should be grouped round the central figure of Love, had, doubtless, its far-off origin in the metaphysical conception of Eros pervading the Platonic philosophy. . . . A stream of kindred sentiment . . . coloured the whole code of chivalrous manners; and, from the new impulse thus given to the ancient Teutonic reverence for women, the troubadours, by the aid of Ovid and of models borrowed from the Arabs, developed the elaborate system of Provençal love poetry. The lyrical fervour of the Provençals, in the cooling atmosphere of the times, gradually became in its turn conventional and didactic; and the long series of allegories following the *Romance of the Rose* is mainly interesting as marking the fall of temperature in the institutions of chivalry (vol. i, pp. 391, 392).

This passage, with its wide sweep of learned vision, shows Dr. Courthope at his best; he gives us an observatory whence we can scan the whole range of fifteenth-century poetry in Scotland, and much in sixteenth-century England. The true method of history is here applied to the life-chronicle of a literary form; it has not been done before, or not so well, in our language, and an example is given from which Mr. Courthope's successors have no excuse for relapsing. His chapter on the ballads needs reviewing in the light of arguments advanced recently by Mr. Gregory Smith, Mr. Lang, and others. The 'Retrospect', at the end of the first volume, which brings the whole story down to the verge of the English Renaissance, is of finer quality, and contains one of the significant thoughts that help to sustain us through the apparent welter and disharmony of late mediaeval verse.

In each class, epic, lyric, and dramatic, we see a movement away from the original didactic purpose of poetry, either towards the direct imitation of nature, or towards the more technical development of art (p. 471). . . . But while the principal forms of modern poetry have their origin in the ecclesiastical and feudal character of the Middle Ages, they are gradually modified by the whole movement of society towards a civil standard of life and thought.

This conception forms one of the texts of the succeeding volumes. Poetry was coloured by the successive polities under which it flourished, and varied according as these were predominantly ecclesiastical and monarchical, or civic and secular. It also varied with its public, which is the most powerful and often the most destructive part of the artist's contemporary environment. The form and soul of our drama varied much, according as this public was the people or the Court. Dr. Courthope's sketch of the setting and drift of early Tudor poetry suffers in proportion. He surveys, at more length than they deserve even as symptoms, the dreary Turbervile and Churchyard, who clear the weeds away so little for the genius of Spenser or Sidney. But the powers of Dr. Courthope, as well as his less fortunate qualities, can best be judged as we approach the poetry of genius, in its two great species, as they pass before us from Spenser to Milton, and from Marlowe to Ford.

V

The weak side of a studious, ambitious essay seeking to *explain* poetry is that, while really doing a good deal, it has the air of seeming to do more than is possible. The book before us is less a history of poetry than a history of certain impersonal forces which from age to age tended to prescribe its form and aim and to beleaguer it about. They play upon each artist in differing proportion, fitfully, and with no steady pressure. But there are other forces that lie beyond analysis, namely, those which move the artist, and decide how he shall *choose* among these floating tendencies in the mind of his time, how he shall combine or alter them, what he shall make of them. Tendencies, it must be repeated, have no real existence, except in the shapes in which the individual mind chooses to submit to them. We only know them through the concrete manifestations from which we then make our generalities. The mind is not a cauldron in which certain ingredients simmer mechanically, so that a certain result can be expected. No, the Time-Spirit says a charm over the cauldron, and unborn shapes arise out of it ; it is only a third-rate writer who can be analysed away into 'influences'. Thus an analyst of tendencies, when he comes to the actual master, and the actual poem, can only make his diagnosis sound up to the last step but one, unless he also has a measure of the divining sympathy, which is a kind of feminine counterpart of the artist's own creative force.

Hence a writer like Dr. Courthope is better in dealing with significant secondary figures like Massinger or Drummond than with larger men ; for his analysis carries him up to the very verge of their comparatively narrow ring of personality, and *they* can be stated in terms of historic tendencies. But the great initiators—Marlowe, Shakespeare, Donne—though from one point of view they absorb and express larger elements of historic growth than the others, are not only harder to diagnose from such considerations, because the forces are more intricate, but actually refuse to be stated in such terms, ultimately, at all. Marlowe is seen in clearer light, certainly, as the embodiment of a ruling mood of the Renaissance, the worship of energy, *virtù*, or, as Dr. Courthope calls it, 'will-worship'; but his real characteristic lies in the form, the voice, he gives to that impulse. And this form and voice are found in the depths of his magic style, in his turn of phrase, in his peculiar tone of passion. No amount of history can give an account of this; nothing, indeed, can ever express it fully; but the nearest approaches can be made by a fellow-poet, like Mr. Swinburne, who writes new poetry upon Marlowe, or criticism that is poetry in all but metre.

Dr. Courthope's scope and limitations are well seen in the case of Donne, on whom he throws new and true light—the light of history, which has never been thrown on Donne so clearly before. It is curious with how little sympathy it is done, and how instructive it is all the same; for Dr. Courthope's account of the historic setting is not in the least brain-spun or capricious; it is solidly based and charged with learning. Donne is taken out of the region of mere anomaly and miracle in which he is too often left by the critics. In him we trace (the phrasing is my own) the logical and dividing habit of the school-divine, a habit applied equally to the sacred matters of faith and fear and to the profaner matters of love and lust; the two worlds, sacred and profane, being

L

joined and confounded at every turn by this pervading
temper that is applied to them. The course of Donne's
thought is traced, perhaps more positively than the
vague dates of his poems warrant, through the successive
phases of belief, of pyrrhonism or nihilism, and of faith
again triumphant; the whole man, in these different
phases, being bound together by the intellectual habit,
carefully defined, of 'wit'. Thus Donne is a sensitive
mirror of many impulses of his time. He remains
a living exponent of the temporary Counter-Renaissance,
or re-emergence of mediaeval habits of mind after the
glow of the Renaissance was spent. All this is to the
good: but there is something more to say, and a passage
that we shall quote later from a different critic, Mr. Saintsbury, will supply what is wanting—the hint of the inner
personality of Donne. Flaubert, in his words on Taine,
put the point very clearly:—

Il y a autre chose dans l'art que le milieu où il s'exerce
et les antécédents physiologiques de l'ouvrier. Avec ce
système-là, on explique la série, le groupe, mais jamais
l'individualité, le fait spécial qui fait qu'on est *celui-là*.
Cette méthode amène forcément à ne faire aucun cas de
talent. Le chef-d'œuvre n'a plus de signification que
comme document historique. Voilà radicalement l'in-
verse de la vieille critique de La Harpe. Autrefois, on
croyait que la littérature était une chose toute personnelle
et que les œuvres tombaient du ciel comme des aérolithes.
Maintenant on nie toute volonté, tout absolu. La vérité
est, je crois, dans l'entre-deux.[108]

I would not saddle Dr. Courthope, whose 'system'
is much sounder than that which Flaubert criticizes, with
the whole of this rebuke, which he often escapes when
he permits himself to give a direct judgement. His words
on Herrick make us ask for more of the same kind. He
thus comments on 'The Funeral Rites of the Rose':—

This exquisiteness of fancy, working on a great variety of subjects—flowers, precious stones, woman's dress, religious ritual, and the like—finds its happiest field in the region of folklore. Shakespeare had already shown the way to this delightful country in the *Tempest*, in the *Midsummer Night's Dream*, and *Romeo and Juliet*. . . . But it may safely be said that none of these creations, not even Shakespeare's description of Queen Mab, surpasses in lightness of touch, or equals in the rich profusion of imagery, Herrick's Euphuistic treatment of the elves (iii. 364).

The whole of Dr. Courthope's survey of seventeenth-century verse, of what I have called the Counter-Renaissance, and of the reassertion of the Latin Renaissance in a fresh and more limited shape during Dryden's time, has the same powers and drawbacks. His classification of the labyrinthine schools of verse under various forms of 'wit' leads to a true and deep analysis of 'wit' itself. His summing up of the influences that went to the making of Milton's *Paradise Lost*, and of the equally complex style which could be its only fit expression, is a triumph of his method, of his skill in bringing many historic rays to converge upon one object. On the other hand, his apprehension of many lesser poets remains a little blank; his connoisseurship, or sense of varieties in accent and gesture, is faint. It is best to illustrate from his chapters on the drama, on which he has spent great care, and which are almost as instructive for what they leave out as for what they say.

Dr. Courthope's high sympathies deaden, it must be said, his understanding of the drama of remote or anomalous passion, however wonderful its style may be. He is capable of quoting the best passages of Cyril Tourneur, with their sombre strangeness of jewelled phrase, at Tourneur's expense. He can slight the fitful but rare tragic talent of Middleton in spite of those central scenes of *The Changeling*, which would have done honour to the author of *Measure for Measure*. He administers an official rebuke to Charles Lamb, for his 'ecstatic' praises of the minor dramatists, on the ground that it raises in the mind 'an idea of the colossal greatness of all the Elizabethan dramatists, which is by no means sustained when their works are examined organically'. Not only is this to visit the mistakes of foolish readers upon Lamb, whose praises are far more carefully defined and qualified than at first appears, but it is to forget how Lamb was moved to his eloquence by that inebriation with language and with a passionate situation well presented, from which Dr. Courthope may be a signed abstainer, but which none the less is the nearest way to reproduce the exalted moods of the playwrights themselves in their creative hour. It is not unfair, it is even refreshing, for the historian to call Marston's *Antonio and Mellida* a 'jumbled hash of bloody recollections'. But nothing can invalidate the happy rightness of Lamb's praise of the prologue to the same play, with its 'passionate earnestness and tragic note of preparation'.

It is right to add that Dr. Courthope falls into his own extreme, not merely from a certain ethical rigidity, but under the sway of one motive that is really and purely artistic. Trained in the classics, he has a real, a sound, and often an offended sense of dramatic structure. Our drama suffers under the test; but suffer it must, and the test is applied with courage. Logic, outline, harmony, consequence—our plays, so often written to be seen and heard, and written under stress, usually fail in these qualities; Shakespeare himself often fails in them. In

English criticism the sense of form and beauty is too often limited to style and expression, and too seldom extends to outline and harmony. Dr. Courthope is always calling aloud for plastic mastery in our drama, and in vain.

VI

Some of Dr. Courthope's conclusions upon matters of fact and authorship, especially in the case of Shakespeare, are sure to excite discussion. He has the right to his own plan, which is not to load his page with titles, learned apparatus, or discussion of the views of other scholars. But it is not always easy to see how far he has studied, and how far rejected, their views. He names Elze and Ulrici, whose simple-minded moralizing of Shakespeare has long been exploded, but he seems to make no use of the contributions of Kreyssig, or Bulthaupt, or Brandes, all of whom would have given him aid. In exegesis he seems to work alone, and to infer easily. He holds that Shakespeare wrote *The Troublesome Reign of King John*, *The Taming of a Shrew* (as well as *The Taming of* the *Shrew*); that *The Tempest*, at all events in its first conception, is a play of the period of the *Dream*, and is identical with *Love's Labour Won*, mentioned by Meres; and that he may dismiss *Henry VIII* as too 'mechanical' to be considered in a history of Shakespeare's art, saying nothing about the deeply-considered view of many scholars that part of it is by Fletcher. Reasons of style and diction, which have to be weighed in advancing a new claimant for the admission to the Shakespearean canon, do not seem to be considered in the case of the *Troublesome Reign* and *A Shrew*, and the other pleas advanced for them, though too elaborate to be discussed here, are weak for so great a conclusion. The dislocation of *The Tempest* from its accepted place not only misinterprets the evidence of language, versification, temper, and subject, but rests upon the frail support of the prologue to *Every Man in His Humour*, in which Jonson refers to storms, stage thunder, and the popularity of 'monsters'. The allusion to monsters is not strong enough to warrant an application to Caliban; and a stage tempest was familiar already in Marlowe. Even if written earlier, as some argue, the Prologue was not printed till the folio edition of Jonson's works in 1616.

In judging the drama Dr. Courthope steadily applies three principles, which are just ones and carry him far. He is on the watch for structure and its absence; he constantly applies the touchstone of a high chivalrous feeling; and thirdly, in tracing the historic pattern, he finds its main theme in the spiritual or moral conceptions that animated the successive schools of playwrights. He has little sympathy with the Marlowesque drama, or seems to admire it unwillingly; but he is right in regarding it, with its concentration on *virtù*, or personal energy desirous and defiant, as a kind of by-product, not really in the main line of dramatic development. And he shows, more clearly than other critics, and even with too much emphasis, how the motive of the old 'Morality', namely, the abstract conflict between personifications of good and evil, strikes deep and far into the drama of Jonson, of Massinger, and to some extent of Shakespeare. Dr. Courthope's incessant and wavering use of the word 'abstract', which sometimes means 'remote from life and reality', and elsewhere suggests moral personifications of virtue and vice, may not be approved; but no doubt, in spite of the elements from Stoical ethics, which came in

later to strengthen and ennoble the bare old forms of the
' Morality ', it is true that there is a real continuity of
moral topic, appearing under many disguises, in the
drama ; so that Massinger, of whom Dr. Courthope gives
a masterly account, derives by a true pedigree, though
unconsciously, from the ruder but genuinely theatrical
forms of art represented in *Everyman*. To unravel this
one thread out of the motley strand of artistic influences
that bewilder the student of the drama, is a service.
The remarks on the nature of melodrama; on the
different notions of love in Shakespeare and in Fletcher ;
on the ' atmosphere of humanity and society' in
Shakespeare's comedies; on Ford, whose ' lack of sympathy ' in dealing with abnormal passion and ' abstract
curiosity' are pointed out with much insight ; and the
account of Dryden's *All for Love* as a Gallicized
Antony and Cleopatra, are but a few examples more
of Mr. Courthope's felicity on his own ground. After
our many criticisms we prefer to end with another
searching piece of analysis, in which the extinction of the
chivalrous idea of love is traced in the work of Dryden.

Love in the poetry of the Middle Ages reveals itself
in two aspects ; it is either a Platonized reflection of the
old Teutonic reverence for women, or it is a school of
knightly manners, where the castled aristocracy may
cultivate a peculiar system of sentiment and language,
distinguishing their order from the plebeian world around
them. Dante's Beatrice and Spenser's Una are the
representatives of one class ; Guillaume de Lorris's new
version of the art of love, in *The Romance of the Rose*,
is the type of the other. The former conception breathes
its spirituality into the beautiful characters of Shakespeare's women, making the unselfishness of Viola, the
patience of Imogen, and the purity of Isabella, at once
ideal and credible. The latter inspires the elaborate
code framed by the female canonists and casuists of the

' Code d'Amour ', which, embodied first of all in the treatise of André le Chapelain, *De Amore*, and adapted to the manners of a later time by Castiglione in his *Cortegiano*, formed the basis of social etiquette in every court of Europe, and was reflected with all the hectic colouring of decline in the comedy of Fletcher (iv. 452).

Dr. Courthope's *History* is thus an experiment of high worth in the philosophical chronicle of literature, revealing as it does the play of many forces, partly ancestral, partly international, partly both, upon literary art.

VII

Professor Saintsbury's *Short History of English Literature* does not show these preoccupations at all strongly, though the author is learned in the writings of many lands. He loses something by this omission; he loses more by almost excluding from his view the intellectual stuff of literature. But he holds finely and firmly to the central clue that writing is an art, and that structure and style are forms of beauty which it is the main affair of the critic to detect and love. He knows that the business of the artist is to give a series of unique pleasures, while that of the critic is to find words for them. Within the limits of the nation, or with only casual references to foreign influence, he has applied the same canon of design and proportion to his own history, laying out in a single volume, which has only been as yet half appreciated, the natural epochs, groups, and outlines, in just perspective. Some drawbacks cannot be ignored. A few errors of detail have been marked down by reviewers with tasteless ferocity. These can be remedied. There is a touch or two of political or ecclesiastical predilection. We hear that 'Hooker's work utterly ruined, from the logical and historical side, the position of the English Puritans'. But if we once begin upon that! The sentence might have been spared in a work where the artistic standpoint is else maintained with dignity. Then, some caprice is shown in the recognition of philological inquiry and its results. They do not profess to do the work of the aesthetic critic, but are there to be used by him. It really does matter to all of us how we sort the poems of the Cynewulfian and Cædmonian schools, and only the linguists can give us the data ; but in the *Short History* the subject is treated with some impatience. Nor is it unfair to point to passages of hasty or parenthetic writing, which might have been spared by an artist in criticism.

Yet Mr. Saintsbury has written the most catholic record of our literature. He has a steady will to enjoy all that is good of every kind, and to give expression to the reason why he does so—a simple creed, and 'pleasant when one considers it', but rare among critics, who are for ever led off either by the British bane of blind whim or by the other mania of vaporous theorizing. Such an open temper— which is the boon of nature nurtured by schooling—ready to perceive the goodness or badness of the handiwork, and the peculiar virtue of the form chosen by each artist, is uncommon. It is present in the *Short History* ; and so is the power of orderly grouping. Thus the vague bibliography, that often does duty in England for a history of letters, falls into an intelligible pattern. It is something to cover the country from Widsith to Tennyson, and from Alfred to Carlyle, in such a spirit. Lightness and cheeriness of step are wanted to carry the pilgrim all that way, and in Mr. Saintsbury they are not absent.

I do not care to compare him with the other scholar

I have reviewed here, save to say that their gifts curiously supplement one another. But, like all good and practised travellers, Mr. Saintsbury has two distinct moods of admiration. There is the general disposition to praise whatever is fair, or even is strangely expressive, whether it be in Hobbes or Newman or Shelley or Drunken Barnabee ; thus obeying the commandment of Plato to ' rejoice wherein we ought to rejoice '. But sometimes the pilgrim is quickened to a different mood altogether, and then his criticism is of the kind which tells us most about both parties to it, and which irritates pedants because it does not pretend to be like a judge's charge. That man is to be pitied who does not get more out of Lamb's sentence that Heywood is a 'kind of prose Shakespeare', than out of the reflection that it is exaggerated. We feel the change quickly when, amid the more level and restrained survey proper to a long history, a critic with ample learning and canons behind him lifts his voice. There are authors we chance on, and find they were always ours ; and we resent that an opinion should be ventured on them by others. Their voice calls up the echoes of our private whispering-gallery. They may not be the greatest of men. But they make us eloquent whether we will or no, and what we say of them is better remembered than the tempered findings of the historic intellect. For want of such passion, much of the criticism of our time wanders away into the useful field of science. Donne, we have seen, is a difficult poet to divine. Mr. Saintsbury explains in what sense he is a ' metaphysical ' poet.

For, behind every image, every ostensible thought of his, there are vistas and backgrounds of other thoughts dimly vanishing, with glimmers in them here and there into the depths of the final enigmas of life and soul. Passion and meditation, the two avenues into this region of doubt and dread, are tried by Donne in the two sections respectively, and of each he has the key. Nor, as he walks in them with eager and solemn tread, are light and music wanting, the light the most unearthly that ever played round a poet's head, the music not the least heavenly that he ever caught and transmitted to his readers. If this language seems more high-flown than is generally used in this book, or than is appropriate to it, &c.

No excuse is wanted! we all wish we could speak of our chosen authors as well. Nay, yet more in this strain would be welcome, upon Donne himself, upon Fielding, upon Tennyson ; all of these Mr. Saintsbury has praised, in one work or another, with his own eloquence. Without some such interludes the mapping of international currents and the watching of impersonal forces become a vain thing. The *Short History* is therefore to be saluted for its completeness within its own scale, its clear historic grouping, its avoidance of crowding, its catholic connoisseurship, and its timely betrayal of preferences. Such books, without seeming to do so, serve in their own way that dream of a federal literature which cannot be too often enunciated.

A WORD ON MYSTICISM

I. Meaning of the Term : the 'Passion for Nonentity'. II. Seventeenth-century Mysticism.   III. Intuition and Error.   IV. The four things illuminated by the Mystics : (1) The Insufficiency of Works; (2) The 'Night of the Soul'.   V. (3) The Claims of the 'Unconscious'; (4) The Desire for Vision.   VI. Validity of the Revelation :   (a) Mysticism proves nothing; (b) Anaesthetic 'Nirvana'; (c) Metaphor taken for Truth.   VII. The Saner Mysticism.

I

Mysticism, in the religious meaning, is the historic title for a special discipline or frame of the soul, through which it seeks to be literally at one with the highest reality of which it knows.   The aim is not merely to understand, but to enter into, or become, this First Reality.   A man may draw close, in sympathy and intelligence, to the mind of another ; or he may see with rapture some crowning truth of science or speculation. But the mystic demands more than this ; *he* wishes to go, by virtue of a faculty beyond reason, higher up the path of knowledge than reason can ever take him ; and the last step of his journey is marked by some act of absorption, communion, or 'vision'.   There is a whole dialect for this breakdown of the personality, which in European mysticism is usually thought of as happening during earthly life, and not as leading at once to another state of being.   Plotinus speaks of 'contact'; his Cambridge recruit, John Smith the preacher, of 'knitting a man's centre, if he have any, unto the centre of divine being';[109] others of *animi extensio in Deum*; Sir Thomas Browne, in his musical enumeration, of 'Christian annihilation, ecstasies, exolution, liquefaction, transformation, the kiss of the spouse, gustation of God, and ingression into the divine shadow';—and these, he says, are a 'handsome anticipation of heaven' to any that have been 'so happy as truly to understand' them. We ask without delay, whether this aspiration is to be thought of as sane, and its hope as valid? Or is it one of the void, self-defeating impulses of man, resting on some illusion that recurs perhaps for ever? Even so, what light does it throw upon the history and pageant of the human spirit? Or is it not a metaphor, misread into a doctrine, but resting on some facts and needs of human nature which we are bound to discover and state rationally? Will any transformed religion simply dismiss, or must it not reckon with and welcome, mysticism? Such questions are prompted by Professor William James's book on *The Varieties of Religious Experience*,[110] where new facts are marshalled and some of the vital issues cleared.

The true type and parent-nerve of mysticism seems to be found in the higher Hindu and Buddhist systems. In these, the First Reality is regarded as a bare abstract unity without differences. The pilgrim puts off, husk by husk, the illusion of this motley world and the evil of phenomenal existence, in order at last to be drawn and merged into the One. The hindrance is desire, which is left behind after a long training. 'If you asked a Hindu, whether priest or peasant,' says Sir Alfred Lyall,[111] 'what is the ultimate good to be aimed at, he would answer, "Liberation," by which he means the freedom of the soul from its bondage of union to the body, to anything that has sensation, and its return to the infinite spirit whence it issued.' The Buddhist philosophy, it is well known, is non-theistic ; its nearest equivalent in the West is that of Schopenhauer, who also measures spiritual progress by the extinction of desire and of all the 'will to live'.[112] But he places the goal, not in any experience that involves a breach with the normal process of thought, but in the dismissal of egoism through ascetic practice and sympathy, and in the perception of the pure Ideas or types that are embodied in works of beautiful art. With the Neoplatonists, the last great masters of Greek thinking, the One figures at the apex of their system, lying beyond not only Soul and Mind but Existence itself; and their chief, Plotinus, had rare and short ecstasies in which he attained to union with it. This 'passion for nonentity', as it has well been called, lies at the heart of much Western and Christian mysticism, but in disguise. The churches have bred and sheltered many varieties of it, which have all had for their aim and pretension a privileged approach to the Highest. But each creed, by precise contracts and dogmas, is for ever defining its own divinity. The old, foreign, pagan First Reality, which often was not named God at all, and which seems all negatives—neither anything, nor everything, nor yet avowedly nothing—becomes specified and humanized. Contact with that rarefied entity had been the ideal limit of contemplation. But in such a blank summit-whiteness the Western mystic, whilst ever pressing thither, can hardly breathe, and he halts on many a ridge and platform, which is tinted by our atmosphere and reached by human sounds from the valleys. Notions of love and goodness, drawn from man, are placed to the credit of God, and 'imputed for righteousness'. And the mystic, when he nears his goal, finds these messengers

duly awaiting him.   He forgets that he sent them there,
and he greets them as though for the first time ; he has
had few consolations by the way.   George Fox became
aware, in such a moment, of ' an infinite ocean of love
and goodness'.   Sometimes the vision vouches for the
truth of pre-existing doctrines : St. Teresa [113] was allowed
to see how it is that God can exist in three Persons.   Or
sanction is given to the special theosophy which the
mystic, on his intellectual side, has already elaborated,
just as the ecstasy of the Neoplatonist had given him, in
a state of exalted feeling, a piece of ontology he had
thought out as a philosopher of this world.   But, typi-
cally, the content of the sacred vision is ineffable and
unrememberable ; there is little left of it afterwards but
an overpowering sense that the boundaries of self were
lost for the time.   To the question, how far this experience
is valid for others, or even for the seer after he has quitted
it, we can return.

II

Great flourishing times of Christian mysticism were
the fourteenth, and again the sixteenth and seventeenth
centuries ; from the latter are drawn most of the illustrations given in these stray notes.   The Roman faith,
so old, so adaptive, and sheltering a thousand types of
humanity, has had more time to breed great visionaries
than the seceding Churches.   But mysticism is plainly
closer to the Protestant principle of the direct relationship of the soul to God, and has been more fully trusted
by Protestantism, and has there clashed less with dogma
and authority.   Heppe,[114] a learned historian of the
Quietism that grew up within the Roman fold, writes
from the evangelical point of view, and treats the Catholic

mystics as working blindly towards a truth which is
alien to their own creed. Quietism is the most thorough
example of mysticism in the West, since it lays fullest
stress on the need of passivity in the quest for truth,
and often specifies very little the precise truth given in
vision. In its well-marked forms, it sprang from the
heart of the Roman Church amongst the great Spanish
saints of Shakespeare's time, St. Teresa and St. John of
the Cross. These were only the chiefs of a multitude.
In the seventeenth century, Quietism grew into a suspected and persecuted heresy. Mme. Guyon,[115] in France,
and Molinos, the author of the *Spiritual Guide*, where
the system can be seen laid out and formulated, were
the best-known victims. Fénelon was hurt in the same
contest, which ended in the suppression of the Quietists
by the Church. Cut off from these Catholic mystics,
but resembling them at many points, are Protestants like
Bunyan and Fox ; and a little earlier come those others of
a more intellectual cast, the Platonists of Cambridge, who
go back to the sources. The general lines of later mysticism within the Churches may be fairly studied from
these records, though its most passionate expression is
perhaps found in the German verse of Angelus Silesius.
Our own 'metaphysical' poets of the same period were
often shepherds or members of the Anglican flock,
avoiding the familiarity and bareness of the Protestants
and also the amorous intensity of the Latins. Crashaw,
who found a home in the old faith, has the headlong
rapture of the Spanish dreamers, and the words in his
Flaming Heart throb like the light in a jewel. George
Herbert lives in his word-play of tender and pious
fancies ; Henry Vaughan is occupied with the wonder,
till then little divined in English poetry, that hangs over
common natural things, the flowers and trees ; he seeks,

by absorption in that, to come nearer to the divine being. Traherne, discovered recently, has more mystical dogma than any others of the generation that came to its end amid an alien age in Norris of Bemerton. The clear-cut pantheism of Traherne keeps him apart from his fellows ; he is a kind of English Scheffler,[116] with far more poetry, and without the 'Silesian Angel's' tedious jingle of impudent, sham-logical paradox. The conceit, which is a worse fault in some of the meaner mystics than their sensuality, could hardly go further than this :—

Ich weiss, dass ohne mich Gott nicht ein Nu kann leben ;
Werd ich zu nicht, er muss von Noth den Geist aufgeben.

But this is nearer to the central nihilistic tenet :—

Wer ist, als wär er nicht und wär er nie geworden :
Der ist (o Seligkeit !) zu lauter Gotte worden.

And so here :—

Mensch, wann dich weder Lieb berührt, noch Leid
      verletzt,
So bist du recht in Gott und Gott in dich versetzt.

This is the true *Gelassenheit*, or tranquillity. Scheffler wrote most of his verse as a Protestant, then went over to Rome, but continued in the same strain—a curious proof of the hospitality of either faith to an outspoken pantheist.

III

But so subtle an essence has often escaped the keeping of the Churches and the poets ; it is not confined to the endless companies of pilgrim-souls, each bent on the same journey. Mysticism does not merely appear in these historic organizations. Secular art and letters are

M

full of it; the rudiment of its temper is in all our lives. Whenever we wait for that which is farthest within us; when we are left alone with it, and lie still, and let it play upon us; when we trust it, and say it is the best, or the truth; and when, at last, in flashes or vision, we believe that it comes from without or from above; then, our state of mind is mystical. The essence lies in this state of mind; the subject-matter, the special truth or opinion resulting, is an historic accident. A daily experience may be cited for the double purpose of exhibiting this, and of noting what are the only terms on which discussion may be judged possible.

Men's intuitions of one another—'first impressions' as we call them—so often false, but also so often confirmed by last impressions, which are the sum of experience, while second thoughts may be warped by theory or foolish tolerance or intolerance, or beguiled by actual intercourse—these judgements seem to tell us, after all, less of what our neighbour is in himself, than of what he is to *us*. Shall we have anything to say to the newcomer, or will he tend to defeat and obstruct us? The shudder of the virtuous maiden or her confidant in popular melodrama, when the villain comes upon the stage, only parodies a fact. Do not women share most in those perceptions of friend and foe which the animal species have survived by possessing, and is not the breed of our race staked on their sagacity? Is it not known that children have a quicker sense of these things, just as they often have of odours, than we have, and that old men of business act wisely on prejudice? Such messages from the animal sensibilities are no oracle, but the fruit of inherited and swiftly registered thought. They are matter for science, though her methods can hardly catch up to these sensible dial-pointers and alarm-calls of the nerves. And the waiting, the flash that seems neither the work of reason nor of ourselves—though it is actually both—the confidence, the readiness to submit, are all marks of the mystical attitude.

But *error !* it will be said ; error and superstition wait on such a temper. The intuitions may be whim or counterfeit, and the trust in them fatal ; the need to correct them is perpetual. Of course—because they are the work of *reason*. Only reason can go wrong. A mere feeling (if the phrase means anything), can tell us nothing but its own existence. Our intuitions, or swifter processes rooted in the latent reason, and our explicit thinking, are congeners, as the hare and tortoise are both animals. The man of intuitions, therefore, is the first who ought to take the oath to reason. He must not be content with half her gifts. He must regulate his faith by the check of normal experience and evidence. His truth did not come to him from some authority that broke with reason by superior right, but from a manifestation, fallible like any other, of reason. He therefore must accept the jurisdiction of the court of reason. But then the ordinary mystic will not take that oath. *His* voices are inspired ; other truth must give way to them ; they are not to be checked by the body of known truth that has accumulated. Such a point of view held good against the old rationalism, which denied any kind of value to the voices themselves, merely saw those aberrations of 'enthusiasm' [117] which they were taken to authorize, allowed in its psychology for nothing but explicit thought, and did not know that mystical intuitions may be the secret and fruitful labour of Thought itself, afterwards to be verified by evidence and reason. The new mystic, if he is to keep any credit at all, must come to terms with the new science. He may learn his path in the darkness, and crave a vision of some ineffable grail or rosy crown of knowledge. But he must see to the cleansing of his own sanctuary, and have his revelations tested, if they are to stand, by the same scrutiny as other forms of truth ; otherwise a formidable chapter of history weighs him down. Many examples for the student of madness, crime, and pathology can be gathered from the chronicle of the mystics ; the well-known old collection of Görres[118] has often been supplemented. False ecstasy, cruel superstitions and crazes, and sexual perversion masking as religion, abound, and insulted nature can hardly be grudged her revenges. In other fields we come upon corruptions of the intellect which are marked by mystical symptoms—the passiveness, the abandonment of mind, the refusal to bear the touch of truth. Many Western theosophists are educated and high-minded. But others are not ; to spend time with them or their books is to be present at a scene of vulgarity and mental weakness. Vulgarity—that is the danger of the cheap mystic, who lacks instruction, and sees no need of it, and presumes on a supposed short cut he has found to truth. Of truth, of *his* truth, he speaks with the familiarity that some people use in speaking of 'the Lord'. The work of rescuing any promising soul from these quagmires ought to be part of a reasonable educational programme. I do not digress to such matters as spiritualism ; much of it stands to the true folklore whence it springs as the sophisticated sister pacing the pavement with her lures stands to the simple peasant, who is left at home and recites a charm to bring her lover.

IV

Among the educated, indeed, it may now be more necessary to plead for the honest mystics than for science. It is well to notice some of the traits or needs in human nature which they, more sharply than any one else, have revealed. Leaving both theosophy and mere wonder-working aside, we may see the value of these records to the beginner in the natural history of man. For that is the true attitude ; we need be neither initiates nor scorners. On four things at least in human nature the mystics have thrown a powerful searchlight:—

1. The protest of the soul against the sufficiency of outer forms, of external good behaviour, of *works*.

2. The tragical experience, termed the *night of the soul* by some writers.

3. The need of trusting the *unconscious* ; the need of *passivity* in the soul's progress.

4. The desire, already noted, for *vision* or revelation.

All these things, we may well hold, must be regarded in any new reading of religion, for they seem, by all the evidence, chronic phenomena of mind. Any creed or code drawn on naturalistic lines will find those who have experience of the needs above specified facing it as patients face a new physician. I speak of a religion for those that are sick, who are a large proportion. For those that are whole a word will be added at the conclusion. Surely the failure, among the people, of a creed like positivism, on many sides so free, so noble, is due to an imperfect psychology that has waived aside the phenomena disclosed by historic mysticism.

1. *The protest against forms and works.* Mystics, unless kept down, are always dissenters. They may obey the rules of their cult, but they win a circle of

freedom within it. They do not deny ritual, but they leave it behind. The authority of their hierarchy soon fails to reach the recesses of their experience. The mystic, left more and more alone with the God whom his Church supplies in the first instance, tends to modify Him; and sometimes a strange new theosophy arises, which the Church resents, as in the case of Eckhart.[119] All this means that the Church in question has not yet found the right food for certain natures; under its shelter, often amid its distrust, an instinct leads them to find their own nourishment. That is well, for it makes for life, for new self-expression, away from officialism, away from the fixed and revered forms, which have *not*, as the event shows, expressed everything. Also, the relation of mysticism to morality has been peculiar. Within the Churches it has usually implied an ascetic, sometimes a savage, discipline, as a preparation for the initiate's journey. And those ideas of supreme goodness and beauty, which already belong to his definition of God, sometimes, as we said, accompany the traveller to the summit of his vision. But it is not essential to him that they should do so. Although many, like St. Teresa, were notable missionaries, still after a certain stage in the journey moral discipline ceases to be prominent, and the aspirant moves in a world 'on the further side of good and evil', out of hearing of the distinction between them. His course of 'contemplation' is, in some sects, technically distinguished from the lower one of 'meditation', which is occupied purely with perfect behaviour. And the theological conception of sin seems to bulk for less among the Roman Quietists than among the Protestants.

And the value of this point of view, the insight it shows into our wants, is evident. What divines call the insufficiency of 'works' (however necessary or desirable these may be) the mystic emphasizes keenly. Take a man of middle life, in strong health, with means enough, and the recognized sources of personal happiness:—love, a family, a good record for honour and charitable practice, a business or career to improve, perhaps the hope of becoming notable. Most of his friends still survive; he has few disasters or estrangements behind him, and his share of natural sorrows has not overpowered him. Let him conform without strain to the ruling religion of his climate, practising its forms much as he takes exercise, or let him dissent from it almost as thoughtlessly. There are many such men, who do much of the work of the world; most of them go on to the end in the same way. But one out of a thousand is different. In his nature there is something unawakened, and he becomes discontented. His peace and complacency are vexed; he sees that the supposed sources of happiness are not enough, that works are not enough. He is led to cast back to the unknown springs and hitherto latent needs of his personality. He must come to terms with himself, and see what he is when alone with himself. To have a good conscience about his personal behaviour is not nearly enough. The sense beats in on him that he has lived with illusions. Even if this sense is itself an illusion, it carries him into a new planet of experience. It is idle to ask him to go back; he must go through. There may be an immense review and transmutation of all the spiritual values hitherto accepted as ultimate. This seems to be a first step that is common to various kinds of mysticism. The form that such an experience may take varies widely. Often one of the authorized creeds, especially of the Protestant kind, is there to satisfy the need, and the change is called conversion. The sense of sin, the consciousness of grace, and final assurance after pain, follow. But this familiar history, though it has mystical elements, is not of the extreme mystical type. Its aim is not to win a beatified vision on earth, but to be at peace about a posthumous heaven.

The chronicle of Tolstoy reveals another course. Part of the picture I have just drawn, of a man who becomes dissatisfied with a life that seems quite satisfactory to others, applies to Tolstoy. He, too, works out, as he thinks, a wholly new set of spiritual values; he preaches the insufficiency of the usual code, the need of a change of heart. He is still more akin to the mystic in his aversion to outward forms and institutions, and in his tragic experience, which consists not in outward drama or misfortune, but is enacted wholly within. On the other hand, Tolstoy leaves the path of the mystic abruptly; he does not work for ecstasy, but searches for a new morality to practise. He tries not to get rid of the real world, but to put himself right with it. But the Protestant, the follower of Tolstoy, and the thoroughgoing mystic, have more in common than their discontent with forms and the common objects of endeavour. In various fashion, they all pass through a phase of feeling, in the record of which we may find their second great contribution to our knowledge of human nature.

2. *The night of the soul.* The mystic has known this: and he who has known it has begun to be a mystic. It is a state of darkness and apathy; not always of acute pain, for the very sources of pain, remedial and curative, as well as of joy, seem cut off. It is a state without tears, without ebb and flow, and without passion; a state as of men drawing hard breath under a low, oppressive sky, and pacing round in the sand without seeming goal or

progress, or even regress, while strange wings brush their faces without their caring; a tonelessness, in which good things once thought of as a possession unforgettable are only remembered as faint in the distance; a *dryness*, to use the special term of the mystics themselves; a form of desperate listlessness or *accidia*, the seventh deadly fault of the old list, figured by Dante [120] under the image of persons buried in the slime and sending only bubbles of air to the surface. The Christian mystics are among our authorities on this condition, which they describe with a power comparable to that of the tragedians. They are the Hamlets of the religious life. The experience, so far from being their monopoly, is common to man; and hence their records are valuable; for they show it in an acute isolation, where we can study it as a physiologist studies an isolated nerve in a conscious living creature.

Professor James gives many instances; another may be added from the merciless and superb St. John of the Cross, [121] who earned the name of the 'Ecstatic Doctor', and died in 1591. St. John carries an air of iron high breeding into his dealings with the Divine, which contrasts well with the unmannerly or enervate familiarity of many mystics; though he revels like them, after attainment, in the usual interpretation of the *Song of Songs*. *The Ascent of Mount Carmel*, a rugged, barefoot climb; the *Obscure Night of the Soul*; the *Flame of Living Love*—the titles of his books hint of his severity and intensity. He wrote within the bounds of the faith, and invented no theosophy. Calvin did not try more wholly to quell every spark of personal pride and life in the pilgrim. And yet, for the journey commanded by John of the Cross, how much of will, of pride, of obstinate self, even while self is being effaced, must be really necessary! With a grandeur of method that becomes insane he strips the soul of one layer of humanity after another, until he leaves it at last naked, abstract, and shivering, but ready for the fierce oppression of divine joys. He carries the soul through a triple night of trial. In the Night of the Sense there is the pain of conquering the vices and appetites, less by direct struggle than by stern diversion. In the Night of the Spirit, not without many snares and lapses, the understanding itself is mortified and killed. In the last Night the pain of abolishing the memory and will must be endured. This is a pitch beyond the world-weariness of Hamlet, who may be called John's spiritual contemporary. The early stages of this journey come nearest to the opiate sorrow of Coleridge, whose ode *Dejection* is the classical utterance in English on the night of the soul :—

> A grief without a pang, void, dark, and drear,
> A stifled, drowsy, unimpassioned grief,
> Which finds no natural outlet, or relief,
> In word, or sigh, or tear.

John of the Cross speaks in the same sense :—

The appetites of sense and spirit are asleep and mortified, without power to savour or relish aught human or divine ; the affections of the soul are oppressed and constrained, without power to stir her or to find a stay in anything ; the imagination is bound up, without force to speak of anything good ; the memory is quenched, and the understanding darkened ; likewise the will is dry and fettered, and all the powers are made void ; and above all this there is a dense and heavy cloud upon the soul, holding it straitened and as though estranged from God.

V

3. The need of escaping from such a state leads all the mystical spirits to see the importance of *Passivity and the Unconscious*. Everywhere they are marked by their insight into that which works upon us without our will taking part and which seems to be not ourselves. In your moments of dryness, they say, wait and acquiesce; struggling will only throw you back to a lower ledge. In a modern figure; a man is in a train, and is being carried forward through a tunnel, without knowing that he is advancing, but only feeling that he is in the dark and is doing nothing. It is not his part to try and jump out of the train and run forward. The same idea is put with dignity by John of the Cross :—

In the hour of the drynesses of this night of the sense . . . the spiritual suffer great pains, not only for the drynesses that they suffer, but for the dread that they have of being lost on this path. They think that the spiritual good has flickered out, and that God hath left them, since they find no stay or relish in anything good. Then they weary themselves, and contrive to find some stay for their faculties on some matter of discourse, after their wont, deeming that when they do not do this or feel themselves at work, they are doing nothing. But they do it not without much disenchantment and inner disgust of their spirit, which was tasting the state of quietness and leisure. And thus, distracting themselves in one wise, they make no way in the other wise; for, by wearing their spirit, they lose the spirit of tranquillity and peace which was theirs. Thus, they are like unto him who should leave the thing that he hath done in order to turn back to it, or to whoso should go out of the city in order to return thither, or, who should give over the chase in order to turn back and renew the chase. . . . And in this season such men, if there be none to understand them, turn back, quitting the path or slackening, or at least bar themselves from going forward. . . . This is excused unto them.

Such a brooding and receptive attitude, in bold contrast with the vulgar advice to strive and cry, is more genially commended by Wordsworth in his counsel of wise passiveness :—

> Think you, amid this mighty sum
> Of things for ever speaking,
> That nothing of itself will come,
> But we must still be seeking?

But it was the mystics who keenly detected, and perhaps were the first to do so, how essential waiting and acquiescence are in the soul's life. A fuller psychology tells us that it is ourselves whom we thus consult and suffer to bear our life onward. The perfectly healthy and opulent mind, no doubt, keeps a kind of balance between its active, missionary, energizing part, and its latent reason, which is suffered to speak in due course. But the old mystics are right in marking how we may go wrong by stirring, by fighting, or by hastening. Where, then, do they find the reward of it all?

4. In *Vision and Illumination.* We are back where we began, with the close of the mystic's book, which opened with a plain, undecorated daylight page of commandment and discipline, and then went forward to litanies and agonies, scrolled round with faint figures of undecipherable pain and colours deepening to black. Suddenly, at last, the page is turned, and a song of escape and triumph follows, with dazzling marginal illuminations ; there is an attempt to paint the sun, which is impossible. Often this wonderful morning of the mystic arrives just after the 'great dereliction', or unpardonable fault. To Bunyan the unlettered, the

severed text has a magical value in procuring his release :—

After I had been in this condition some three or four days, as I was sitting by the fire, I suddenly felt this word to sound in my heart, 'I must go to Jesus.'   At this my former darkness and atheism fled away, and the blessed things of Heaven were set within my view. While I was on this sudden thus overtaken with surprise, Wife, said I, is there ever such a scripture, 'I must go to Jesus'?   She said she could not tell, therefore I sat musing still to see if I could remember such a place. I had not sat above two or three minutes, but that came bolting in upon me, and to an innumerable company of angels, and withal, Hebrews, the twelfth about the Mount Sion, was set before mine eyes.   Then with joy I told my wife, Now I know, I know!   But that night was a good night to me.   I never had but few better.[122]

Bunyan's endless adventures before reaching this goal are like those of the more high-born mystics translated into his quick Saxon of the roads.   His experience, however, is less ambitious and metaphysical.   St. Teresa was allowed 'to see in one instant how all things are seen and contained in God', as in one immense transparent diamond.   'The Lord said these words unto me: She [the soul] unmakes herself, my daughter, to bring herself closer to me.   It is no more she that lives, but I.'

The approaches to this indescribable state are variously told by the mystics, always with a fixed confidence in its reality.   Two centuries earlier, in the German school, the touch of Nihilism is more strongly felt.   The author of the *Theologia Germanica* verges upon it:—

For if the soul shall rise to such a state, she must be quite pure, wholly stripped, and bare of all images, and be entirely separate from all creatures, and, above all, from herself. . . . In the heart [of the man who has attained] there is a content, and a quietness, so that he doth not desire to know more or less, to have, to love, to die, to be or not to be, or anything of the kind. . . . A man cannot find satisfaction in God, unless all things are one to him, and one is all, and something and nothing are alike.

So Tauler, yet more frankly :—

[The soul] should be bare of all things, without need of anything, and then it can come to God in his likeness ; for nothing unites so much as likeness, and receives its colour so soon. . . . Thus its union becomes so intimate that it does not work its works in the form of a creature, but in its divine form, wherein it is united to God. . . . Then, while it beholds God and thus becomes much more united to him, the union may become such that God altogether pours himself into it, and draws it so entirely into himself, that it has no longer any distinct perception of virtue and vice, or recognizes any marks by which it knows what itself is.[122a]

Hegel's account of Nirvana, in his *Philosophy of History*,[123] shows how near these Germans were to the East. 'In this condition of happiness, virtue or vice is out of the question ; for the true blessedness is union with nothingness.'

VI

Many such accounts could be cited of the mystic's goal and prize. The nearer it is to the pure Oriental type, the less talk is there of goodness, or even of happiness. But in many visionaries this indeterminate state is bathed in organic feelings of joy. Wordsworth's reports of the hour when ' Thought was not ', and his experience by Tintern Abbey, are of this kind. And Professor James has gathered reports from a number of persons, many of whom, apparently without any preceding discipline at all, went to the length of having it revealed to them in one instant that this universe is good in essence. Professor James shows that optimism is a frequent feature of the mystical temper. A reason will be offered presently for believing this to be true of an amended, and, if the term may be used, of a rational mysticism. It also seems actually to hold good of many recent visionaries, in the sense that the contents of their vision have been a message of encouragement about the world. On the other hand, in strict logic, as well as in history, optimism is not a necessary ally of mysticism. However it be with Christian initiates, the Buddhist founds his aspiration to Nirvana on the essential evil of life, in which he believes, not as mysteriously revealed, but as a dogma of reasoned truth. He therefore seeks the removal of all bounds that are implied in the terms good and evil, pleasure and pain. And if it is correct to hold this 'passion for nonentity' as the distinctive mood of the consistent mystic, then all conclusions as to the nature of the world, for good or evil, which are drawn from the supposed information furnished in vision, cease to win any further credit from that circumstance. For all such conclusions show that the vision in which they seem to come deviates, or declines, from the pure pattern. Mr. Inge,[124] a refined Anglican scholar, wishing in some way to legitimate the mystics, has treated pure Quietism and the 'negative way' as erratic types. But what, then, is the normal type? It cannot be that which happens to corroborate, as the result of vision, your or my particular doctrine, or theory of the world. To make this point clearer, it is time to come back to the question, Is the mystic revelation valid, and what light does it throw on the needs of the human spirit? The first of these issues, I repeat, can only be argued amongst those who fully admit the tribunal of thought and reason, before which alone it can be heard. On this head three considerations may be urged.

(*a*) Mysticism proves nothing; it adds nothing to the force of a proof which is not already complete. The thoroughgoing votary doubtless tries all other truth by its conformity with his own revelation. It seems to be nearer to him than anything he has ever known. Newman, in whom there was a deeply mystical element, was as certain of the being of a God as of his own existence; millions of Buddhists, and others, are not. There is no common ground. We therefore cannot argue with such a mind; we can only plead with those who admit our tribunal; who, perhaps, may also have thought that they have had a revelation, but who may now doubt, and wish for assurance; who may say with the poet—

> We have played,
> We likewise, in that subtle shade.

And such persons may come to feel that every articulate thought or judgement, which appeared to be given them by vision, was really brought thither, and *imputed* to vision. Revelations differ. St. Teresa's intuition of the Trinity might as well have been of a Duality, had she been brought up in the appropriate heresy. The supposed perception of a pervading goodness in the world, experienced by Mr. James's witnesses, is simply a theory or hope that goodness is thus pervasive, carried up into a rare state of sensation, which is then naïvely taken to prove it. It is conceivable that a man could bring with him into a condition of this kind, and there fully realize, a conviction that the essence of things is evil. Whatever theory of life is true, the point for emphasis is that vision cannot give it more likelihood, or more claim upon us, than it had before, or without. It may be said that the revelations of the mystic are valid *for him*. *De facto*, yes, if the mystic is invulnerable to argument even when he has emerged. But *de jure*? That is just the question.

(*b*) The state of rapture or ecstasy bears one highly suspicious mark when confronted with some analogous states which are artificially induced without any religious aim or moral discipline, or without any purpose at all except to escape the pain of surgery. We are told that a book has been written, in America, on the ' anaesthetic revelation '. We may wake from the dream of nitrous oxide or chloroform with the well-known sense of an unspeakable secret, so near us, lately won, but hopelessly and painfully lost ; our words for which, when we wake, are gibberish so far as they do not merely express ideas which we had before sleeping. Some lines may be quoted, the author of which must have been reading a popular description of Nirvana ; no doubt they embody the afterthought, or the reading, rather than the dream itself ; but they also express the kind of longing, permanent in human nature, for which mysticism seeks to formulate some satisfaction.

NIRVANA AT THE DENTIST'S

I drank the subtle fire ; the engine roared :
The voices long resounded deep and clear.
Pain wrestled long with pleasure ; then I soared
In spirit up into the seventh sphere.

I keep its secret, like the moth that flew,
Seeking more life, into the heart of flame.
But first, ere quite submerged by dark, I knew,
In one wild flash, the hands, the window-frame.

Then forward rolled the sea of nothingness ;
With my weak arms I beat its billows back ;
The voices tinkled far and meaningless ;
By delicate degrees the monstrous, black,

N

> Merciful sea of Being without bound
> Came; I was one with every drop of it.
> Then first I felt that Eastern saw profound:
> 'Brother and sister, All and Nothing sit.'
>
> Such death be mine! No memory of joy
> Or doing good, and none of sin or woe;
> No waking to this finite crude alloy
> Of soul and substance in their ceaseless flow.

Professor James seems to imply that in such a state there may be a true revelation, especially from those latent parts of the mind, for which the word 'subconsciousness' has been found as a metaphor for their imagined sphere or receptacle. But the nonsense talked at waking suggests that the feeling of the 'great secret' lost is akin to hallucination; that there has really been nothing to lose, except a dream-state, which itself is only a mass of waking ideas without their rational co-ordination, and which offers a sham fruition to the passion for nonentity.

(c) It agrees with this point of view, that the alleged fusion with God, or with the First Reality, involves a rupture in the process of thinking. Up to a point, nothing is so systematic as mysticism. Goethe has well called it 'the scholastic of the heart, the dialectic of the feelings'. But at an arbitrary point the dialectic stops; there is a sudden snap in the chain. The aim is not to comprehend the First Reality, or resemble God morally by purity of will; it is virtually to become God. Professor A. Seth [125] has dealt with this aspiration simply and steadily. 'Mysticism,' he says, 'does not distinguish between what is metaphorical and what is susceptible of a literal interpretation.' Hence, 'it is prone to taste a relation of ethical harmony'—let us add, emotional and imaginative harmony, since ethics tend to vanish in the visionary state—' as if it were one of substantial identity or chemical fusion ; and, taking the sensuous language of religious feeling literally, it bids the individual aim at nothing less than interpenetration of essence '. This criticism answers broadly to that of Hegel, in the passage already quoted, upon the ambition of the Hindu and Buddhist. The generic principle of the former, he says, is ' Spirit in a state of Dream '. ' The sensuous matter and content is in each case simply and in the rough taken up, and carried over it into the sphere of the universal and immeasurable.' [126] The logical limit of the mystic's progress, were his hope sound, would be not vision but death, with the dissolution of personality and of the body.

But it is not enough to suspect such mysticism on philosophical grounds ; it is philosophical to ask what it tells us about the history of our own nature. Man, in his desire for the infinite, seems sporadically liable to the supreme illusion that he can merge himself in the supreme reality. This is one of the self-defeating impulses in his nature ; but it also is entangled with other impulses that may make for his advance. What really justifies the mystic, nay, what actually spurs him on his way, is not the quest for the great illusion—which is only, after all, an imaginative way of stating an ideal term—but the need to express those other powers and cravings, some of which have been noted here. He thinks he is led on by *vis a fronte* ; he is really driven by *vis a tergo*. He wants to get beyond mere outward good behaviour, to shatter old forms which his feeling has outgrown, to put due trust in the latent and salutary powers of his nature, and to find his way through the darker experience of the inward life. And he wants, above all, to aspire ; and if he cheats himself with metaphor in his tireless pilgrimage, at least he succeeds in aspiring.

VII

Trying to speak of all this, not without some historic and dramatic sympathy, I may end by remarking that one kind of mystical attitude, less dangerous and lonely than those referred to above, has yet to be named. The moral indifference attributed to Pantheism is more a matter of supposed logic than of recorded fact. Such a temper as that of Giordano Bruno or Walt Whitman has ever been allied with a love of the broad and generous life of the world; or, in more technical words, with an inclination not to strip away the manifold of sense and get down to bare unity, as in the paler Eastern systems, but to grasp as much of the manifold as is possible at once, in the light of the One. Even without any Pantheistic doctrine, the better impulse of the mystic may be bent towards breaking down the barrier, not between man and the supposed First Reality, but between man and his fellows, whose reality is less questionable. The ideal limit, which is the total identifying of our personality with that of others, can only be partially approached. But the old Eastern formula, ' This art thou,' so often invoked by Schopenhauer [127] in his nobly impersonal system of ethics, may be addressed by the mystic to himself in presence not only of human beings, but of the animals; not to speak of the rest of the organic and inorganic world. It is the formula which thins the barrier made between individuals by the selfish will, and it implies a release from the cravings of that will. While the body and the life remain, such a fusion can only be approximate. This old formula does not profess to reveal any new truth in ecstasy, such as that the world is good; it only realizes what is believed already; but life and self-training tend to make the truth effectual. Hence, it stands with a higher authority than the optimistic raptures cited by Professor James. In so far as the aim is achieved, the personality is enriched and dis-imprisoned.

Schopenhauer founds his discipline upon pessimism ; logically, it need imply neither pessimism nor optimism ; but it is more nearly linked in the actual evolution of man to the latter.   It certainly produces a more hopeful and humane temper than the ordinary discipline of the religious mystic, even although many of this class, such as St. Teresa, were, as has been said, practical organizers. We may go to the doctors of the soul for the virulent drugs or soft nepenthes or slow surgeries required for sick humanity.   But they give no adequate rule for a life of laborious health, of sanguine and creative energy. The poets of a joyous and victorious cast find the ideal expression for such natures, whom a rush of force and affirmation carries past the reefs on which the others founder.   Professor James devotes two chapters [128] to de-scribing persons of this type.   They are biologically better than their opposites.   For they tend to increase the sum of life ; and it is the actual survival of mankind that shows them to be nearer the mark, while the isolated mystic, whose scheme of existence often leaves him celibate, is a self-destroying species ; although that species at present always recurs, the causes for its origin lying deep in humanity.   We must cherish the hope that one day the bitter experience and illusory vision which are at the root of official mysticism may tend to die out, at any rate in the West.   The process may be as long as the step from primitive idolatry, and meantime the regular mystics and their dispensaries must hold a regarded place.   But science now forces us to think in long periods of time.   Translating into the mood of poetry, we may say that we are most truly our-selves, and nearest to truthful vision, when we happen to be one in heart with our kind, or feel that we are borne along as a bubble, whose bursting is a matter of indifference, on the everlasting tide of life and fertility.

TENNYSON:

AN INAUGURAL LECTURE

I. Character of Tennyson greater than his Ideas. II. His Freshness, 1830–40, and Intellectual Frustration afterwards.   III.   Metrical   Power;   Warnings.   IV. Fiction a Truer Medium of the Best Ideas (1850–1900) than Poetry.   V. The Achievement of Tennyson: (1) Sound, Landscape, Imagery.   VI. Rendering (2) of Shadowy and Morbid Feeling; 'In Memoriam.' VII. Skill in (3) Hellenics; Conclusion.

I

Tennyson, of whose life we have all read, leaves a strong impression of natural force, to which his poetry bears less perfect witness. He lived in a time and a land needing the resistance of any artist who would not wish to resign his title and become afraid. He was a figure in our stable, immemorial, dignified English society: he was ever in a deep harmony with its ruling caste; a way of life which makes more clearly for practice and high civic uses than for unimpeded poetry, and more for the contentment and accomplishment of the intelligence than for its free and daring, or even its disinterested, play. The last half-century of his life was a phase of high formative value in English thought, but is already stamped in intellectual history with something of what the Germans call *Halbheit*; and this Tennyson expresses. He expresses the fluid theorizing which is also found in men so different as Maurice and Jowett, with their liberalism in one case hazy and in the other canny, which helped to dissolve the passing order of ideas, while shrinking from perfect faith in speculation. Their work served education well. Thoroughly English figures, answerable for who shall say how many well-trained minds that were in turn to train others, they help, on retrospect, to intensify that sense of *Halbheit*, of which Tennyson, who stands near their group, remains the exponent to a far larger audience than theirs. Their battles were fought less on final principles than on the frontier-ground of this or that article of subscription, or in the effort to adjust new lights with doctrine, so that many minor heresies by which society was much stirred have now become options. The effect of this peculiar spirit on poetic art was marked and disastrous, especially with men of high faculty like Tennyson: and the same might be said, with a difference, of Browning. They gave a wonderful gathering of early spring flowers; and then, like Proserpine, they retired into a land of unseizable shadows, for a longer night than hers, and with briefer reappearances. They ceased to be true to art. They fell into the national vice, which claims also the transient parts of Milton and Wordsworth, of producing something which is neither pure art nor pure thinking. High of purpose, they busied themselves with moral and religious ideas, which Tennyson had not the force to put strictly, and Browning not the gift to shape poetically. What is to become of *La Saisiaz*, or of 'Who loves not knowledge' (*In Memoriam*, cxiv)? They served up those ideas, under forms and shows of art, yet inartistically, so that the work makes straight for oblivion and drags down the ideas with it. This, in reference to Tennyson, is the main seeming paradox of my address, so far as I am led to speak against him; or rather against his public. It is a course which can give no offence, for no individual is ever a member of the public.

Das Publicum will wie Frauenzimmer behandelt sein ;
man soll ihnen durchaus nichts sagen als was sie hören
möchten (Goethe).

So firm a nature was not readily subdued to its surroundings. Tennyson turned now and then, though
seldom powerfully, against the world he lived in. He
withdrew in part, and watched the still surface, nothing
more! of English society, with its beautiful and graceful
persons, as he might have watched the lilies in a pond ;
and he sometimes made believe that they lived in the day
of King Arthur ; a pretence which gives most of what
life is yet retained in those faint unrealized allegories,
the *Idylls of the King*, with their thin strange morality
and beautiful curiosity of rhythm. He once made a
poem, his best, the frustrate masterpiece of *Maud*, which
his own public and the official press were shy of accepting. But history shows that a life like his of orderly
happiness is not the soil for every kind of poetry. Think
of poor Verlaine, whose touch moves us thrice as often
as Tennyson's, sinking from hospital to hospital, and
shattered by nature with a recklessness she often reserves
for her rarest lyrical instruments! The wonder is that
Tennyson did so much. He held with a single mind
to what he thought was his business. Despite his
monarchical place in the public eye, he easily remained
a man amid all his temptations to become a personage.
Many a writer of equal gift might have needed a sharper
experience to make him do what Tennyson did. Some
early struggles ; a long waiting for the admirable wife,
who was his companion for forty years, and outlived him ;
one chief loss, his other constant companion, which finally
diffused itself through his intellect and fancy, and found
ease in intricate expression, somewhat after an old Italian
manner ; much chafing, in default of worse things, over

press notices, often at first of the rowdy, half-lettered kind ruling in our earlier Scotch journalism ; such, in the main, we are told, were Tennyson's trials, in a life otherwise outwardly like that of some absorbed landscape painter or lapidary ; any curious, delicate, and strange elements, and any wilder ones, coming out, as best they might under such conditions, into his work.

As we read the *Memoir*, we are aware of quite other elements than these, serving surely as excellent practical shelter to them ; of many oaken outworks and defences of character, which make the better part of the Englishman. Tennyson appears in the dealings of life as a sane, strong-witted, sardonic companion, with plenty of gaiety and sagacity. He was the comrade of Carlyle, who has drawn him :—

A fine large-featured, dim-eyed, bronze-coloured, shaggy-headed man is Alfred, dusty, smoky, free, and easy; who swims outwardly and inwardly with great composure in an inarticulate element of tranquil chaos and tobacco-smoke; great now and then when he does emerge; a most restful, brotherly, solid-hearted man.

The picture might be that of a Red Indian chieftain, sitting wisely through the silent hours of the calumet. His few personal faults were such as might beseem a chieftain. For the utterance of Carlyle's Tennyson, we had best look to Tennyson's prose, in his talk, maxim, and correspondence. That, certainly, is ever entirely natural, masculine, and well-cut. He uttered, declared his friend Fitzgerald, no adoring critic, ' by far the finest prose sayings of any one.' The best of them concern the literature that came home to Tennyson; but there is greatness in others that are on record.

I thank you for your kind congratulations about the peerage ; but being now in my 75th year, and having lost almost all my youthful contemporaries, I see myself, as it were, in an extra page of Holbein's *Dance of Death*, and standing before the mouth of an open sepulchre where the Queen hands me a coronet, and the skeleton takes it away, and points me downward into the darkness.

We come there on a temper and an intellect of large design more clearly than in many of his metrical works. Like Ben Jonson, he is a prose writer, who is barely saved to us. He might hardly have liked the comparison, for he has worded perfectly the dissatisfaction that Jonson leaves in us, while we admire his immense voracious faculty and animation. Tennyson is reported to have said, ' I cannot read him. I feel as if I were moving in a wide sea of glue.' So, in reading *The Lord of Burleigh*, or *In the Children's Hospital*, we might feel like those who mock their thirst with distilled water, lacking the race and iron and sparkle of the spring. But he was a born critic of all the audible part of poetry, in which he excels, and in which it were no small thing to say that his chief excellence lies ; for the power of verbal fullness and harmony, in such a measure as he has it, presupposes, and alone can make articulate, many another quality of the soul. He said of Mr. Swinburne, that he is ' a reed through which all things grow into music ' ; of Browning, that ' he has plenty of music in him, but cannot get it out. He seldom attempts the marriage of sense with sound, although he shows a spontaneous felicity in the adaptation of words to ideas and feelings.'

II

' The adaptation of words to ideas and feelings ' : the consonance, that is, of expression with some delicate mood of scenery or of reverie ; and the promise of the subtle or regal utterance of these moods in sound—such qualities, together with others more widely captivating, struck on the sensitive readers between the years 1830 and 1840, who, like similar readers now, were busy waiting for the new poet, and asking themselves whether they had found him. There was something, it might be felt, in the face of England, some play of her current mood and temper, as yet unrecorded ; something which Byron and Shelley, the exiles, had been too alien or too impatient to express, and missed by Wordsworth, so impervious in his hill-bound hermitage to contemporary thought. To these readers, the volumes of 1830 and 1832, with *Claribel* and *The Lady of Shalott* and *The Dream of Fair Women*, might have come like this hope of theirs made articulate, as 'the buzzings of the honied hours'. I must quote what Tennyson afterwards nobly said of Keats : 'There is something of the innermost soul of poetry in almost everthing he ever wrote.' Well, we hear from a critic of that day that

Since the death of John Keats, the last lineal descendant of Apollo, our English region of Parnassus has been domineered over by kings of shreds and patches. But, if I mistake not, the true heir is found.

The writer is Arthur Hallam, and he continues, from *The Winter's Tale* :—

The mantle and jewel about the neck! The letters whose character is known! The majesty of the creature in resemblance of its father, the affection of nobleness and many other evidences, proclaim him, with all certainty, to be the king's son.

Nay, with the book of ten years later, containing *Ulysses* and *Break, break, break,* he might have felt in presence of such a freshness of tint and purity of temper—not yet hardened into the versified expression of opinion about

purity—as reminded him of the youth of Milton. The
poetic youth of Keats and that of Milton, I must say in
passing, are subjects which have never yet been duly
treated, and, therefore, I would hope, await the hand of
my predecessor, Mr. Raleigh, who has already shown
his power to speak of both poets. But such a reminiscence those older readers may well have felt, for we feel
it still, we feel it here :—

> and though
> We are not now that strength which in old days
> Moved earth and heaven, that which we are, we are ;
> One equal temper of heroic hearts
> Made weak by time and fate, but strong in will
> To strive, to seek, to find, and not to yield.

Such new gifts, a new and strange manner of rendering
natural beauty, a bright abundance of experiment, and
a noble bent of expression, led another judicious reviewer,
Monckton Milnes, later Lord Houghton, to declare :—

> It rests with Mr. Tennyson to prove that he can place
> himself at the head of all these his contemporaries. His
> command of diction is complete, and his sense of the
> harmonies [of words]. He has only to show that he
> has substance, what Goethe called *Stoff*, worthy of his
> media.

The next forty years saw Tennyson's unceasing efforts
to show that he had substance. In poems like *L'Allegro*
or *The Lotos-Eaters* we do not resent the lack of any
matter which can be put into intellectual statement ; the
poems vanish, when we try to make such a statement of
them, into a pinch of dust. That is only to say that
they do not betray a great experience of life passed
through the re-creative process of expression, which may
have been what Goethe meant by *Stoff*. Still, a profound life circulates through them, which is the life of

rhythm, of a musical mood. We are aware of a surprising instrument of melody fitted to memorize dream, or picture, or delicate and passing phases of pensive feeling. Tennyson tried to fit this instrument to countless other things. Besides four ambitious works, *Maud* and *The Princess*, *In Memoriam* and the *Idylls*, he has left a mass of verse more widely accepted than that of any modern English poet after Byron. I wish to take the best, and there is much that it would not be fair to treat at length. There are his plays, which often have the virtues of his undramatic verse. One of them, *The Cup*, shows a true power of romantic invention springing up in old age, while another, *The Promise of May*, is so weak intellectually that it ought not to have been republished by Lord Tennyson's friends. Many of his other pieces trust to their pathos and to the appeal they make to the simpler emotions. Saving for a few lyrics, I think that Tennyson must lose his hold as a poet of the simple emotions ; for his true skill is to elaborate emotions not simple at all. The pathos of *Dora* or of *Elaine* is not much more to be trusted than that of *The May Queen*, which is to be trusted very little and has a certain sickliness of sound and metre, one of the surest warning-signals of easy sentiment.

III

Tennyson has a curious, a noble, and a various invention in metre, and his use of it would ask for a long discourse. *Boadicea*, and the *Lines to the Rev. F. D. Maurice*, and the *Lines to Virgil*, and much else, show how seriously and skilfully he set himself to administer this his province of sound. He paid the deepest attention to his blank verse, and is usually called one of its supreme masters.

Lucretius, for instance, takes our breath away, not only by its superlative admired rhetoric and tesselations, but by its metrical craft, until we think of Lucretius himself and his hexameter.   But Tennyson's blank verse is so far from infallible, that if its glories are melody and fullness, its fault is slothfulness.   It is dominated by monotony, despite the endless ripples and modulations. Indeed, Tennyson's method is to charge and clog his line, whatever its measure, with little intricacies of sound, and this nearly always makes it slow.   Sometimes, again, he allows a metre which is naturally strong to tumble continually into a weaker one, as in *Locksley Hall*. Compare the effect of the following lines, where the real and powerful scheme of eight beats in ' falling ' or 'trochaic' rhythm is heard :—

Déep in | yónder | shíning | órient, | whére my | lífe be-| gán to | beát. . . .
Ríft the | hílls, and | róll the | wáters, | flásh the | líght- nings, | weígh the | Sún.

And then listen to these, where the cantering or sham- bling effect is heard, and where the scheme is or tends to be a four-beat one in ' rising rhythm ', the feet being either ' anapaests ' or of the four-syllabled type here exem- plified :—

In this hóstel, | I remémber, | I repént it | o'er his gráve. . . . |
But the jíngling | of the guínea. |

This difference will be audible enough even to those who may not care for the technical language.

But the sound, once more, warns us most surely in the high-uplifted *Rizpahs* and *Despairs*, which make a furious attack upon our feelings, and handle very solemn matters by the method of invective.   Tennyson in a mass of his

writings uses a strain of hollow fierce diction for denun-
ciation or appeal.   It was an error ; in all this kind of
work he is far inferior to Dr. Johnson, who wrote the
Vanity of Human Wishes.   And if that condemnation
holds good, how much of Tennyson falls under it ! There
is the shriek of *Aylmer's Field* ; the shriek in *Locksley
Hall : Sixty years after,* against Celtic Demos, French
novels, and the future of science :—

Chaos, Cosmos ! Cosmos, Chaos ! Who can tell how all
    will end ?
Read the world's wide annals, you, and take their wisdom
    for your friend.

There is, in the sanctimonious kind, the oration of the peda-
gogue Arthur to his Queen.   There is the other oration
in which the Prince expounds his own magnanimity to
the Princess Ida.   It is a speech to which the whole of
The Princess leads up, for that curious piece of playful
and petty carving, ' laborious orient ivory,' is not allowed,
unhappily, to lead to nothing.   Thus he speaks to his
promised bride :—

> The new day comes, the light
> Dearer for night, as dearer thou for faults
> Lived over ; lift thine eyes . . .
> Look up, and let thy nature strike on mine,
> Like yonder morning on the blind half-world ;
> Approach, and fear not.

That does not show the possession of what Goethe meant
by *substance.*   What a degeneration from the frank,
youthful, undoctrinal cry in the earlier, the real *Locksley
Hall*, the only poem where Tennyson shows felicity in
expressing anger :—

Drug thy memories, lest thou learn it, lest thy heart
    be put to proof
In the dead unhappy night, and when the rain is on
    the roof.

IV

Tennyson has gone down with thousands as a great remedial thinker ; but from the first there were signs and omens, as in *The Palace of Art*, that this was an illusion. That poem is admirably decorated ; but it preaches the strangest piece of faithlessness which is possible to an artist, namely lack of faith in beauty. Such is the necessary danger in a puritan country ; but a poet should go about to escape it. No words are better than those of one of the clearest-witted among the older critics—a man, let us remember, much occupied with the idea of moral nobility in poetry. John Sterling, the disciple of Goethe and friend of Carlyle, thus wrote :—

The writer's doctrine seems to be that the soul, while by its own energy surrounding itself with the most beautiful and expressive images that the history of mankind has produced, and sympathizing wholly with the world's best thoughts, is perpetrating some prodigious moral offence, for which it is bound to repent in sackcloth and ashes.

But instead of piecemeal attack, let me cast about a little and confess the broader reasons, as I find them, of Tennyson's inaptitude for the position his admirers, who take him so seriously, give him. What if he, the widest-known retailer of ideas in English verse, was all the while in a backwater where only the fainter wash of the larger currents reached him ? And what, then, are those currents of thought, I do not say as abstractly shown in pure philosophy, but as expressed in literary art ? What forms of art bring us nearest to them ? The last question may be answered soonest. It is idle, perhaps, to try and rate the new literature now being made,

o

or rather weltering; idle, not merely because it is so close to us, but because that familiar cry for the new writer, the new poet, who has not come, is only a recognition that all great mental forces are dark until we see them in a sufficiently great individual, nay, do not even fully exist until he appears, and that until then we had best not be estimating forces at all. But if we look back at the work of the living veterans, not in England only, we begin to doubt whether the last half-century will be primarily remembered in the history of letters for its verse. Its truest and deepest vein runs through fiction. We must use the term *fiction*, through the poverty of our language, not only for the novel but for the drama, which describes actual life and is now usually though not always written in prose. The time of Shakespeare put its main literary energy into drama; the time of Pope put its main energy into rhyming or other combat. The recent age put its main energy into fiction. I am the last to forget the school of impassioned artists in verse and colour who found their centre in Dante Gabriel Rossetti. But they triumphed by partly shutting away the outer life of their time, as it was their business to do. It is chiefly in fiction that we seem to find two opposing currents which have yet to measure their strength fairly. One is pessimism, which found brilliant form and system in Schopenhauer, and has since penetrated the modern view of life like an acid. Who has not felt it in the portrayal of the Russian world by Tolstoy, both before and after he found the remedy which now contents him? The living novelist of Western England, to whom his style promises such safety, shows us his discouragement alike with what nature has made of man, and what men have made of one another. There are other voices abroad, in Italy and elsewhere, from Leopardi and the early romantic writers downwards, which utter the same tones, sometimes in lyric, like the author of the *Poems and Ballads* of 1866, but oftener in fable or fiction. Before such an energy, such an analysis, the complacencies of Tennyson and his world wither; his Whig complacency, which is so immovable in spite of a few tirades against marrying for money, over the social arrangements; his British complacency over what he calls 'the Saxo-Norman race, which breeds, methinks, the noblest men'; and his complacency over sham-chivalrous morality, with its nominal adoration and secret patronage of women.   Once or twice, in *Maud*, he is faintly attacked by the true malady.   It has to be met by some sharper cure than can be given by him or by his thinking, which no one sensitive to these influences can take seriously.

Some help is forthcoming in fiction.   The literature of hope, of faith in the known life of man, and of a hard-won optimism, has veteran and trained commanders beside whom Tennyson is only like an amateur aristocrat permitted to accompany outlying portions of a campaign. Scarred and gaunt, sometimes harsh of style, a little overwhelming to the men of intellectual diplomacy and compromise, unscared, strong-headed, they stand, with most of their work ready for judgement, reaping a few long-grudged honours for which they cannot care.   It would take long to draw out the lines of connexion between minds so divergent as those which created the poem of *Brand*, the epic story of *La Débâcle*, and *The Ordeal of Richard Feverel*.   But their united thought and aspiration spans the same quarter of the heavens. The courageous irony and deep-mining thought of Ibsen, and Zola's noble trust in human concert and the franker community of the future, are allied with one another and

with the spirit of their English compeer or superior.
And each furnishes something of his own; for Mr.
George Meredith is distinguished by a hopefulness
which arises, as with Goethe, out of severe experience,
and by a spiritual energy in the representation of mortal
love, which hardly belongs to the Gallic genius with all
its invaluable faith in gaiety, in fraternity, in happiness,
and in reason. If I am to find in one word the chief bond
between these minds, with their different ways of work,
I should name the great business of our time, science—
yes, *science!* I do not mean the crude transference
of physical images or theories to matters of life and
character. The spirit of science is seen in the region
of art by a particular temper, by openness of vision, by
the determination to exhibit reality and to hope for just
so much as may be expected, by the bold use of such
hypotheses as can be brought to book, and by the steady
temper that has

> power to fright
> The spirits of the shady night.

This is the central current in the literature of our time.
I must not follow it further, for it is a digression from
my theme of Tennyson.

V

But I am faced now by a famous saying, to the effect
that true criticism deals not with a man's failures and
erroneous experiments, but with what he has achieved,
and I wish to name three or four things which I suppose
Tennyson to have achieved.

Poetry, though not the widest kind of poetry, can
easily live without any distinct intellectual or moral
drift; but no poetry can live unless it is rooted in that

nobler animal part of man, honoured by Milton under
the term 'sensuous', on pain of being blind and deaf and
without motion.   This is why the poetry we call didactic,
that is, mere metrical precept cut off from images, is
apt to be a diseased kind.   Tennyson—and this is his
primary excellence—is never cut off from images, and
they often revive our interest when his ideas are dead-
ening it.   Works still continue to be written on his
landscape, and on the outfit of nice and alert senses with
which he watched and listened.   He was much alone
with the inarticulate world; and his mind was always
like a perfectly true lens, or enchanted crystal, in which
everything is carefully mirrored small, yet with a pris-
matic strangeness and variableness.   Some of his earlier
verses we call romantic, meaning they are in the direct
line between *La Belle Dame sans Merci* and *The Blessed
Damozel*.   Such a poem is *Mariana in the Moated
Grange*, which prefigures many of the qualities and
the rare peculiar turn of words that we think of as
Rossetti's;—a connexion with a younger and bolder
school, which becomes intelligible enough to those who
know the pictures by Millais and Hunt in the volume
containing *The Lady of Shalott*.   *Mariana* is truly—
to recover the true meaning of a jaded word—an *intense*
poem.   Its minute flashing pictures and its slow returning
metre foreshow, as has often been said, some things in
In Memoriam.

> About a stone-cast from the wall
>   A sluice with blacken'd waters slept,
> And o'er it, many, round and small,
>   The cluster'd marish-mosses crept.
> Hard by a poplar shook alway,
>   All silver-green with gnarled bark;
>   For leagues no other tree did mark
> The level waste, the rounding grey.

The verse plays the same tune on us as the scene itself, or as the few lines in *Measure for Measure* by which Shakespeare magically isolates the original Mariana within her moat from the world of Vienna.   Tennyson's way of wording landscape has its history.   At first it has the playful or intimate fancy which a child might own or recognize ; the four-handed mole is heard scraping in the darkness, the sudden laughters of the jay (or the ' scritches ', for the poet wavered delicately between the words) ring in the damp holts, the bearded meteor trails light in the heavens.   Later, nature becomes the truest occupation of his art, and the chosen sphere of his felicity in style.   Of the waves tumbling about the bows of a steamer, he said at once, ' they are swift, glittering deeps, sharp like the back fin of a fish ' ; ' and so,' adds the reporter, ' they were.'   The critics wrongly said he was inaccurate ; he was always right, and his landscapes are often built up indoors out of notes taken without, after the way of some painters.

Lying among the [Pyrenees] before a waterfall that comes down one thousand or twelve hundred feet, I sketched it (according to my custom then) in these words :—

Slow-dropping veils of thinnest lawn.

When I printed this, a critic informed me that ' lawn ' was the material used in theatres to imitate a waterfall, and graciously added, ' Mr. T. should not go to the boards of a theatre but to Nature herself for his suggestions.'   And I had gone to Nature herself.

All this shows much study, but it was not the fatal study of words apart from sound or images, and we have the sense that it was not a painful, active kind of labour.   At his best Tennyson seems to have waited for his expression to come to him ; to have brooded before a scene with its orchestra of sounds, in a kind of intense passiveness—closely akin to that mood of mystical withdrawal, which he often describes—until the thing beheld became greatly different from what it was at any other moment or to any other man ; and, late or soon, the words arose which still fix for us, as though seen by summer lightning, its haunting principle.

> To-night the winds begin to rise
>   And roar from yonder dropping day :
>   The last red leaf is whirled away,
> The rooks are blown about the skies.
>
> The forest crack'd, the waters curl'd,
>   The cattle huddled on the lea ;
>   And wildly dash'd on tower and tree
> The sunbeam strikes along the world.

That is almost poetry striving to go over into the art of Claude. It may be that Tennyson is best in homelike and pensive English places, for there he can play a little ; and the element of play is present in almost all his dealings with words at any time, to his pleasure and his peril.

> By night we linger'd on the lawn,
>   For underfoot the herb was dry ;
>   And genial warmth ; and o'er the sky
> The silvery veil of summer drawn.
>
> And bats went round in fragrant skies,
>   And wheel'd or lit the filmy shapes
>   That haunt the dusk, with ermine capes
> And woolly breasts and beaded eyes.
>
> While now we sing old songs that peal'd
>   From knoll to knoll, where, couch'd at ease,
>   The white kine glimmer'd, and the trees
> Laid their dark arms about the field.

And if what we there perceive is nature dreaming happily, or breathing in her sleep, rather than her wilder

or more oppressive music which Mr. Thomas Hardy has
written down, yet the poet's full compensation comes in
his lyric, which is nearly always touched by scenery and
thus wins much of its worth.   The cold grey stones,
the happy autumn fields, the sound and foam in *Crossing
the Bar*, give a support and local habitation to the
feeling, in that handful of unassailable songs which place
Tennyson, for several instants, near Shakespeare.   For
in poems like *Come not when I am dead* and *Break,
break, break*, those unconscious elemental powers which
Tennyson habitually educates away into elaboration, or
strives to conjure back by mannered simplicity, gain free
flight, and play as if without his will, so that in a few
words he says everything, instead of spending long
misguided toil in saying far less than that.   We would
sacrifice many eulogies of the Prince Consort for more
like the four lines out of which *Maud* was built
originally :—

> Oh, that 'twere possible
> After long grief and pain
> To find the arms of my true love
> Round me once again.

These lyrics might be soliloquies cried suddenly in the
open air, and they give the actual fugitive essence or
virtue of the South of England, with the perfumed
exhalations of its earth and its plaintive or happy
melancholy.

VI

It is natural, secondly, that Tennyson should, with
this endowment, show himself a master in representing
feeling which is difficult and shadowy, and often morbid
and remote ; and the more fully he lets himself go in this

direction, the better he is. He is much less surely at home in moral and religious ideas than in this bottomless and shifting region. In *Maud* he visits it oftenest, and shows that he has received the freedom of the city of dreams and the keys of the house of distraction, where all men sojourn in sleep, and where abides the truest reality of many prose-bound lives. The half-obliterated language of those places is only recalled by the words of poets like De Quincey. And, in his degree, Tennyson also does his best with words when he has to express something not of necessity tragic, but elusive, unstrung, or visionary; and this is a very high excellence, for he can measure these moods with the same sort of precision as the features of a daylight landscape. *Mariana*, once more, is wholly a record of such subtle waking misery, in its essence the same as that familiar antinomy of dreams, where some penance, at once impossible and necessary, set by the unknown taskmasters of sleep, lengthens out before the mind and crushes it:—

> The sparrow's chirrup on the roof,
>   The slow clock ticking, and the sound
> Which to the wooing wind aloof
>   The poplar made, did all confound
> Her sense; but most she loathed the hour
>   When the thick-moted sunbeam lay
>   Athwart the chambers, and the day
> Was sloping toward his western bower.
>
>   Then, said she, 'I am very dreary,
>   He will not come,' she said;
>   She wept, 'I am aweary, aweary,
>   Oh God, that I were dead!'

Elsewhere there is the resolution of vague into connected dreams:—

All those sharp fancies, by down lapsing-thought
Stream'd onward, lost their edges, and did creep,
Roll'd on each other, rounded, smooth'd, and brought
Into the gulfs of sleep.

Or there are the nightmares of the fiend-haunted religious fanatic on his pillar :—

Abaddon and Asmodeus caught at me ;
I smote them with the cross ; they swarmed again.
In bed like monstrous apes they crushed my chest;
They flapped my light out as I read ; I saw
Their faces grow between me and my book.
With colt-like whinny and with hoggish whine
They burst my prayer.

The third number of *Maud* illustrates all the gifts of
Tennyson for which I have thus far pleaded he should
claim remembrance ; especially his power of prolonged
and concerted music, used for the rendering of nature,
of fevered feeling, and of dream. It may be rhetoric,
but it is right. It is the rhetoric of the overwrought
heart whose energy overflows into the restless fancy.
The speaker goes out into the dark after the slight
passed upon him by his mistress :—

Cold and clear-cut face, why come you so cruelly meek,
Breaking a slumber in which all spleenful folly was
    drown'd,
Pale with the golden beam of an eyelash dead on the
    cheek,
Passionless, pale, cold face, star-sweet on a gloom
    profound ;
Woman-like, taking revenge too deep for a transient
    wrong
Done but in thought to your beauty, and ever as pale
    as before
Growing and fading and growing upon me without a
    sound,
Luminous, gemlike, ghostlike, deathlike, half the night
    long

Growing and fading and growing, till I could bear it
    no more,
But arose, and all by myself in my own dark garden
    ground,
Listening now to the tide in its broad-flung ship-
    wrecking roar,
Now to the scream of a madden'd beach dragg'd down
    by the wave,
Walk'd in a wintry wind by a ghastly glimmer, and
    found
The shining daffodil dead, and Orion low in his grave.

This and the songs in *Maud* show Tennyson's fullness of
hectic or languid feeling, which links him to poets of the
tribe of Spenser, Coleridge, and Keats, in so far as he
wisely yields to it ; a poetical voluptuousness of which
The Lotos-Eaters and *Fatima* are the best examples,
but of which he may have become ashamed, feeling himself called away to express more abstract things.

    Part of the same comment applies to *In Memoriam*.
This is one of the hardest poems in the modern English
language ; it is set with small thorns for the interpreter ;
and it calls for no intelligence less fine and serious, and
for no scholarship less nicely-dividing, than have been
bestowed on it by Professor Bradley—a successor may
be permitted to say thus much—in the book he has
founded on discourses once given in Liverpool. It is
hard through its compressed intricacy of style, rather
than for any display of the sterner speculative power for
which the subject calls and which other writers have
shown in urging a like conclusion. And it is hardly in
the English, or the German, or the Celtic temper. But
an Italian might more willingly listen to Tennyson's
methodized grief, which is presented in a way suggesting
Petrarch's. The sense of loss, so far from having ' no
language but a cry '—which is a misdescription of the

poem—becomes a straining prisoner of the discursive fancy, and the stuff of sorrow is beaten out into a thousand curious filaments. It is well if feeling, on these terms, does not shrink into an occasion for talking about feeling, and if none of the poignancy is spun away in the care for finish. To intrude on the private audience of *In Memoriam*, to whom the ever-brightening course of the poet's plea commends itself, and who find in it the history of their own consolation, would mean an excursion through the very windings of the argument, on a certain side so sceptical. It appeals to those who do not lean on such hopes of immortality and reunion as are offered by the common reasonings, but find the truth of those hopes pledged by the invincible assurance either of the heart or of mystical revelation. But its real power is won by the perfection of some of its single poems in point of sound, by its grey pageantry of dreams and memories, and its adjustment of scenery to lyric mood, although these things are chequered by an odd rhetoric and by a great fallibility in style. It is distinguished by its special excellences from other studious elegies, like Milton's or Dryden's. It is never safer, possibly, than in passages like the following, which show why I bring it, profanely as some may suppose, under the chapter of Tennyson's triumphs in strange psychology :—

> I cannot see the features right,
>   When on the gloom I strive to paint
>   The face I know; the hues are faint
> And mix with hollow masks of night;
>
> Cloud-towers by ghostly masons wrought,
>   A gulf that ever shuts and gapes,
>   A hand that points, and palled shapes
> In shadowy thoroughfares of thought;

And crowds that stream from yawning doors,
  And shoals of pucker'd faces drive;
  Dark bulks that tumble half-alive,
And lazy lengths on boundless shores;

Till all at once beyond the will
  I hear a wizard music roll;
  And through a lattice on the soul
Looks thy fair face and makes it still.

VII

Lastly, Tennyson, like Gray and Landor, is a poet of the classical Renaissance, and this is another of his titles. *The Lotos-Eaters*, *Tithonus*, and *Ulysses* are what we call Hellenics, although *Ulysses* is full of Dante and *The Lotos-Eaters* of Spenser. Such a following of older poets implies a distinct gain of originality. This may be said of the whole mass of echoes, imitations, and noble or gracious reminiscence that scholars have sought and found in Tennyson's works. In his Hellenics, Tennyson starts with an immense advantage which he is always forfeiting elsewhere. I mean that his aim is pure beauty, that he has not one eye on his application, that he is not writing what can be quoted at congresses, and that he is throwing himself on his real gift and his real temperament. We find a mixture of ancient feeling with his own, and we find the same gifts as in the best of his other work. The dissolved melancholy, the wail of a shadowy soul in an indistinct other world, with its faint cry as of a bat or a bird, its longing to finish, its faint clinging to life, all receive expression in the slow labouring movement of the verse, which penetrates even the heroic strain of *Ulysses*:—

The long day wanes; the slow moon climbs; the deep
Moans round with many voices.

The essence of all such antique or half-antique feeling is gathered into the *Lines to Virgil*, who of all the ancient poets gives us most of it. Those lines show the heart of Tennyson as a poetic artist, just as the lyrics give us the best of his landscape, and *Maud* the best of his human insight :—

Light among the vanish'd ages, star that gildest yet
　　this phantom shore,
Golden branch amid the shadows, kings and realms
　　that pass to rise no more ;

Now thy Forum roars no longer, fallen every purple
　　Caesar's dome.
Tho' thine ocean-roll of rhythm resound for ever of
　　Imperial Rome ;

Now the Rome of slaves hath perish'd, and the Rome
　　of freemen holds her place,
I, from out the Northern island, sunder'd once from
　　all the human race,

I salute thee, Mantovano, I that loved thee since my
　　day began,
Wielder of the stateliest measure ever moulded by the
　　lips of man.

I have wished to speak broadly of Tennyson, leaving out lesser counts on either side of the reckoning. In trying to put aside his superabounding glory, which forms a gross refracting medium, we only follow in his own path. He was full of an honourable apathy to the flatteries of the English-reading world, and also to literary fame, which wilted away to something inconsiderable in view of the 'next glacial epoch'. Yet the far future, as he said so simply, was his home always ; and he was unlike some of the slighter Elizabethans, who were sure of poetical eternity, and are lucky if they receive a limited reprint from a learned society. But if, as I come to think, he is not a great remedial thinker and leaves no

great imaginative whole, and if his ruling conceptions are
vanishing into a past of shadows and his style fluctuates
in value with his matter, then the collection of ruined
palaces and pleasances that we call his works may seem
to us a kind of rich man's Folly.   And to say this is not
altogether a slight.   In vain, perhaps, the surprising
ambition of the mausoleum, in vain the top-heavy allegories that load the ceilings.   What we turn to, what we
wish to save, are the little outlying kiosques and summer-
houses, a scrap here and there of dignified if mannered
statuary, a few fountains of fresh water, a plaintive corner
of garden landscape, and a thousand happy gleams of
colour on the fast-wearing frescoes.   Best of all, there
are corners of wild undergrowth ; it was Mrs. Oliphant
who well said of Tennyson : ' In reality, there is a rough-
ness and acrid gloom about him, which saves him from
his romantic appearance.'

MR. SWINBURNE'S POEMS

I

After a generation, Mr. Swinburne's verse comes out in a collected form, happily under the author's care, and without alteration of the text. There is 'nothing that he could wish to cancel, or to alter, or to unsay, in any pages he has ever laid before his reader'. This is very well, for his earlier writings, at any rate, are now historic, and any change, even for the better, would change their nature. His preface on his own poetry is a happy example of his critical prose. It is untouched by the flagrant volubility of enormous panegyric or superlative damnation which often covers up the clearness and gravity of Mr. Swinburne's judgements on literature. Well we know that style, where the shot is so weighty and well aimed, but is discharged with a furious waste of powder, and even at times with an inconvenient recoil. But in this preface, with its proud and unfailing dignity of retrospect, one of the greatest critics amongst English poets judges himself and makes awards, as few English poets have done, between his own works. We need not expect

that his choice should be ours. Such pieces as *In
the Bay* and *On the Cliffs*, which he singles out from
amongst those 'inspired by the influence of places'
as of deeper appeal to himself, may perhaps belong, in
point of performance, to the large class of his lyrics
that can be termed self-echoes—beautiful enough, but
with a beauty that the author has himself already excelled
in its own kind, and therefore not so much alive in our
memory as their predecessors in our love.   But *A Forsaken Garden*, which he ranks as to its associations with
those others, had a new freshness of landscape and a new
intensity of rhythm, which brings it into a different class
of lovely things.   The poet's re-reading of these pieces
has begotten a passage of lyrical prose that stands with
A Forsaken Garden itself:—

Not to you or any other poet, or indeed to the very
humblest and simplest lover of poetry, will it seem
incongruous or strange, suggestive of imperfect sympathy
with life or deficient inspiration from nature, that the
very words of Sappho should be heard and recognized
in the notes of the nightingales, the glory of the presence
of dead poets imagined in the presence of the glory of
the sky, the lustre of their advent and their passage felt
visible as in vision on the live and limpid floorwork of
the cloudless and sunset-coloured sea.

Some words from the same preface touch on the
species and aspirations of the ode, 'considered as something above all less pure and absolute song by the very
law of its being', and defined, if not rigidly by the corre-
spondent forms of strophe that are based on Pindar's,
still so as to exclude the sham Pindaric and such 'law-
less lyrics of irregular and uneven build as Coleridge'
used.   They throw light on Mr. Swinburne's conception
of his own highest task as a poet as well as on his fundamentally Hellenic sympathies as a lyrist.   Whether, in

the nature of things, one kind is inherently greater or more central than another kind of lyrical perfection, his own briefer songs, 'Love laid his weary head' and *A Match*, even when confronted with the *Ode to Victor Hugo* and the choruses in *Atalanta*, may leave us questioning. Any primacy that the ode may possess, it possibly gains, not only from the larger sweep and more elaborate resonance of its form, but from the suggestion, whether overt or underlying, of some great and public emotion uttered by a throng of performers to a larger throng of responsive hearers, and celebrated in triumphal or burial procession. From this point of view, which seems to imply some actual event or the memory of one, in order to awaken sufficient resonance in the heart, those odes, where, as in Wordsworth's on the *Intimations of Immortality*, the poet is his own audience and the subject is a pure idea, however legitimate and splendid they be, would fall furthest from the original and fullest conception of the species; not because of their irregular measures, but by the restriction of their imagined audience, to one person, who is the poet himself, and by the failure of the mind's eye to furnish any scene or visible centre for their emotion. By Mr. Swinburne no such experiment is ever risked; for the choruses in his Greek plays, and his *Hymn of Man*, and his *Ode to Victor Hugo*, one and all presuppose, if not always an actual occurrence, still some unison of many spirits in a common admiration or passion, which is of the essence of the ode ; and in these pieces, whether they be more or less perfect than the little lyrics and elegies, we should be dull to ignore a special pride of rhythm and ambition of wing, that answer faithfully enough to the poet's now expressed promotion of the ode above all other forms of song.

II

Mr. Swinburne began his poetic life as a member of a school; and by a school of artists more is meant than when we speak of a school of herrings, darting and gleaming about in one place indistinguishably. It is a band of men, working so as to stamp their separate souls, be it through forms or colours or melodies (which may themselves often enough betray an inner likeness), upon moods or ideas that animate them all: so that their work as a whole may without absurdity be regarded as a single poem, or work of art, conceived in honour of a single series of ideas. The stronger each member of the band, the firmer his hold, though the greater his individual expression, of those ruling ideas. So it was with William Morris, Rossetti, Burne-Jones, and so with the youngest-born and youngest-natured of them all, who is still with us and at work. The more they diverged, the plainer was their engrossment with pure beauty, with visible beauty, and especially with the beauty of the feminine form, which came to be looked on, even by the halest of the four, as a typical vesture or symbol of Beauty herself, and perhaps also as the 'sovran shrine' of Melancholy. Common to them all, therefore, was the mystical will to go behind Beauty and have its meaning; and here they parted company and each of them spoke for himself. Rossetti saw the spiritual call in face and form, and desired the spirit through his desire of the body, and at last did not know the one desire from the other, and pressed on, true mystic as he was, in ever-narrowing circles, to some third thing that seemed to lie behind both desires. Some such impulse, as we have said, was not absent in Morris, though it hardly went urther than the delicious complaint and unrest of the *Earthly Paradise* ; but after a time, in his prose romances, he came to find little more in beauty than the object of natural human longing, and the shrine, not of melancholy, but of affections and tender graces. The frank desire that is told of in these stories is that of the young man for young-eyed beauty. A third of the group, the painter, feeling that 'soul is form, and doth the body make', embodied abstract emotions or dreams, after Spenser's way, but embodied them in figures of his own dream-life, figures in which the two sexes are not always markedly contrasted ; and he exhibited different phases of Love—Love weary, or Love cruel, or Love incurably remote ; or, more often, Love at pause and transparent and void of quality, like a clean empty cup of crystal. Akin to this, but less seated in the dream-world and more stinging in expression, was the conception of beauty that inspired the first series of *Poems and Ballads*. Thus in the work of the four artists there is enough unity to earn them the title of a historic school, whose flowering-time was from about 1855 to about 1880. No other school has since arisen in Britain, except that slighter but authentic one of the young Irish writers, whose vision of beauty, and the manner of whose mystical utterance, is very different. The prologue and the epilogue to Mr. Swinburne's lyrical writings show the endurance of his affection for the two friends, to whom he pays noble tribute in lines that fly lightly like birds from crest to crest of the breaking wave. Written in the same measure, both are offered to Burne-Jones, with whom, in the new dedication, is joined the name of William Morris. The purged ethereal pathos of this utterance is more than a renewal of the writer's poetical youth.

No sweeter, no kindlier, no fairer,
   No lovelier a soul from its birth
Wore ever a brighter and rarer
   Life's raiment for life upon earth
Than his who enkindled and cherished
   Art's vestal and luminous flame
That dies not when kingdoms have perished
   In storm or in shame.

No braver, no trustier, no purer,
   No stronger and clearer a soul
Bore witness more splendid and surer
   For manhood found perfect and whole
Since man was a warrior and dreamer
   Than his who in hatred of wrong
Would fain have arisen a redeemer
   By sword or by song.

III

In his preface Mr. Swinburne recalls his past amusement over those critics of the first *Poems and Ballads*
who 'insisted on regarding all the studies of passion and
sensation attempted and achieved in it as either confessions of positive fact or excursions of absolute fancy'.
This is a remark that might warn some of the critics of
Shakespeare's *Sonnets*, who either sneer at them as a
literary exercise or paw over them as Pepys-like confessions. To treat a poet as a diarist, or again to imagine him
building his creations out of no experience, is to be blind
to the first conditions of artistic handicraft. The critic
has to do, not with the actual experience of the poet,
but with the experience that the poet presents to him,
blended as it is of memory and dreams and invention
inscrutably. We had better not pry into that chemistry.
Even if we were the Recording Angel, or God's spies,
and knew the evidence, it would not help us to detect the
creative process. Goethe, it has often been observed, left

volumes of self-portrayal, and we are no nearer the secret of his work. The conception, in its greater or less nobility and clearness, and the execution, in its greater or less unity and rightness, are all that concern us in presence of a piece of art. From this, the only point of view, it may be fairly said that many of Mr. Swinburne's earlier pieces remain, to adapt a phrase of Poe's, not only poems of obscure emotion, but obscure poems of emotion, and the *Note* upon *Dolores*, *Hesperia*, and the rest, ought all the more to be now republished, if only as a prose poem in its own right. The pressmen of that earlier time, red with muddled and excited protest, often treated Swinburne as one of the writers called by Baudelaire ' brutaux et purement épidermiques '. But he was, in fact, a poet of the emotions, and not merely or mainly of the sensations. Look at D'Annunzio's *Il Peccato di Maggio*,[129] where the sentimental hardness of the Latin, the solemn inventory of the woman's body, the callow particularity, only suggest the first amour of a collegian ; and then turn to *An Interlude*, with its light step and backward wistful look. One is a poem of sensation, the other a poem of emotion—of emotion that comes short of anything highly spiritual, but of emotion still :—

> I remember the way we parted,
>   The day and the way we met,
> You hoped we were both broken-hearted,
>   And knew we should both forget.

Even in the poems that are a pure record of delirium mingled with the foretaste of heavy regret for its transiency, like *In the Orchard*, the advantage remains with the English poet, for the taste of expected loss is as strong upon his lips as the taste of present pleasure. And the harsher and stranger among those

Poems and Ballads were studies of idea as well as of emotion and sensation.   They are the first verses in England since those of Donne to utter faithfully certain youthful moods of sick revulsion, or of acrid satiety, or of hope idly recurrent, or of passion on the ebb and self-regretting.   They chronicle the invasion of hatred amid the triumph of pleasure, and the stranding of light love on its own shallow rocks ; the balance of the soul in apathy, like the slow fluctuation of a weed in the stream languid after the tidal wave ; the cold-handed visit of Retrospect, and the revulsion to the dreamy peace of the Garden of Proserpine.   These things are part of our youth, and it was Swinburne who gave them words. They are far behind, and yet they come back again in his art.   It is an error to treat these poems as literary followings of Baudelaire and Gautier, in whom some of their moods and themes may doubtless be paralleled. The feeling, that recurs oftenest and seems to govern all the rest, is easily definable and perfectly real, and is most fully set forth in *Ilicet*.   It is that love of death which is felt in youth or adolescence.   It is a feeling much derided, and wholly unaffected.   Age looks on the end as an intruder, or as a timely gift of nature, or as a natural process, or it does not think at all of the end, which comes on before it is realized.   But to youth in its dark hour the end is a treasure lusted for, it is the desire of no consciousness, it is the release from irritation, it is the crown of the garland of sleep.   This is the burden of *Ilicet* and of *Félise* :—

> No memory more of love or hate,
>   No trouble, nothing that aspires,
> No sleepless labour thwarting fate,
>   And thwarted ; where no travail tires,
>   Where no faith fires.

And again—

> Not for their love shall Fate retire,
> Nor they relent for our desire,
>   Nor the graves open for their call.
> The end is more than joy and anguish,
> Than lives that laugh and lives that languish,
>   The poppied sleep, the end of all.

As old in poetry as Catullus, this permanent or recurring cry of mankind is repeated in *Poems and Ballads* with unwearied energy. The slightest curb on the feeling would spoil everything. There is no curb except on the expression, and this is why the verses live ; for the controlled expression of uncontrolled feeling is essential to high lyric. No doubt there is a loftier weariness. Shakespeare was tired, not merely of the mirage of desire, but of that bitterness of mature experience, which in these young poems is wholly absent. Yet not for that is the right of the hastier and less-tired soul diminished to sing of its lightlier-earned fatigue, or to set into rhyme the strange measures of joy and grief that it has trodden.

IV

The repetitions in the first series of *Poems and Ballads* show that the poet was dissatisfied with his subjects, and was moving forward to larger ones. He ceased to find true matter for his imagination in the pathological idyll, or in the theme *Amor Mortis conturbat me* ; for the frame of mind that inspires such themes cannot, in its nature, last long, although it had called out his portentous creative power as a metrist, and had uttered itself in caressing triple rhymes, or undulant long stanzas unknown before. Some pieces in the same book announce the heroic age of Mr. Swinburne's poetry, which ran its course (if we exclude his dramas on English subjects) between the *Song of Italy* in 1867 and the *Erechtheus* of 1876. The lines to *Victor Hugo* wind a clear horn of onset amid the amorous Asiatic timbrels of 1866; and the honours paid to Landor, the 'oldest singer that England bore', show the temper that was to animate, and perhaps to release, the genius of the youngest. The delicately pure and more than Sicilian grace of Landor's own elegy and idyll, and also his passion for the noble antique, sank into his scholar. The earliest creed of Mr. Swinburne may perhaps be read in the Greek memorial lines preceding *Atalanta* and addressed to Landor. The praise of the old man's potent passion for liberty, and of his stately talent for poetical sculpture, suddenly closes upon the note of *Ilicet*. The enthusiasm of the born Hellenist mingles with the spirit of the Preacher—who surely, contrary to common opinion, must have been a young man—as in some sad refrain of Theognis. But the English piece, already mentioned, written in Landor's honour, has something of Landor's own strictness in outline and high-bred beauty of phrase; and these were salutary stars for the poet of the *Triumph of Time*, with its beautiful profusion and verbal ebullience, to steer by. A clear political strain already exalts the verse of the younger republican aristocrat, and it is also heard, with less restraint, in the *Song in Time of Revolution*. Mr. Swinburne's style at this time was greater and stronger than anything he had found to say. The result was that it often wreaked itself upon the air.

The full inspiration came from Italy, and the compelling voice was the voice of Mazzini, to whom the *Songs before Sunrise* and *A Song of Italy* are dedicated. Mr. Swinburne never offered any mere echo of Mazzini's doctrine.

I never pretended to see eye to eye with my illustrious friends and masters, Victor Hugo and Giuseppe Mazzini, in regard to the positive and passionate confidence of their sublime and purified theology.

Nor did he ever try to set forth in verse the whole of Mazzini's social and political religion. In this abstinence he was true to his lyrical and odic gift. A ruminative poet like Wordsworth—if ever Wordsworth could have risen to appreciate Mazzini's creed—would have covered a high tableland of leisurely blank verse with the abstract exposition of it. But in song and ode only a certain measure of such thinking can dissolve : if more is attempted, the result is a dreadful and dulling sediment of doctrine. The large emotions of fraternity and self-sacrifice and ultimate hope are the lyric poet's true material, apart from all programmes and tactics. Also, Mr. Swinburne gave more expression to the revolutionary cry than his master. To Mazzini the overthrow of the existing order and the clamour for freedom, for freedom undefined, were a mere preface to the real work in hand.

We invoke (he says) a social world, a vast harmonious organization of the forces existing in undirected activity in that vast laboratory, the earth ; and, in order to call this new world into being, and to lay the foundation of a pacific organization, we have recourse to those old habits of rebellion which consume our forces within the circle of individualism.

Not all of this idea is absorbed by the English poet ; but some of it flowers in *The Pilgrims* and in the *Prelude* to the *Songs before Sunrise*. The *Prelude* tells of the poet's escape from the exotic or orgiastic dreams of his younger fancy ; but with the lure of the names—*Thyiades, Cotytto, Bassarid*—a gust of the old airs blows across the

scene ; and then, at the end, he turns again to the future
and utters the public impulse of a whole era with
a buoyant lyric passion that makes its own tune and
flows without waste or riot and breaks into a beauty like
that of the morning.   The same is true of the *Eve of
Revolution*, a poem of transcendent hope and insuperable
will.   Mazzini's vision is that of a perfected and pacified
society ; but his scholar rather dreams of such a vigilant
heroic thinker as Mazzini himself, who risks his life but
keeps his spirit free of fear and doubt during the unresting labours of his mortal lease.

These poems are surrounded by many more, which
keep pace with the stages in the battle for Italian unity,
or serve as inspiriting marches of comradeship in the
pauses of the weightier music.   *Dirae*, a sonnet-series
that followed, is a frantic imprecation on the successive
anniversaries of Garibaldi's check at Mentana, and is
marred by Hugoesque virulence.   The two worst influences on Mr. Swinburne's art have been Victor Hugo
and the Authorized Version of the Bible.   If only he
had chosen Alfred de Vigny for his worship, what lapses
and effusion had been spared !   And almost every transference of scriptural style, by way of parody or irony,
to erotic or anti-clerical rhetoric, has been a failure.
There is no good reason why the noble manner of our
old translators of Hebrew poetry should be thus misused.
There is no cruder weapon for the expression of invective.
One exception may be found in the poem called *Before
a Crucifix*, where the rhetoric, if it does not quite find
entrance, calls and clangs at the gate of the heart owing to
the splendour of the rhythm.   But among these odes
and poems of liberation are found the highest and finest
of Swinburne's lyrical writings.   They are an eager,
young-hearted accompaniment to the public events of

the years 1866 to 1870.   If at times they run to formless overflow, they are pure in phrasing and infallible in cadence.   Of this poet it may too often be felt that his 'strength's abundance weakens his own heart'.   The stream is so high in flood, that the banks are lost and the boundaries blurred, though the course is true and the higher landmarks visible.   The series may be said to close with the *Ode on the Proclamation of the French Republic*.   Unity in Italy was won, but without the republic dreamed of by Mazzini; and Mr. Swinburne, who may not have felt drawn to celebrate what seemed a triumph marred, kept his paean for the France of 1871. In his later volumes there are many political verses, but not so many as might have been hoped that are fresh, adequate, and beautiful.   Some, like those on Nelson, speak to all.   The comminations on Gladstone and the Boers are not likely to please even fanatics.   But the hopes declared in the *Songs before Sunrise*, if at some seasons they have faded out of sight, are in their nature lasting, like that high expression of them to which Mr. Swinburne rose in his fortunate hour.

V

The abstract and moral passion for mankind does not always wear long in an Englishman.   Mr. Swinburne gave it voice in 1870; even in 1875, in the *Songs of Two Nations*, it is heard.   It had not come to him from Comte with his quaint hierarchies, so dangerous if they were not mere nightmares, but from those Republican ardours of Mazzini, from the emancipation of Italy and France.   Then Mr. Swinburne came back to themes which seem to have lain deeper in his blood; to Mary of Scotland, to our Renaissance drama, to Britain and her present hopes.   But meanwhile he took leave of

those free artists of France with whom his own affinity
was strong. Rossetti had translated from Villon with
even a more intimate sense of words than the younger
poet, but his pent and searching spirit must have cared
far less for that bright and blackguardly ballad-maker.
Mr. Swinburne's *Ballade* on Villon might have been made
on a friend or companion who died yesterday :—

Poor splendid wings so frayed and soiled and torn!
    Poor kind wild eyes so dashed with light quick tears!
Poor perfect voice, most blithe when most forlorn.

It does not appear whether personal acquaintance inspired
the laments on Gautier and Baudelaire ; we hardly
trace it in the faint and acrid immortelles that are laid
upon their tombs in the Second Series of *Poems and
Ballads*. There Mr. Swinburne is back once more in
the land of inquisitive passion, of absorption in form,
on the further side of good and evil. His public and
political enthusiasm is in arrest. Few men cared so
sublimely little for the general fates of the world as the
authors of *Les Fleurs du Mal* and *Le Roi Candaule* ; and
rightly, for the world was not their business. It takes
a Frenchman to be thorough, whether in his devotion
or in his apathy to the hopes of man. There had been
signs in *Félise* of the study of Baudelaire ; and Gautier's
best-known and strangest, though not his greatest, piece
of decoration, 'the golden book of spirit and sense,' had
received a sonnet from his English brother ; but the
elegies of Mr. Swinburne on both poets ring deeper than
those tributes, and rarely has a foreign writer earned
a more glorious valediction from an English mourner
than Baudelaire in *Ave atque Vale* :—

For thee, O now a silent soul, my brother,
    Take at my hands this garland, and farewell ;
    Thin is the leaf, and chill the wintry smell,

> And chill the solemn earth, a fatal mother,
>   With sadder than the Niobean womb,
>   And in the hollow of her breasts a tomb.

This part of the Second Series of *Poems and Ballads* is an elegy of the poet on himself, a farewell to his youth and its early masters, a pagan wayside ritual, an *ex voto* before he travels on, restless-hearted, with a scornful look askance at the peace of the Christian graveyards.

The Second Series appeared in 1878; and meanwhile more had been done. The two Hellenics, *Atalanta* and *Erechtheus*, belonging to the golden youth of the poet, are significantly reprinted, not amongst his plays, but amongst his lyrics and narratives. Their interest is far more than purely musical; but no poems leave a surer conviction that the untouched musical resources of the language are infinite; that no measure is so old as to be dead, and that when the right player comes the long burden of the metrical past is as nothing. And most of their glory lies in the rhymed measures of the choruses, which attain a longer sweep of line and a fuller rush of movement than all but the best of the *Poems and Ballads*. In his new preface Mr. Swinburne records his own preference to *Erechtheus* on the score of 'the whole being greater than the parts', while of the constructive power in *Atalanta* he can hardly say so much.

The two best things in these two Greek plays, the antiphonal lamentation for the dying Meleager and the choral presentation of stormy battle between the forces of land and sea, lose less by such division from the main body of the poem than would those scenes in *Bothwell* which deal with the turning-point in the life of Mary Stuart on the central and conclusive day of Carberry Hill.

Charged as these poems are with reminiscences of Greek tragedy, and carefully as they are laid out on the

Greek convention, their predominantly lyric tone, over-flowing even into dialogue and monologue, keeps them from being Greek in essence, and leaves them only the more original.   They are, in soul and spirit, not so near even to the more decorative kind of ancient drama as *Samson Agonistes* is to the plays of Sophocles.   It is less the thought than the sure mastery of swift-footed and magnificent cadence that remains upon the memory—a cadence new and young that has not yet spent itself in myriad self-echoes.

VI

Four years after the second *Poems and Ballads*, in 1882, came the romance *Tristram of Lyonesse*.   The lyrical poet is trying, in a narrative metre, to sing and tell a story at the same time.   The verse goes apace, but the manner is so expansive and diffusive that the tale goes slowly.   The same tale can be stripped and presented in a short ballad, the leisurely psychology disappearing, and giving us instead the quick strokes of vital passion.   There is an old Icelandic ballad on Tristram, where the refrain of seven words gives the heart of the story : *their doom was nought, save to part* ; and this method is one for a concentrated, economical artist.   But the old regular way, the spacious, tardy, and not less beautiful way of romancing, as it is seen in Chaucer's *Troilus and Creseide*, or in Morris's *Story of Rhodope*, is used in *Tristram of Lyonesse* : but here the movement is vehement and quick, there it is gentle and leisurely.   The surging rollers of its rhyme advance rapidly and break loudly, but the shore is sometimes invisible, and the faces of the personages, the situation at a given moment, are obscured in the rumour and the spray.

Our old heroic couplet has never been so hastened by the devices of overflowing line and trisyllabic bar and by the lightening of accent. Yet all such comparisons, which try to convey the impression of rapid *tempo*, are really out of place. For *Tristram* is a true romance, where the conception of time is abolished altogether. This is the distinguishing mark of a story where the real persons are only two or three, and the active world is a far-off murmur, not suffered to intrude otherwise. For time can only be measured in such a story by the interruptions of the world, and these are never suffered to happen. At the crises, no time passes ; but the rapid absorbed life of a few instants in the heart of Iseult or Cressida belies all measurement by beats of the clock. Nor are the characters distinctly shown ; for the subject of *Tristram* is not so much the long-canonized lovers as Love itself, and the epilogue on 'the light and sound and darkness of the sea ' is in concord with their fates.

VII

The *Tale of Balen*, printed fifteen years later, is a greater poem and better done than *Tristram*, though its theme is not so great. It reaches the heart, through the ear, more surely, and the versification has a clearer beauty. It is another story of guilt, though fate is the guilty party and punishes the good and noble as if the guilt were theirs. The story is one of the large heroic episodes—the predestined, innocent, and mutual death of brother at the hand of brother, beguiled and environed by treacherous black magic. Tennyson tells the story too ; but it is less suited than some other chapters of Malory to his far-sought felicity of decoration and his various but slowly-wheeling blank verse. Mr. Swinburne rides, as he tells us,

> Reining my rhymes into buoyant order
> Through honeyed leagues of the northland border;

and the gusty airs and thrilling scents of his own country-side pass into the aspiring fourfold rimes and pathetic refluent close of each stanza. The old harmony by contrast which pervaded *Poems and Ballads*, of the sense of joy with the countervailing sense of doom, is here with a difference: for it goes to a proud and manly march. Balen, *fey*, but jaunting with a high heart through omens and the invisible smiting foes that leave their prey in his path and vanish, and ever nearing the fratricidal field by the accursed castle, is he not the latest and perhaps the last creation of those romancers of a renewed Middle Age who first spoke in the *Defence of Guenevere*, now close on half a century ago? Yet, from the severe and rigid concentration of the youthful Morris, to the copious ease and generous magnificence of his friend, the step in workmanship is far. *Balen* shows that vigour of the Northern blood, wild-hearted and strong-headed, which befits a teller of tales in rhyme. The exotic and plaintive moods of the *Poems and Ballads* are still present, and intervene in undertone, and save the story from being no more than a capital Walter Scott ballad of killing and foray and perfunctory romance.

So long, so voluble, an interval after *Tristram*, and then, in *Balen*, a sudden resurrection of lyric power! The *Roundels*, with their odd, often ineffectual refrains, like childish gestures; the Third Series of *Poems and Ballads*, and *Astrophel*, and its companions, hard to remember; *A Midsummer Holiday*; all again and again stirring dimly the old fascination; many of these are the work of a wonderful improviser, so sure of doing his feat that he cannot fail if he tries, and his skill becomes involuntary and monotonous; he is heard at

Q

last with more surprise than pleasure. The composition is empty, the executant infallible; as if he had wagered how well he could do—nothing. The exertion of great skill *in vacuo* always becomes at last supremely painful. We blame ourselves for wearying of that with which no fault can be found, except that it is faultlessly null. Much of Mr. Swinburne's song and lyric for twenty years has been performance rather than creation. No one else could write it; it is sincere; but it perishes like the scud or the cloud-wreath, in the act of formation. His true power during that long interval lies in prose and drama. The present edition does not give the critical papers; the English dramas are contained in a separate one. Both justify a reissue more loudly than much that is here reprinted. The noble early commentary on Blake, now republished, is written with the sanity of a true poet; and the articles on the playwrights from Chapman to Heywood, produced mostly in the eighties, are even better as criticisms than the companion sonnets, superb in harmony and strenuous in effort but not always fortunate as poems. The reader of the prose and verse eulogies on Hugo sickens at the calls on his admiration; but *A Note on Charlotte Brontë* and others of the English studies abide, in their essential justice, their splendid praise, and their poetic insight. The evolution of Mr. Swinburne's dramatic style can be traced from the lyrism of *Chastelard*, through the epical tragedy of *Bothwell*, to the curt strength of *The Sisters*— where the phrasing is only just within the liberties of verse—and of *Rosamund, Queen of the Lombards*. This change has meant a sterner hold on character and historical truth, and an increase in pure brainwork. But his plays, like his prose writings, are very nearly a life-work in themselves, and would call for a respectful and a separate notice. Nor is the time yet ready for the final anthology which will be made by Time from the six volumes before us, with their rich variety, here so scantily chronicled, of landscape, and sea-piece, and ballad, and memorial ode. The fame of a profuse and unequal and unresting writer has of necessity to wait longer than that of one who, like Dante Gabriel Rossetti, winnows his work and saves only that which possesses the utmost intensity and perfection, and who is thus his own anthologist. Yet the ultimate garland of the more spendthrift singer may prove to be not less in quantity, as it will certainly not rank lower in beauty of its own noble order.

MR. GEORGE MEREDITH

I. Delay of Popularity; Remoteness from Pessimistic Fiction.   II. The Social Scene of the Novels; The English Country House, and Italy.   III. Women in the Novels; Analysis of Tragic and Obscure Feeling. IV. The 'Comic Spirit' as an Implement.   V. Creed; the 'Earth' in Poetry.   VI. Style and Epigram; 'Dark with Excess of Light'; Contrast of Verse and Prose.

I

Who really cares for what I say? The English people know nothing about me. There has always been something antipathetic between them and me. With book after book it was always the same outcry of censure and disapproval. The first time or two I minded it, then I determined to disregard what people said altogether, and since then I have written only to please myself. But even if you could tell the world all I think, no one would listen.

Mr. Meredith, who is reported thus to have spoken some years ago, has notwithstanding won the only kind of fame for which he can be supposed to care. Not only has he received the Order of Merit, the last official *imprimatur* set by English society upon brains that are pronounced to be eminent and also harmless. He has the honour paid him by all his fellow craftsmen, and by thousands of other persons. In such a case the good of fame is greater to those who proffer it than to the possibly weary winner of the fame. Mr. Meredith is now a kind of Field-Marshal of English letters. He is the man who

has done most, and seen most service. To the general
joy he is amongst us and still upon the watch. His first
verses were printed in the year (1851) after Wordsworth's
Prelude. His poetry is still being commented, proclaimed, and defended, it is alive and singing in our ears.
The Odes in Contribution to the Song of French History
were collected in 1898. Last year (1906) saw his jubilee
as a novelist; for in 1856 appeared *The Shaving of
Shagpat*, which disclosed the costly treasure-house of
his fancy and the overrunning springs of his wit. *The
Ordeal of Richard Feverel* came out in 1859, the same
year as *Adam Bede* and *The Origin of Species*; *Lord
Ormont and his Aminta*, in 1894. Some thirteen novels,
besides short tales, criticisms, and poems, are the fruit of
those forty years. Mr. Meredith wrought unweariably
through the later day of Dickens and Thackeray, through
the day of George Eliot and the jaunty revulsion against
her, and now through the day of Mr. Hardy and Mr. Henry
James. He was neglected or patronized by many of the
critics in the sixties and the early seventies, and perhaps
the habit of feeling induced by this treatment may linger
in the words quoted above. The bigger reading public,
the masses of the English community overseas, no doubt
are still recalcitrant. Mr. Meredith has never struck
home to them, as Dickens struck home with his splendid
humanity, his uncertain art and moderate education, and
his true wealth of genial and farcical type. Some, too,
of those devoted to Thackeray's vast and populous canvas,
to his occasional classic sureness and constant elegance of
speech (amidst much that is merely journalistic fiction),
and to his half-dozen scenes of vehement human drama,
may have shivered at the refreshing east wind and
shrunk from the mountain sickness that the reader of
Mr. Meredith must face. To read him is like climbing,

and calls for training and eyesight ; but there is always the view at the top, there are the sunrise and the upper air. Nor is such a tax always paid him willingly by the better-trained, serious public of escaped and enlightened puritans, the dwindled public of George Eliot. Nor has he much in common with the novelists, English and other, of a later day.

For he, like Goethe, ' bids you hope,' while *Tess of the D'Urbervilles* and *The Wings of the Dove* do not. The movement of later fiction is towards pessimism, and its best makers, Guy de Maupassant, Gorky, D'Annunzio, agree in their want of hopefulness if in nothing else. They have been catching up and expressing in fiction ideas that found a nobler expression, philosophical or lyrical, nearly a century ago, in Schopenhauer and Leopardi. The same discouragement lay at the base of Tolstoy's thought, before he found his peculiar salvation, and it still tinges his fiction when he forgets his creed and remembers he is an artist. The history of this pessimistic movement in fiction is still unwritten, and the movement itself is unexhausted.

But the groundwork of Mr. Meredith, with his forward look, his belief in love and courage, is different. It is stoical rather than pessimistic ; and in that he resembles Zola, whose method—laborious, serried, humorless—is the opposite of his. Mr. Meredith grew up on the high hopes fed by the revolutions of the mid-century, and the most heroic figure in his books is Mazzini, the ' Chief' in *Vittoria*. He has a moral and spiritual afflatus of the nobler order, peculiarly and traditionally English, in that line of the great English prophets which comes down from Langland and Sir Thomas More to Carlyle. His creed does not depend, visibly, on formal doctrine for its force, but neither does it rest on any preoccupying enmity

towards doctrine. His inspiration plays in various moods
—strenuous, ethereal, ironical—rarely serene, over his
vision of 'certain nobler races, now dimly imagined';
and casts a new interpreting light, above all, on the rarer
forms of love and patriotism and friendship. Yet there
are none of the airs of the prophet, for the media preferred
by Mr. Meredith in his prose are wit and aphorism, situation and portraiture, and to these the lyrical and didactic
elements are subordinate.

II

Mr. Meredith has run a course of his own, and has
owed little to any man of his own craft. It may be
guessed, indeed, that the author of *Harry Richmond* had
before him in *Copperfield* the example of a new, humorous,
natural, and beautiful form of autobiographic fiction.
And Thomas Love Peacock, to whom Mr. Meredith's
first book was inscribed, may have lent a happy turn
to his generous and repeated and witty praise of wine,
and have supplied some hint for those country-house
gatherings of humorists and fantasts of which a specimen
is found so late as 1890 in *One of Our Conquerors*. In
such a gathering the inmates and visitors are endowed
with a surprising point, wit, and agility of soul in their
tongue-combats. But Peacock's humorists all come from
London, or from the void, for the week-end, and go back
on the Monday. These are minor debts, and Mr. Meredith
stands apart from all the recognized groups of schools of
English novelists. For his true and chosen background
is the real, feudal, Tory, country world of old Victorian
England, with its ineradicable shades of caste-feeling, its
surface gallantry, its reluctance to think, its vigour of
physique, and its excellent manners. It is not likely that
such a world, which is still alive, and long will be, should

trouble much about its own countenance as reflected in the 'steel glass' of the novelist. His favourite characters are the bravest and fairest that such a society can breed, or at least cannot prevent from being bred, in its midst ; and his frequent subject is the struggle of these favourites to rise above the spiritual and mental level of their world. Many of his personages are real gentry, rooted in their estates, persons of the upper untitled or the lower titled classes, or else in some defined social relationship to these— great dames, young soldiers, eldest sons of the land, naval commanders, scholars of the strenuous or the portly type, parsons of good estimation, usually ponderous, and the babbling society mob. In natural connexion with these are the tenants, oaken old yeomen or farmers, Fleming or Blaize, often the fathers of fair daughters, who rise by natural selection, like Lucy Feverel ; or gentlemen proved such by trial of circumstance, like Evan Harrington the tailor's son. There are, further, the retainers, butlers, intelligent handmaids, sporting coves, and prize-fighters like that admirable light-weight Skepsey, the servant of Nataly Radnor. There are the ladies of clouded fame, who serve the unauthorized amusements of gentlemen, and who are somewhat unreal, though tragically-conceived, characters. Mr. Meredith, by choosing within this province an immeasurably higher range of interest and passion than the accurate patient Trollope, has added a new stratum of semi-barbarian territory to English fiction.

It may be called the Empire-making stratum, and the profound feeling for the work and future of our race that throbs through Mr. Meredith's writings provides him with an outlet into a freer air. He is, I have said, a liberal idealist, whose hopes are rooted in the tenacious, the Norman, the constructive aspirations of the Englishman. And his faith is strengthened by his outlook upon the European stir for freedom, which carries him beyond the political creed of the class he portrays. A rare reconciliation of ideals, that may perhaps hereafter be noted as prophetic! In *Vittoria* he finds a subject that is free from any of the limitations imposed by irony. Music and freedom, the freedom of Italy and its signal, the singing of the heroine in La Scala, are its animating powers. The compass of his gifts, both as an epical narrator and a painter of noble character, are best seen in the pair of stories that take us from the humours of the English lawn to the struggle of Italian liberation. In *Emilia in England*, otherwise *Sandra Belloni*, and in *Emilia in Italy*, otherwise *Vittoria* (all three being names for one woman), he has described, as no English writer ever yet, a true artist-soul, with a patriot soul behind it of equal stature. The companion-book is Mr. Swinburne's *Songs before Sunrise*, for the spirit of Mazzini breathes in both. And in other stories Mr. Meredith has found an air freer than that of England. There are bright and keen glimpses of France in *Beauchamp's Career* and in the gracious Renée de Rouaillout. The study of Lassalle and Helène de Racowitza, made from the authorities, in *The Tragic Comedians*, does not fully reach the high-strung purpose of the writer, in spite of the elemental or tidal energy of Alvan-Lassalle. But Alvan is a relief after the manly, self-restrained, pattern Englishmen commonly invented by Mr. Meredith in order to find some one worthy of his heroines.

III

He seems to have 'reversed the order of Paradise', and to have created his women first, and so to have had less clay at disposal for fashioning their mates. Renée,

Emilia, Carinthia, Lucy, with their musical names—in
their talk, and his talk about them, his style is at its
purest and clearest, and the colours of the portraits are
unfading. Women are nearer to nature than men, and
the power to paint them can only come straight from
the breast of nature—from experience lived through and
transmuted into artistic form. Indeed, the business of
' reading the female heart ' has not often been practised
in English prose without a dispiriting effect. The
tradition of unreality is old and obstinate. It runs far
back to the Renaissance romance, like Sidney's *Arcadia*—
where, indeed, there is one tragic feminine figure, the
queen Gynecia ; and to the long-winded books in French
and English consumed by our seventeenth-century an-
cestresses. But those old romances were apt to be made
either by courtly, artificial men or by spinsters without
any profitable experience of humanity. One of these
spinsters, Samuel Richardson, succeeded once, despite
his fussy morals and clammy rhetoric. The laborious
knife of George Eliot sometimes bites deep. But a man,
if only he is great enough and can rise above the
natural barrier ('La haine entre les deux sexes,' says
Joubert, 'ne s'éteint guère') is the best and kindest
painter of women and of their ailments of the soul, and
the best describer of them. Or so the event seems to
have proved. This is not a reflection upon women ; for,
after all, it is better to belong to the class that is
pictured than to the class that paints pictures.

Balzac and Mr. Meredith, diverse in almost all ways,
have both left behind them a portrait gallery of actual
and living women. Balzac excels with older, harder,
and stranger natures. The Englishman, more of a poet
at the heart, prefers to celebrate youth and beauty that
are victorious after long inward and outward trial. But

he has, more than once, his Hermiones as well as his
Perditas, figures of the 'sanctissima coniux', September
faces, thrown into contrast with those fresher ones without loss of charm. The friendship of Diana of the
Crossways and her 'Tony' is an instance. *One of Our
Conquerors* essays the hardest and nicest problem in
Mr. Meredith's later books, as *Rhoda Fleming* does
among the earlier. It is a demonstration of the mystery
of pain in the hearts of a mother and a daughter. The
mother dreads the disclosure, which the daughter
has to face, of their socially unauthorized position. The
girl is illegitimate, owing to a foolish marriage made by
her father long ago. Words are found for her discovery
of the circumstance ; for this is required the delicacy of
the great masters. The mother dies, the girl becomes
a magnificent spirit, a sworn defender of the unfortunate
among her own sex, and her own happiness is at last
assured, a handsome and chivalrous hero being provided
for her with some surface failings that make him possible.

But for such work Mr. Meredith has had to invent
his own dialect. He sets himself, continually, to realize
motives that have their life only in the antechambers of
consciousness, and sensations that fade in the effort to
give them words. Here he forswears whim and witty
fancy ; in the best passages, all is attention and grave
precision. The bending of English prose to this finer
purpose is one of Mr. Meredith's substantial glories.
Undiscovered forces of vanity, of self-protection that is
sure of its danger but not of its reasons, of self-regard
and self-distrust, find their calculus. He is taxed with
obscurity, but he is as lucid a writer, in this province, as
the nature of the subject permits. He moves as safely
in the dark as Dostoieffsky, the great specialist ; and
though, unlike him, he is sometimes hampered by the

satiric aim, and is less content to let the nakedness of our nature plead for itself, he is also free from the wildness and mirage and crazy touch that prove refracting elements in *Crime and Punishment* or *The Idiot.* In the scientific dissection of motive, filament by filament, Mr. Henry James ranks beside him, and in the power to realize deeply-plotting, ambiguous natures, may be his superior, just as his hold on beauty of style is more certain and steady. But the characters of Mr. Meredith are fuller than any other novelist's of strong, natural vitality; they fight, and swim, and wander in scented forests, and wipe the sweat from their brows, and intercept mad dogs, and make love in their youth beneath the wild cherry-blossom, and give their lives to save some ' little mudlarking waif ', like Beauchamp ; and his words accordingly ring and rush as the blood runs faster. Out of this kind of strength comes the power that lies behind the finer, tenderer passages that interpret obscure matters of the heart. The intellect remains the master while threading the mazes of unuttered painful feeling. In the episode already mentioned, Nataly, the nominal wife, who is caught in the birdlime of a false social position, asks a friend for the counsel which yet she fears to receive.

She bowed to her chastisement. One motive in her consultation with him came of the knowledge of his capacity to inflict it and honesty in the act, and a thirst she had to hear the truth loud-tongued from him: together with a feeling that he was excessive and satiric, not to be read by the letter of his words : and in consequence, she could bear the lash from him, and tell her soul that he overdid it, and have an unjustly-treated self to cherish. But in very truth she was a woman who loved to hear the truth ; *she was formed to love the truth her position reduced her to violate* ; she esteemed the

hearing of it as medical to her; she selected for coun-
sellor him who would apply it: so far she went on the
straight way : and the desire for a sustaining deception
from the mouth of a trustworthy man set her hanging
on his utterances with an anxious hope of the reverse of
what was to come and what she herself apprehended;
such as checked her pulses and iced her feet and fingers.

Mr. Meredith's analysis, in serious romance, is nearly
always *moral* analysis; it is concerned with complex
refinements of the profounder pieties and veracities. He
is always testing human nature with his finger, like a
glass, to see if it rings clear and right.   Or rather, to
read him, before the heart is hardened, is like going
to the dentist, who does not spare to touch the nerve.
This is another reason for his incomplete popularity ; but,
inasmuch as his science is genuine, it is also a reason for
his name enduring.   In his dramatic, ironic way, he is
one of the masters of the spiritual life :—not the life of
the lonely mystic or thinker (for such persons do not
figure in his books as they do in Balzac's) but the life
of men and women in contact, snared by instinct or
egoism, but capable of emerging with made souls, marked
and scarred but ready to begin afresh.   Historically, this
kind of special power leaves him somewhat solitary
amongst English novelists.

IV

There is, however, no monotony of tragic note.
Mr. Meredith's chosen weapon is comedy, and his discourse *On the Idea of Comedy,* given in 1877 at the
middle of his career, throws a backward and forward
light upon his artistic practice.   It is a classic piece of
criticism, written by a fellow of Hazlitt, with the
advantages that the craftsman, like Dryden in the

Discourse of Satire, is speaking of his own craft ; and that, like Dryden, he has ample reading and scholarship as well as the memory of his own creative processes. As we read, we feel that since Goldsmith the higher comic spirit, as distinct from that of farce or irony, has fled from the stage to the novel. Mr. Meredith is not popular, because he is full of the comic spirit as he conceives it. It is not the high and bare cynicism of Congreve, the emperor of phrasing. It is distinguished from farcical humour by its different treatment of the victim.

If you laugh all around him, tumble him, roll him about, deal him a smack, and drop a tear on him, own his like-ness to you and yours to your neighbour, spare him as little as you shun, pity him as much as you expose, it is a spirit of Humour that is moving you.

But even this is not the whole of the comic spirit. Lessing had said that ' Comedy is laughter, not derision ' ; and derision with a moral purpose is still further off from comedy than farce. Even irony is only part of its essence.

If instead of falling foul of the ridiculous person with a satiric rod, to make him writhe and shriek aloud, you prefer to sting him under a semi-caress, by which he shall in his anguish be rendered doubtful whether indeed anything has hurt him, you are an engine of Irony.

In the view of Mr. Meredith the comic spirit, as distinct from inferior or allied forms of humour, cannot flourish except in a disinfected society where manners are highly trained. Like most honest readers, he finds the Restora-tion and Revolution comedy, which records quite another society, generally dead and tiresome, presupposing as it does an audience not a little inhuman. The flowering of the comic spirit is bound up, he insists, with the due position and honourable estate of women.   Where they are the cheap butts, rather than the arbiters and voices of the comic spirit, there is no hope for it.

Now, comedy is the fountain of good sense, not the less perfectly sound on account of the sparkle; and comedy lifts women to a station offering them free play for their wit, as they usually show it, when they have it, on the side of good sense.   The higher the comedy, the more prominent the part they enjoy in it. . . . Celimène is undisputed mistress of the attribute (of common sense) in the *Misanthrope*, wiser as a woman than Alceste as a man.   In Congreve's *Way of the World* Millamant overshadows Mirabel, the sprightliest male figure of English comedy.

It may be replied that Alceste, with his passion for Celimène conflicting with his passion for sincerity, is the higher of the two; but in respect of pure wit he is doubtless the smaller.   It may also be added that Mr. Meredith's women are not often witty, or that when they are their wit is strained.   But good sense, barbed with disconcerting smiles, they have in a supreme measure. We can best understand Mr. Meredith's idea of the comic spirit from the malady which it is intended to show up and, if possible, to cure.   That is ' sentimentalism'; and by the term is understood, not the simple movements of the heart in simple persons, with their untrained expression, but the impulses of vanity or selfish craving, masquerading as those of the heart and uttering phrases too big for the occasion or false to it.   Sentimentalism implies the absence both of clear reason, and also of the one other thing, besides religion and country, that the comic spirit respects, simple and healthy passion.   *Evan Harrington* and *The Egoist* are built upon this conception of a vanity which is the target of thoughtful glancing ridicule, and which is at last exposed, if not cured, by the daylight of reason—and banished, if at all, by the warmth of authentic love. *Evan Harrington* is a second *Book of Snobs*, the air being some hundred feet higher of social elevation, and the scene being laid amidst the classes where the sense of rank and caste, at the era depicted in the book, is Chinese in its strictness. It is the lightest and blithest of Mr. Meredith's English tales, and in it his tragic force is sleeping, while his heroic force is at play. *The Egoist*, with its more intricate and mature subject, is now long established in all our affections, and answers best to the author's own ' idea ' of the comic spirit. Here he writes intoxicated with his own wit, in the way that is so rare in Englishmen. He is like some irresistible executant, unafraid of the most discordant or fantastic witch-dance of words, and yet striking continually into impeccable expression. The same relish is felt in all his later books, but never for so long.

V

Though no one speaks less from a chair or pulpit, Mr. Meredith stands to be judged as a teacher and prophet. He is not content to be an observer. Comedy and morality are in history old and lawfully wedded lovers. If we cannot have the perfectly free poetical life of Arden, then give us that *L'École des Femmes* or *The Egoist*. In *The Amazing Marriage*, in *One of Our Conquerors*, and everywhere, the pleasure of the educator is apparent. The characters are plunged into trial, they are beaten and tempered and annealed, partly by ridicule, partly by their own passion ; and this is done in the name of Nature, to see how they will stand the shock. Mr. Meredith's ethic is best applied in his prose and best expounded in his verse, though his verse comes, far less

often than his prose, to rightness of form. He has his
own divinity, pagan by name. Where other writers
appeal to God or to Humanity, he speaks, somewhat
insistently, of the Earth; and the Earth is not the
malign stepmother of pessimistic theory, but a stern
genial mother, if at times something of a governess.
In Mr. G. M. Trevelyan's clear exposition of *The Poetry
and Philosophy of George Meredith*, there is heard
a welcome note of caution:—

Some may think that the value of the lessons he would
enforce is not much enhanced by the alleged sanction of
Earth. They may think that it is really much the same
as the more usual formula of the sanction of Heaven, and
that it has equally much or equally little weight.

Earth, however, is less a 'sanction' than an emotional
symbol of Nature, and its incessant recurrence does more
harm to Mr. Meredith's art than to his thinking. Earth
lends us our bodies, our fund of power, and our capital of
instinct, which may be turned to uses fruitful or sterile.
Our life is the adjustment and realization of the forces
that Earth has given us. It is love, rightly understood,
that tasks and rewards our power of directing those
forces. Such love helps us, in its better forms, to the
vision of those 'nobler races', for out of love they must
be begotten. The creed is not unlike Carlyle's in its
courage, but it is more possible, less savage, and less
solitary. There is to be no tampering with the intellect
by soothing illusions; 'we must do,' as George Eliot
said, 'without opium'. The volume called *A Reading
of Earth*, and the poem therein called *A Faith on Trial*,
give us Mr. Meredith's religion. Whatever the power or
complexion of the enemy, whether it be ignorance, or
languor, or bereavement, or self-deception, he is always
in the attitude of the challenger; like Ivanhoe, who rode

R

up the lists, and in token of mortal combat touched the shield with the sharp end of his spear, despite the well-meant hints of ' some of the lower classes '.

VI

Soon or late has to be faced the hindrance of Mr. Meredith's verbal strangeness, which is still supposed to warrant or explain his slow acceptance by the public. The robust older critics, who were still flourishing when he began to write fifty years ago, made much, it is said, of this hindrance. But they did not try to understand. Their idea was to decree rewards and punishments to an artist—so many stripes of the cat on the shoulders balanced by so many of good conduct on the sleeve. The author, if not a criminal who had to come up for punishment, was a kind of ticket-of-leave man who must report himself under suspicion. And if the sentence was capital, the executioner wore a mask of blue or buff, according to the complexion of the journal that sheltered his anonymity. It was the kind of criticism that trained its readers to lose the instinct for literary power, and it is now nearly dead. No doubt there was, at first sight, colourable matter for reproach. In every book by Mr. Meredith, from *The Shaving of Shagpat* to *The Amazing Marriage*, the outline of the figures and even of the events is more or less veiled under a sparkling mist or spray of commentary, an emanation of bewildering light. Self-suppression does not enter into such a method, as it does into that of Flaubert, and there is as much choric interlude as drama. There is a heady, subtle element, which beguiles and dislodges the reader, and dazes him with myriads of epigrams. The epigrams of Mr. Meredith might be fairly divided into those which leave a headache behind them and those that do not. So great a rapidity of comment does not make for proportion and composition. But take the story, and strip it, at whatever momentary sacrifice, of all but the actual narrative and dialogue, keeping also the passages that expressly describe motive and sensation, but leaving out the chorus of aphorisms, and the test will be nobly met. We can then go back again and put in as much of the rainbow as we will. The difficulty of style is felt most keenly in Mr. Meredith's poetry. There, in its most restless form, is the swift intellect, working for the writer's cherished ethical or spiritual ideas, and working through a torrent of images, sometimes turbid and sometimes abstrusely delicate, but huddling on one another as fast as in the dying speech of Romeo. As Lamb said of Shakespeare, 'before one idea has burst its shell, another is hatched and clamorous for disclosure.' But the poetry also often suffers (the prose less, because prose will bear more of such vagrancy than poetry, and yet remain true to the law of its art) because the intellect, so far from being content to let the sensuous matter clear itself and rely on itself, as Keats in his finest passages is content to do, is always interposing and enlisting that material in the service of the 'criticism of life'. Many are the verses where the issue is doubtful, or rather not doubtful; where the night-long wrestle with words is continued from sheer courage rather than in the hope or possibility of victory. Many, again, for instance in *Modern Love*, are those where the result is impeccable and the sense of strain is lost. More seldom are the imagery and the music all-sufficient to one another, in a kind of Goethe-like repose, as here :—

> The pine-tree drops its dead ;
> They are quiet, as under the sea.
> Overhead, overhead,

Rushes life in a race,
As the clouds the clouds trace chase:
And we go,
And we drop like the fruits of the tree,
Even we,
Even so.

But commonly, in Mr. Meredith's verses, imagination is at war with and outraces its own power of expression, and thus is too frequently defeated, though its triumphs are not rare, and would, if selected and arrayed together, form a 'golden treasury' large enough. But, as with some older poets like George Chapman, words, lines, and passages, which are informed with lofty and gracious ideas, are so variably cast that the innermost soul of poetry must alternately repudiate and welcome them. In the novels the proportion is different; the pages that go quite amiss and do violence to the writer's own ideals of form are relatively fewer. The diction of Mr. Meredith in his prose is, for long spaces, pure, chosen, and simple. The oddness is produced by slight dislocations of historic English, an unusual order of words, a curious disposal of particles and abstract nouns, which in cumulation give a superficial effect of freakishness. As so often with Latin or Italian, the decipherer finds himself gazing at a sentence made up of common words without getting to their sense. The subject may be commended to some young Germanized American for a golden or leaden dissertation. There is, indeed, no reason why a classic author should not be treated by the usual methods of scholarship, if they are applied with tact, as Mr. Trevelyan applies them. This is only a sign of respect, which we offer to Chapman or to Donne. But it may be well to have the transpicuous page of Fielding open before us, that we may keep our heads while we study the heir of his noble art.

THE NOVELS OF MR. HENRY JAMES

I

THEY have a novelist with pretensions to literature, who writes about the chase for the husband and the adventures of the rich Americans in our corrupt old Europe, where their primaeval candour put the Europeans to shame. *C'est proprement écrit*; but it's terribly pale.

These words are imputed, by the ingenious 'novelist with pretensions', in an early tale of his own, to an imaginary Frenchman travelling in the States. They give a true if a jaunty account of the theme to which Mr. Henry James devoted himself with an almost constant affection between 1876 and 1888. By that theme the larger public still know and define him; they seldom read, unless with perplexity, the books which he has written from 1892 onwards, and wherein he has come to his own. *Roderick Hudson* and *Daisy Miller*, *The American*, and *The Portrait of a Lady*—we do not name them to slight them; we know them; they are domesticated pleasures of old standing; but, above all, they explain their successors, and in their light we read the later, more enigmatical, sometimes murkier stories, which the critics either let off with general empty praise, or handle with suspicion like some strange fruit that might appear on a familiar tree. It is really the same fruit enriched by new graftings. 'The adventures of the rich Americans in our corrupt old Europe' are revived, with a difference, in the later masterpieces, *The Wings of the Dove* and *The Golden Bowl*. The author has travelled far; but he is the same puritan, half-escaped, who made *The Portait of a Lady* the deepest of his earlier works. He is not a cosmopolitan even yet; he never was one. He is better; he understands other countries, but does not adopt them, for his last heroines, Milly Theale and Maggie Verver, the 'Dove' and the 'Princess', are of his own land.

On the threshold of that earlier time, Mr. Henry James hung out several clues to the temper in which he wrote. The *Essays on French Poets and Novelists* (1878) show a certain recoil from the great models, Balzac and Flaubert. He was hardly just to Balzac then, missing in him, perhaps, the still small voice, and preferring the fine and recondite class of artist, to which he himself belongs, before the hearty and assertive creators. There was much in Tourgénieff, on whom Mr. James wrote with sympathetic zeal, to quicken his own congenial talent; there was the sad reserve, the pessimism, the delicacy; also the interest in heart-breaking, ineffectual persons, like Dmitri Rudin or Roderick Hudson. We have no right to say that Mr. James was much affected by George

Eliot; but he was writing during her full vogue, and shared with her a certain atmosphere, perhaps at first familiar to him in his own country. The weight of distressing and severe scruple is felt in his early tales. Osmond, the egoist and alleged fine gentleman in *The Portrait of a Lady*, who fetters and torments a generous wife with invisible chains, is of the race of Grandcourt in *Deronda*. The wife, Isabel, instead of accepting the fierce offers of her American suitor, who is at least a man, in her folly goes back, though childless and untrammelled, to the conventional life of wifely duty and misery. It may be in keeping that she should do so, but the author seems to approve. And Mr. James loved, like the Russian, to close his scene in discord and failure. *The American*, Newman, robbed of his French bride by the caste-rancour of her family, sees his revenge, but sees that it is not worth taking, and finds at the last that his enemies had all the while counted on his good nature not to take it. This kind of ending, which baffles men at the last moment by some malign turn of fortune, was to become characteristic of Mr. James. He is fond of the cruel slip between the cup and the lip.

Moreover, he stands with the writers I have named by virtue of his power to draw women and of his keen feminine insight into men. Some few of his young girls are painted in our memories beside Helena and Lisa. Often, while we see only the actions of the men, we are told the feelings of the women, or at least of the good ones. Several of the stories are narrated by a girl or spinster, or by some nondescript, felinely observant man of letters, who understands things that are hid from the virile. And there is nearly always passion. In the early books, that of the men is intimated rather as it presents itself to the women, while that of the women is more deeply felt. Such distinguishing marks continue into the later tales, but are transformed in colouring. And along with this special sort of analysis went the higher mood prevailing in the middle Victorian years, the mood of George Eliot, of Browning, and even of Tennyson. They and their aims were noble, and their nobleness informs their best work, while it cannot save the rest. Not on any time in our literature has the national stamp of moral vigour been so clearly printed. It was a century of preachers, and we are only now turning round to ask what, after all, they had to say. Their praise has been inscribed by Mr. James in words he wrote after the death of Browning :—

He played with the curious and the special; they never submerged him, and it was a sign of his robustness that he could play till the end. His voice sounds loudest, and also clearest, for the things that, as a race, we like best . . . the fascination of faith, the acceptance of life, the respect for its mysteries, the endurance of its charges, the vitality of the will, the validity of character, the beauty of action, the seriousness, above all, of the great human passion.

Such, we may say, was the clear charter of Mr. Henry James himself for the first fifteen years of his artistic life. He was too true a craftsman to let idealism jar his hand. He never rushed in a black coat upon the stage amongst his own actors in order to harangue the house with what the age of Addison called 'the sentiments'. But the idealizing spirit is there, and it finds somewhat simple expression. There is a conflict in nearly every story ; and it is, in the first instance, the conflict waged between American and European, the latter usually preying on the wealth and simplicity of the former. But there is another conflict behind, and we are almost led back to religious parlance in describing it. It is the conflict of complication and corruption with what is simple, single-hearted and fresh. The world and the spirit are at odds; the intricate world, with its deeps of old energy, so much more telling and resourceful than its victim, and full of swagger and colour and craft and will; and the spirit, in some frail or quaint, but brave embodiment, relying only on itself. 'Lady Barberina' is a dumbly stubborn, almost malign, English girl of rank who carries back her New York husband in his own despite from his country to live among her aristocratic friends. Daisy Miller is deliberately exposed to fatal malaria by the little Italian suitor who has no hope of winning her. Isabel Osmond is married for her money and utilized. In *The Europeans* the theme is pleasingly varied; the dull-eyed Gertrude, alien in mind, follows her foreign cousin and husband away for ever from her charming, rectilineal home. But in most cases love and hope are defeated either by evil or by circumstance—by conspiracy, or the unfitness of the object, or prejudice. The struggle, therefore, lies rather between the *dramatis personae* than within their characters, and there is no perturbing of the sympathies. Indeed, there is a touch of emphasis about the adventuresses and hard old women that makes them stand out in a rather suspicious brightness beside the quiet and lucid truth of the American portraits.

If Mr. Henry James had ceased to write about 1890, he might have been remembered for his choice of this fresh, distinct plot of ground, and for his happy and varied cultivation of it. The flowers were a little 'pale', but full of tender, clear colour, unlike any others in the garden of fiction. There was humour; and the pages were full of a softly stinging wit. The English was that of the easy classical tradition, a little chequered, as befitted the scene, with the French and American tongues. It was careful; it flowed and did not stick; it did not first of all try to express embroiled feeling or imperceptible changes of temperature. In a few pieces, like *The Aspern Papers* (1888), the style might have seemed more tense, and the subject bizarre and a little ghostly. But few would have prophesied the growth of the novelist's talent in this direction. *The Princess Casamassima*, with its wonderful opening scene of tragic rage, wandered into some extravagance. These were experiments; the account might seem to have been closed.

II

But the century wore out, and over our fiction there came the breath of a stranger temper, different from that of the gallant Victorian crusaders. It was natural that no writer of English should be quicker than Mr. James to feel any artistic current from the mainland that might tardily wash our shores. And, in fact, amongst his later books we find ourselves in presence of the much-talked-of 'decadence', of the mood that speaks so variously in the *Master-Builder* and *Jude the Obscure*, in *Pelleas and Melisande* and *Là-Bas*. Many are the dialects, but we feel that there is one fundamental idiom, which the literary historian must seek to state hereafter, just as he is now trying to state that of 'realism' or of the older romance. We are still in the 'decadence', and can see little more than the confusions of the term. It might signify, of course, the general decay of plastic power; but the art of fiction is not at present suffering from that. It may mean, again, a failure of largeness and nobleness in the treatment, a decline of spiritual energy; but no one can seriously ascribe such a failure to Maeterlinck or Sudermann, or, we add, to Mr. Henry James. Lastly, 'decadence' may imply a love of subjects which are aloof from the general lot of man, of dark and confused moral issues, of the study of problematic or twisted natures, in contrast with the daily open life of the world; in a word, it may presuppose the temper of the specialist. Much of the literature now being written has these traits; but 'decadence' is not the word to describe it; there is only a fresh lease, a diversion, a different concentration of talent. Donne was not a decadent; he was a renewer and explorer. And so, in the case of Mr. Henry James, the question is in what ways the new temper has come to tinge his expression, or to deepen and restate the comparatively simple issues that once engrossed him.

During the last fifteen years Mr. James has printed some fifty or sixty stories, of which eight or ten are long enough to be called books. They are not all equally significant; some of them tease the reader more than he deserves. But there is no monotony; the design is different and peculiar in each, deriving from some curious and cruel knot that has never been tied before. The rigid intellect is always at exercise, though at times upon matter all but impalpable. There is the surface intricacy that is produced by a web of fine threads intently complicated; the texture is firm as well as dense. Strength of passionate situation, always with a certain oddity, an intense curiosity for rare cases, is everywhere present. Sometimes the passion is softened into the mood of high comedy, but it is never far away. 'Lord Beaupré,' a rich young heir, in order to stave off the pursuit of a fortune-hunting girl, gets his friendly cousin to consent to a mock engagement between them. The strains and delicacies of the position all come out ; the cousin is kept all the more by this very device, in pure modesty, from showing her real heart to Lord Beaupré. She accepts an American ; Lord Beaupré falls to the fortune-hunter. The style adopted for this kind of tale (1893), light, fine, and sensitive, is not very different from that of 1876 ; the full change in the author's style has come during the last five or six years—the change to an instrument of registration still more responsive ; parenthetical, colloquial, elliptical, unpopular, full of new difficult music, that repays while it taxes the ear.

The stories of Mr. James are liable to raise an obscure discomfort in the English reader, resembling that caused by want of air. They are tales of the private life only ; and men of our race are not quite easy under that limitation. Across the page of Tourgénieff, of Balzac, of George Eliot, of George Meredith, of Stendhal, there blows the wind of historic events and national aspirations. Reading them, we think of the liberation of the serfs, of 1848, of the Reform Bill, of Mazzini and Italy, of Waterloo, of the world's destinies. But for the characters of Mr. Henry James no such things exist; there is a void, a darkness that can be felt, surrounding their particular lot. We have no right to complain of such an exclusion, though we want sometimes to open a window and listen to the clamour of the bigger life. What is odder in an artist and thinker, the world of art and thought is hardly to be detected at all in these novels. Mr. James's painters and men of letters are merely so ticketed ; they never say anything to show their talent, or get out of their personal affairs into the intellectual region that they are supposed to speak for. They are mostly examples of failure ; they die before they have expressed themselves, they work for the profit of others—

perhaps of publishers. We are told that they are eminent ; but the interest is, in fact, centred on some one by their side who admires them or suffers for them.

On the other hand, the able editors, small pressmen, journalizing ladies lunching in bread-shops, and reporting Americans, dance across the microscopic 'field', and are lively creatures indeed ; never yet so deftly captured by any collector for exhibition. Innocent or shady Bohemia, sinking down to penury and silence, or clambering up into the recognized classes ; wealth that is just outside those classes, but wishes to enter them on the strength of having beauty to offer ; the stable, placid, English orders themselves, in their country houses, on their lawns, with possibilities of woe and excruciation there also ; the routes of travel, the great capitals, Venice, Paris, Rome, New York, serving as the background for these same persons on their voyages ; and London, to which they all return ; London, whose murmur is caught again and again, as a kind of tragic refrain to the curious chant ; over all this world Mr. Henry James moves with prac- tised step, knowing quickly where he wishes to arrive, and wasting no time on what he does not know. His essay on our great city, written some while since, gives us the stage on which many of his romances are unfolded. Lovers of the poetry of London and of the heady London spring, with the fumes that rise from the earth into the brain amid a chorus of innumerable wheels and horse- hoofs ; those who feel her landscape, who hear the rhythm of her call to her children, offering them both the best and the worst ;—such will know that her setting of dim noise and her canopy of softening mist, with the sense of infinite life—thrown into distance and not intruding— just serve to relieve and enhance these peculiar dramas, so personal, so remote from the ordinary, and for that

very reason possible nowhere but in the heart of the place
where all things happen ;

> Chronicle at once
> And burial-place of passions, and their home
> Imperial, their chief living residence.

The natural heart of London is the parks, with their
' smutted sheep ' and grassy distances ; and the parks often
are the scene of drama. Here, in the northern alleys,
with life moving breathlessly between them, Kate Croy
and her lover, in *The Wings of the Dove*, pace together
full of hope and defiance and exchange their vows :—

Suddenly she said to him with extraordinary beauty :
' I engage myself to you for ever.'
The beauty was in everything, and he could have separated nothing . . . couldn't have thought of her face as
distinct from the whole joy. Yet her face had a new
light. ' And I pledge you—I call God to witness !—every
spark of my faith ; I give you every drop of my life.'
That was all, for the moment, but it was enough, and it
was almost as quiet as if it were nothing. They were in
the open air, in an alley of the Gardens ; the great space,
which seemed to arch just then higher and spread wider
for them, threw them back into deep concentration.

III

The tide of actual life is beating there. But, on the
other hand, the gift and scope of pure fantasy in this
countryman and student of Hawthorne have hardly had
proper recognition. Mr. Henry James has perfected a
certain kind of preternatural story. The use of an
uncanny motive for the purpose for light and scarifying
satire is well shown in *The Private Life*. A distinguished
writer is introduced, who is oddly common and second-
rate in society, so that his friends wonder how his books

are written. But there are really two persons: the other is the hidden familiar, genius, or double, who writes the books, and who plays hide-and-seek with his earthly companion in a style that even the observant can never quite bring home to either. Beside the man of letters, moreover, there is another personage—a man of the world—who is composed of nothing but infinite tact, a social leader who never says anything in particular, but always the right thing. But it is only in society that he has even a physical existence ; when he is alone he *goes out*. He is a hallucination suffered by other people. His wife has her suspicions of this rather perplexing attribute of nonentity, and tries to fend off inquiry. Here the supernatural is only a symbol ; we have all known such persons, or something like them. But in *Sir Edmund Orme* there is an actual ghost, haunting the woman who has wronged him during life, and threatening to repeat the same curse upon her daughter if she repeats her mother's fickleness. The daughter just escapes incurring both the blame and the curse.

Mr. James has put still more force into *The Turn of the Screw*, one of the hideous stories of our language. Is any limitation placed on the choice of an artist by the mere measure of the pain he inflicts upon the nerves ? If not, then the subject is admissible. It is a tale where sinister and spectral powers are shown spoiling and daunting the innocence of the young. There is at first sight something wanton in the ruthless fancy—in the re-invasion of our life by the dead butler Peter Quint and his paramour ; in the struggle with these visitants for the souls of the two young and beautiful children, a little boy and a little girl, whom in life they have already influenced ; in the doubt, raised and kept hanging, whether, after all, the two ghosts who can choose to which persons they will appear, are facts, or delusions of the young governess who tells the story ; and in the final defeat of hope by the boy's death just at the moment when he may perhaps be saved. But on reflection we see that all this is the work of a symbolist, who is also a kind of puritan. The ghosts play their part in the bodily sphere as terrifying *dramatis personae* —neither substance nor shadow; they are *there*, as Gorgon faces at the window ; while, spiritually, they figure as the survival of the poison which they had sown while living in the breasts of the innocents. And when this influence reawakens, the earthly forms of the sowers gather visible shape, at once as symbols and as actual combatants. The full effect is won by Mr. James's peculiar gift of speaking in the name of women. The whole visitation comes to us through its play upon the nerves, its stimulus to the courage, of the young English lady who, desperate and unaided, vainly shelters the children. The tension is heightened by the distrust with which others regard her story, and the aversion towards her inspired by the ghosts in the children themselves.

Mr. Henry James is skilled in the feat of drawing children or very young persons, either prematurely oppressed by tragedy or otherwise abnormally alive. The more we think, the less we feel that he is attracted by the mere pathology of such cases. But he once more recalls Tourgénieff by his strained acuteness of hearing for the quickenings, the forebodings, and the half-aware discoveries of the tender mind, during its morning twilight, as the walls of life loom and close about it, in their oppressive tyranny, too soon. Like Tourgénieff, he conveys these things by the method of reticence, by omissions, pauses, economies, rests in the talk, and speaking silences. There are, however, more ways than one of reticence in literature. In *First Love* Tourgénieff illustrates one of them; it is the reticence, the silence of startled Nature herself retreating to her fastnesses in the mind of a boy. Mr. Henry James is possibly over-prone to mystify by scattering restless hints and practising elaborate steps in order at once to hide and express what is brutally simple. In *What Maisie Knew* there is something too much of this method. Maisie is a little girl who has to spend half the year with each of two parents, who justly detest each other and are equally at fault in the eye of the law. The question ' what she knew ', to which the answer soon appears to be that she knows everything, is happily resolved into the question how she shall escape ; and the solution for once is not mere discomfiture. In *The Awkward Age* there is just as much to ' know ', and known it certainly is. We are glad that this particular interest does not too long detain so fine an artist, for though it gives curious chances to his gift, it is not illimitable. In the gay, clean-cut, sad little anecdote of *The Pupil* the effect is less sinister. A family, who just struggle to be presentable and flit impecuniously over Europe, find a tutor, a poor collegian, for their boy, who is charming, precocious, and delicate. They trade on the tutor's love for the boy in order to defer the question of salary. The child sees everything, and dies just as he is hoping to escape with his friend. There is the sting of real life in this, and happily it is a short story ; for the endless folds and doublings of analysis in some of the longer books demand a specially trained and scientific attention, and fatigue us like a race in a labyrinth. Mr. James, it may be feared, loses more readers by this peculiarity than by any other.

In some of these sketches Mr. James crosses the border between the serious comedy of manners and high tragedy. *The Beast in the Jungle*, issued lately in the

S

collection called *The Better Sort*, might easily have been matter for some dramatic monologue of Browning. It contains, perhaps, the nearest thing in all his prose to a great and superb 'bravura' passage. He tries rarely—too rarely—for such effects; language always responds to him when he does try. A man is haunted by the fear of some unnamed disaster, or mortal harm, leaping on him out of his own nature—out of the 'jungle' —and he seeks the good and friendly offices of a woman to listen to him and comfort him. He is wrapped up in himself, and does not see until she is dead that she has loved him. Over her grave he finds it out, and he discovers also, in the face of a passing mourner—a stranger —what the tragic loss of love once enjoyed may really mean. He sees that the beast has leapt upon him indeed, in the form he least suspected. It is clear how the conception of tragic futility, which has been present to Mr. Henry James ever since his first sketches, remains, in a sense, the same; but with what an extraordinary transformation! Let us be thankful for the 'decadence' that brings these gifts. And it has also to be said that the happier and more peaceful tones of poetry are not absent. *The Altar of the Dead*, though not dramatic in form, is like a pensive play of M. Maeterlinck in its unencumbered impulse towards beauty. And *The Great Good Place* is a kind of cloistral dreamrefuge for the tired artist from the clatter of London; a house of the fancy, whence all that jars or wearies or sterilizes is resolutely banished. The soft rhythms of the prose make us wish for more like it, even to the loss of the stories of a few 'trivial sphinxes' and adventuresses :—

The fragrance of flowers just wandered through the void, and the quiet recurrence of delicate plain fare in a high, clean refectory where the soundless, simple service was the triumph of art. That, as he analysed, remained the constant explanation : all the sweetness and serenity were created, calculated things. He analysed, however, but in a desultory way and with a positive delight in the residuum of mystery that made for the great artist in the background the innermost shrine of the idol of a temple ; there were odd moments for it, mild meditations when, in the broad cloister of peace or some garden-nook where the air was light, a special glimpse of beauty and reminder of felicity, seemed, in passing, to hover and linger.

But of *The Sacred Fount* (1901), so full of faint mazy figures that the superscription might have been 'Come like shadows, so depart!' a single scene is left surely on the mind—a summer garden at evening, with a desolate feminine shape sitting in its useless perfume and silence.

IV

Each of the larger novels published since 1895, *The Other House, The Spoils of Poynton*, and *The Awkward Age*, would be worthy of studious review. It is curious how the passion for the scenery of the English country house and 'grounds' recurs in them, as in the delightful *Covering End*. But the fresh gifts, the motives, the newly modulated style that they reveal are all more perfectly apparent in *The Wings of the Dove*, the most remarkable book, apart from *The Golden Bowl*, that Mr. James has written. It has been little noticed amid the mart of dreadfully competent fiction. But, wherever it has penetrated, it is likely, after the manner of certain plays of Ibsen, to leave a long wake of disputation, partly over the question as to what actually happens in the story, and partly about the rights and wrongs of the solution. Hence, a fuller analysis may be pardoned ; for the book resumes so much that went before in the author's production, and intensifies so sharply the changes in his temper, that to know *The Wings of the Dove* is to know much of Mr. Henry James. He has gone back to his old topic of the rich American in Europe, and the contending parties have, in a sense, the same symbolism as before. The world and the spirit are afresh in conflict on the trodden battle-ground. But the arts of war, offensive and defensive, have been transformed in the interval ; there are forces in the air that were unknown to the Osmonds and Madame Merles of an earlier day. And, chief alteration of all, the sympathies are entangled with both sides. The puritan dualism, so to call it, of the older books is greatly blunted ; and the artist, borne along by his own discoveries, comes to bend his intensest and finest light upon the arch-conspirator, who nearly supplants her intended victim in tragic and intellectual interest. Moreover, there is no sharp solution by the sword of justice, moral or 'poetical'. The mental movement of our time, as Matthew Arnold well said, is a 'lay' one ; and nothing could be more wholly of this life, without hint or doctrine of a second world, than the tales of Mr. James. And this, one of his two deepest books, is 'lay' indeed. Very seldom, with a still questioning irony, something else seems to be indicated. The dove-like heroine dies, and the event is canvassed by a worldly old lady and the man who might have been her husband.

'Our dear dove, then, as Kate calls her, has folded her wonderful wings.'

'Yes—folded them.'

It rather racked him, but he tried to receive it as she intended, and she evidently took his formal assent for self-control. 'Unless it's more true,' she accordingly added, 'that she has spread them the wider.'

' For a flight, I trust, to some happiness greater——'

'Exactly.   Greater,' Densher broke in ; but now with a look, he feared, that did, a little, warn her off.

But this is to forestall the history itself, which tells of a fray unprecedented enough.

The world first !   The tale opens in the back, shady regions—surely on the south side of the Thames—where Mr. George Gissing moved so easily, knowing them as a man might know his own house in the dark.   The hard and grey tones lower the pulse of the spectator. Mr. Henry James, when he wishes, can visit the same scene ; but it is with the fresh-edged perceptions of one coming from another society altogether, and not yet accustomed to the voices and smells and tints of this one.   In a small room in ' Chirk Street ', Kate Croy awaits her impossible, jaunty father, who has done some-thing which reticence cannot specify, but who is ' all pink and silver ', with ' kind, safe eyes ', and an inimit-able manner, and ' indescribable arts that quite turned the tables '.   Here Kate tastes ' the faint, flat emanation of things, the failure of fortune and of honour '.

The interview is a triumph of acrid comedy.   This nameless parent (her mother has died of her troubles) stands aside from the story, but is necessary in order to explain Kate.   He is that from which she flies ; yet she has sprung from him.   She flies, by instinct, upwards in society, on the wings of the hawk, not of the dove ; no mere kite, but a predatory creature of a larger sweep, with nobilities, with weaknesses after all.   She flies to the only life where she can imagine herself to breathe— where there is room for her will, room for her beauty— chances for her marriage, chances for winning money, and station, and love as well, and not one of these things without the rest.   When she leaves the house we know something of Kate ; her exhalation of silent power, her disregard of all cost to herself in pursuit of her quest, her mysterious, undeniable nobleness of stamp, which we must reconcile as best we can with her later piracies and perversities. Already she has got away from her father and her weariful widowed sister, whom she supports with her own inheritance. Her aunt, in Lancaster Gate, Mrs. Lowder, the 'aunt Maud' of the story, has seen the social value of Kate. She is a girl who might, and must, marry a 'great man', and so satisfy the dowager affections and long-delayed ambitions of her aunt. Thus they would both escape from the amphibious society in which they move, into that region of the London world which is really 'great'. Fielding would have rejoiced in this view of 'greatness'. Their ambition, at bottom vulgar, is embraced by them with a religious gravity. The author himself almost seems to take it too seriously, at moments.

Kate, in her revulsion from Chirk Street, is ready enough for this programme, but for one obstacle. She loves a man who can never be great at all. He is merely a journalist of some parts, with a foreign education, Merton Densher, who from the standpoint of Mrs. Lowder is quite inadmissible. It would seem that Kate must either resign Densher or her expectations. She is weak, she cannot give up her expectations. But she is also strong ; for she is prepared to play high, and to wait for an opportunity of winning both, should such present itself. It does present itself; and there is the story, but there also is the tragedy. Meantime let her have her precarious, whole-hearted, stolen happiness, walking pledged in Kensington Gardens.

The difficulties sharpen. Densher is visiting on terms of sufferance, which are dissected to the thinnest point, at the house in Lancaster Gate. The hostess accepts him because she feels she can crush him at any moment, but she positively likes him all the while. A certain 'Lord Mark' who is asserted rather than proved to be uncannily clever, but who is wanted for the conduct of the tragedy, is on the watch; and in any case Kate must tarry for the great man who is not yet forthcoming. At this point Densher is sent by his newspaper office to America to make articles. Kate's opportunity for high play is not ripe till his return. Unaware she waits the coming of the 'Dove'.

Milly Theale, strangely and richly left, the dying flower of an old wild family, carrying in herself the seeds of an undefined malady, and also the memory of three calls paid to her in New York by a young Englishman, Densher—Milly Theale is found in Europe, whither she has restlessly fled with a lady escort, a simple, but not foolish, little New Englander, by profession a furnisher of novels. Fled, from what? and whither? From the fear and from the memory, which accompany her nevertheless. The method of reticence, of dumb actions and silences, is here followed triumphantly. The reader, as well as Milly's companion, Mrs. Stringham, are cunningly let into the secret, which is stoically kept by Milly. It comes out by degrees, on a wooded pass, in the little parlours of the inns; and before England is reached the charm is felt by the reader, who knows the pale face, coppery hair, and the radiation, strong, soft, and beneficent, of the lonely, wealthy woman, who well knows that she has *not* 'really everything'. To England they go; Mrs. Stringham remembers an old friend, Mrs. Lowder, now high in the world; and with her the Americans are next found in company. At first it is not known that Densher is a common acquaintance.

The Dove has to fly over fresh waters, which later will prove cruel and hungry enough, but which welcome her more than graciously at first. The opening dinner-party is described, from her point of view. It is described with Richardsonian prolixity, and the dinner itself could hardly take longer. But this is Mr. Henry James's way of enhancing his illusion. The persons move, through a strange, turbid medium, towards a dramatic comprehension of one another. We hear slowly how the two girls, Kate Croy and Milly, become intimate; how they discover, without words, that both know and think of Densher; how Milly betrays her passion to the ' onyx-eyed Aunt Maud '; how Densher returns, visits the National Gallery with Kate by secret appointment, and is thus beheld by Milly as she sits there forlornly ' counting the Americans '. In one scene which precedes this incident the physical doom of Milly is foreshadowed. She is taken by the fortune-hunting Lord Mark, who is trying to wrap invisible nets round her, to a great house, in order that she may be seen in his company. He brings her up to an old picture, ' by Bronzino,' of a fair, dead lady to whom she has a surprising chance likeness.

She found herself, for the first moment, looking at the mysterious portrait through tears. Perhaps it was her tears that made it just then so strange and fair—as wonderful as he had said: the face of a young woman, as magnificently drawn, down to the hands, and magnificently dressed; a face almost livid in hue, yet handsome in sadness and crowned with a mass of hair, rolled back and high, that must, before fading with time, have had a family resemblance with her own. The lady in question, at all events, with her slightly Michelangelesque squareness, her eyes of other days, her full lips, her long neck, her recorded jewels, her brocaded and wasted reds, was a very great personage, only unaccompanied by a joy. And she was dead, dead, dead. Milly recognized her exactly in words that had nothing to do with her. 'I shall never be better than this.'

This is only one of many passages that show how Mr. James has shared in the special impulse towards beauty which distinguishes the new generation of writers. An American like Milly Theale becomes, by her rich ancestry, by her affinity of type to the master-painting, a member herself of an old world, no longer merely simple-minded and delightfully puritan, but with all kinds of complicated stirrings and concessions that might surprise her countrywomen. And the style of Mr. James gathers the dignity of an old master's as it rises to the expression of these deeper and more dramatic things. It has become more and more charged with beauty; it marches with slow, intricately measured paces, as in a dream; and, in this book, even the harsher incidents and cruelties of the story do not prove too much for the style. It would be idle to credit younger Belgian or Celtic symbolists with a definite influence in any direction upon the author. This kind of enchantment is now in the air of literature, and Mr. Henry James, in the fullness of his powers, has returned spell for spell.

Soon Milly knows how she stands. A big, clear-witted physician, Sir Luke Strett, with a 'fine, closed face', comes into her life. It is implied that she will die, or die the sooner, unless she has the happiness, the marriage that she needs. The doctor tells her, significantly, to 'live', and she wishes to live. The scenes in his consulting-room form one of the accessory perfections of the book. Soon Sir Luke sees that Densher is the man of her heart. Soon they all see, they all crowd round her from different sides. Mrs. Lowder is willing

that Densher should be tempted away, so that Kate may
be free for greatness. Kate herself has to act, and the
critical episodes begin.

V

Mr. James has tried hard to render probable the bold
and ugly scheme which Kate devises on behalf of herself
and her lover. It is seldom that the artist can say of
the critic,

O, what is this that knows the road I came?

For that road he often cannot retread himself, and the
critic can know it still less. But in this case a theory
may be offered which is conceivable though probably
wrong. Might it be conjectured that Mr. James, having
first thought of the central motive, proceeded to invent
backwards explanatory antecedents for Kate Croy, which
should leave her capable of a crime even against her
own passion; that he made her, nevertheless, a woman
of large build, of sympathy, full of heart and pieties of
her own kind; and that when the moment came for
unscrupulous action, behold, she was too good for the
work? So Chaucer, when his authorities tell him that
the time is due for Cressida to be false to Troilus, has
himself spent too much kindness on her to believe it, and
refers, somewhat shamefacedly, to the 'books' to prove
the fact. Kate goes wrong, but not in Cressida's way.
At this point there is a change in the method of painting
her, which serves to cover any violence in the transition.
We are never again in her confidence as before; the
curtain is dropped, and the story becomes a diary not of
her feelings, but of the feelings of Densher. Thus any
struggle in the mind of Kate is unknown. The second
great difficulty is to make Densher, who is a man of at

least average decency, her accomplice, and to incline him
to acquiesce in the false report that, while he is desperate
for Kate, Kate is averse from him.   On this footing of
a person to be pitied, he drifts by delicate degrees into
the position of an intimate with Milly, and one whom she
is quite ready to console.

The plan is a kind of dubious, low insurance job;
Mr. Henry James has never invented anything so extraordinary.   Densher, while privately pledged to Kate, is
to 'make up to a sick girl' who wishes to gain him, but
who may die, after not too long an interval, leaving him
well endowed and free to marry Kate.   He is to pay
certain premiums, for a term, in the way of simulated
love; but he pays them on a 'bad life'; when that life
'determines' (these images are not used in the book) he
is to receive the millions for which the policy has been
taken out.   The full position only comes home to him
slowly; by the time he realizes it the action is ready for
the most startling turn of all.   At first, man, woman,
and fate conspire for the success of the plot, and the
scene shifts to Venice, which 'plashed and chimed and
called again' in sympathy, until cold and wicked
weather, also in sympathy, set in.   All the characters
are on the stage.   For their beauty and strange grace,
these Venetian chapters, let us prophesy frankly, may
come to be thought a classic in their kind.   For the
Dove, as her frail body fades in her palace, begins, in
ways unforeseen, to prevail; though she seems to be
deceived, and for a while she is deceived, with the hope
of 'living'.   It is upon Densher that the strain tells.
He knows what manner of man he is, when Milly, 'in all
the candour of her smile, the lustre of her pearls, the
value of her life, the essence of her wealth,' gazes across
her own hall at himself and Kate as they are furtively

discussing the profit that her death may bring to themselves. Densher is not easy in mind, and his next act
makes the knot insoluble indeed.

He cannot go on with his part in the game without
an instalment of payment. There, in the palace of Milly,
he tells Kate what encouragement she must give him.
She has ruled his action thus far ; it is now the turn of
the male. He has a lodging, a little dim old place, on
one of the canals. If she comes to him, he will be
immutably forced to go through with their programme.
Kate sees, and blenches ; but consents, and goes. This,
by a deep but sound paradox, is the first sign that
Densher is shaken by the influence of the Dove. For
anything like this conception, and the way it is faced,
we must go back to the freedoms of Jacobean tragedy.

The visit of Kate to the lodging is not narrated,
though some inferior authors would have felt bound on
theory to narrate it. Economy is in its place here.
Tolstoy would have forborne to tell it ; but, as in
Anna Karénina, he would at once have informed us
that there was an after-taste of sick humiliation. But
there was not. Nothing at all is told us but the preliminary compact ; and then the man's after-taste, in the
lonely lodging, of glory and absorption. At this point
we remember that psychology is in the blood of
Mr. Henry James. The present, in such a case, is
scientifically indescribable ; it is an illusion, indeed it is
nil if abstracted from its sequel ; its life is in hopes and
memories ; their faintness, their vividness renewed in
rhythmical fashion, their sudden chasing away by a new,
black train of associations. Densher is left alone in
Venice to carry out his agreement.

Then appears the heavy cruelty of the new situation for
all parties. The Dove, now dying, and waiting vainly for

her hopes, acts upon Densher in another paradoxical but natural way. To win her seems, after what has passed, to be more than ever necessary, if he is not utterly to cheat Kate ; but it seems less than ever possible, the Dove being the noble person that she is. After a little the very possibility of winning her is denied him. ' Susan Shepherd,' Mrs. Stringham, who has followed everything silently, like some clairvoyant animal, comes to give him a last chance ; she will accept any terms if only her friend's last ray of happiness may be kept alive. Densher is restrained from going through with his bond by a host of little chains of belated conscience and distaste ; and soon it is too late. He has a final, astonishing interview with the dying lady, in which she receives him with invincible style, in full dress, refusing 'to smell of drugs, to taste of medicine'. What passed no others know : the interview is only mentioned in a later conversation with Kate ; and Kate is not the person to hear its details—does not wish to hear them. But we gather that Milly, while knowing much, and divining we know not how much more—knowing certainly, since a malicious, finally killing revelation by Lord ‚Mark, that she had been lied to, and that Kate had really cared for Densher throughout—Milly *pardons*. And this divine impression is left on Densher : her last words

Enforce attention, like deep harmony.

Thus Milly prevails. Having lost all, she regains everything—not practically, but in the sphere of love, soul, and devotion, in which she moves, and in which Densher must henceforth be said to live a kind of absolved existence. Yet even practically, as the sequel shows, she exerts a decisive influence, she wins.

For the memory of her is now fixed in Densher. His experience of power and craft, of passion secular and unshrinking, is overborne by an experience yet stronger. The waft of the Dove's wings as she fled has altered him. He has, in a sense, killed her; he would not have her; now she, and not Kate, is mistress of *him*. By the same token, he is false to Kate. Where, then, is there an issue?

VI

Nothing so vulgar is suggested as that possession had cooled Densher towards Kate: that is not the point at all. But another power, 'through creeks and inlets making,' controls him. He comes home to England, and the final act is played. All that went before is really nothing as compared with his present complication with Kate. And the last beneficent action of the Dove adds another coil to the tangle. He resumes, with a difference, his old wanderings with Kate; the difference is expressed in his phrase that they are 'damned civil' to each other. Kate is strong still, is strong to the last. She guesses that she has gained her end, though he has not married Milly, and that she has gained it without having had to pay the expected price of seeing him Milly's husband for a time. So far she has guessed right. Milly has left him a great fortune. Her last letter comes, in which he would have seen, had he ever read it, what a wonderful and gracious turn she would have given to her bequest. The reader never sees the letter either. When Densher puts it into her hand, Kate burns it unopened, under the sway of an wholly new feeling, which is out of her usual reckoning altogether; jealousy of the dead. This is one of the many profundities of the tale. Kate could bear to see her lover

marry Milly without love; she cannot bear to see him
in love with Milly dead.   But she sees that the centres
of his life have shifted; his heart and mind are entirely
with the dead, with the unread letter that is ashes.   But
in act he is still true to Kate.   The business letter an-
nouncing the fortune comes from America; he sends this
letter to her to ' test ' her; she is positive-minded, she
does not understand the 'test', and she reads it.   Densher
refuses to read it, and the final crisis comes.   He
pursues his last sad advantage with Kate.   He will
not touch the money for himself.   There must be a kind
of expiation.   Either she must marry him poor, as he
was of old: or, he will make over the money to her; but
in that case he will not marry her.   Such at least seems
to be the meaning of the latter pages.   Thus the spirit
of the Dove penetrates material life, as the ether penetrates the most stubborn substances of the earth.   The
strong, consistent woman is now at a disadvantage; the
half-baked man, who has a conscience but had not nerve
enough to carry the plot through, is, in his converted
state, the dominant partner.   In the last sentences of the
book Kate taunts him with being in love with the dead.
He makes no answer, but says :—

   ' I'll marry you, mind you, in an hour.'
   ' As we were? '
   ' As we were.'
But she turned to the door, and her headshake was now
the end.
   ' We shall never be again as we were ! '

   So the tale ends.   It is easy to ask the wrong question,
to ask, What happens?   Do they marry, or does she
take the money?   Probably she marries Lord Mark.
But all that is of no consequence.   It is the end of two
personalities, the final unsoldering of the alliance so

exquisitely sealed in Kensington Gardens. The irruption of forces from another and a spiritual world has done this. Other questions, equally hard but more profitable, we are forced to ask. What has the Dove accomplished by her high generosity?—Spoilt what she wished to mend! She had made the bequest in order that the two might be free as they desired. But they have no use for freedom. With whom, then, does the sympathy finally rest? With the man, who through his very weakness, his two-sidedness, has been in a sense regenerate? Or with the partner, proud, strong, and true to her strange self, who has given herself unflinchingly, and is now dispossessed of her reward? Let us say that our sympathy is with her, as it would never have been had she simply succeeded.

We can put such questions without end. The book is not like a great tragedy of the older kind, which ends in some ennobling resolution of errors through death. But it ends in a deep, resonant discord. Such a discord equally has its place in art, for it might actually close just such a passage of significant, tumultuous life. The conflict between the world and the spirit, with which we started, has ended drawn; the spirit has conquered in its own sphere; the world has been disconcerted and baffled. But Kate, the embodiment of the world, is not wholly eclipsed. She remains pathetic, dignified even after her failure, and above all strong. The last word is hers. The interest, almost the benediction of the author, goes with her. Here we notice, as in so much else, the long slow change in his way of facing life. The victims in his earlier novels were the clear-souled and innocent. Milly Theale is such a victim, certainly; but the sufferer, the protagonist, foiled by forces beyond her scope, yet holding firm, and remaining, in her own style, noble, is Kate,

the daughter of Lionel Croy. Thus the interest, and even
the beauty, begin to gather at last to the side of the will,
craft, and energy, which have failed in part and are now
thrown back with little but themselves to live upon. In
current political theory the cult of will and craft is just
now evident. Art must be touched by it as well, and
more legitimately. In this way, with his share of the
specialist's temper and his love of strangeness in beauty,
Mr. Henry James, aloof as he appears, is trebly representative—one of the finer voices that may be heard telling the future for what our time cared.

VII

For relief, there came a year or so later the gently
ironical comedy, with its graver passages, of *The Am-
bassadors*, in which an elderly, autumnal American, a
local man of letters, fine and good and rather weak, is
sent over to Paris to save a young countryman from the
witchcraft of that city, but falls himself under the charm,
and begins his education. There is the same old quest for
American money, and the usual lacework of intrigue and
psychology ; but the book is the book of a *penseroso*, full
of the power, denied to youth, of tasting rather than
devouring enjoyment. But the respite was not for long ;
in 1905 came *The Golden Bowl*, a complex story of
adultery—though such a word does not occur in its
pages. Thicker, even, than in *The Wings of the Dove* is
the tangle of issues and the confusion of sympathies ; the
plummet has gone deeper. The book, no doubt, suffers
from some defects that spring from its power. It is long ;
a scene always takes longer to tell than to happen ; for
the commentary, the afterthoughts, are spun out so
lengthily that we often lose the sense of the text itself,

which is pretty long also; we cannot say that, like Merlin's charm, it is 'no bigger than the limbs of fleas'. Moreover, at many a critical point the silence and reticence of the personages themselves leaves much to the analyst. But that is part of the method. A kind of *hantise* is produced by the ever-deepening sense of matter unspoken and of the fine invisible nets that imprison the passionate sufferers. There are four chief persons: the Italian Prince; his American wife; her friend, who becomes his mistress; and the wife's father,—who is also, notice! the friend's husband. For a long time all four pick their steps more nicely amidst the dynamite than seems allowable to flesh and blood. We are every moment expecting some light concussion that should make each and all of them flare up, after standing a moment aghast, and join in open internecine combat. This moment never comes; but the failure of it does not imply any want of power in the writer to rise to such a scene. The lurid sparks that fly from the Princess forbid any such doubt.

The Golden Bowl is a study of a slow and strange turning of the tables, but this primary theme is so much overlaid that it almost vanishes. The punishers, the Americans, suffer nearly as much as their punished partners, and suffer much more than one of them. Our sympathy, at the last, turns away from the rightful avenger to one of the culprits, while the other culprit has the best of it all in the end. This is very like life; as a summary—which must always be poor and bare of so endlessly complex a story—may begin to show. The book opens with the marriage of the Prince, Amerigo, with his bankrupt fortunes and high shady ancestry, to the heiress, Maggie Verver, young, straight-minded, trustful, much in love, and 'nice enough'. So the Prince is rescued, he has reached 'the port of the Golden Isles'.

Maggie is inseparable from her father, outwardly a spare, gentle little man and mildly humorous, but, so we are told, a mighty maker of dollars, a musing, impassioned connoisseur of art, a collector planning a palace of art in a distant 'American City'. Father and daughter are one in soul and essence, and it becomes part of the bargain that the Prince marries Mr. Verver too. Maggie does not know that Charlotte Stant, her bosom friend, a brilliant, effective, and eclipsing lady, but penniless, has already come into the Prince's life. They have met in Italy. Charlotte has refused, for the sake of the Prince's fortunes, to take him in marriage, and, for her own sake, to take him without it. Thus they are declared but unsatisfied lovers, and they have parted, and the Prince is to marry Charlotte's pretty little rich friend. But Charlotte, by instinct rather than purposely, drifts back on the scene before the wedding, and meets the Prince at the house of a genial, expansive lady, a Mrs. Assingham, who is the maker of the match. Mrs. Assingham plays chorus to the plot, and comments endlessly (when the author is tired of doing so in person), in her talks with her husband, Colonel Bob, another admirable figure, who manages his Club, and also 'edited for their general economy, the play of his wife's mind, just as he edited, savingly, with the stump of a pencil, her redundant telegrams'. Charlotte induces the Prince to take a last private walk together that they may buy her wedding gift for Maggie. In Bloomsbury they enter the 'low-browed' shop of a dealer in curios, and parley over a certain Golden Bowl of great beauty; but, the Prince detecting a flaw, it is not purchased. The vendor, a sharply fantastic personage 'with an extraordinary pair of eyes', like some wizard purveyor in a fantasy of Balzac, understands their compromising talk in Italian, and never forgets their faces. He will be heard of again. The Golden Bowl is the symbol, and is also to be the means of a catastrophe. It is the happiness of Maggie Verver, gilded over and wonderfully wrought and precious—but there is always the crack.

A year or so after the marriage, the threads of the plot tighten. Maggie wishes her father, for his happiness, and also to make up for her partial absorption in her own happiness, to remarry. He chooses, or is chosen by, Charlotte, who marries him to establish herself, and also (we think) to be near the Prince. She acts, however, in good faith ; she offers Verver, before they are married, a clue to the unknown past relationship with the Prince, but Verver in his innocent delicacy puts the offer by. At this stage he seems, it must be said, a little of a fool, and we are not well prepared for his ominous later development. The two couples live in London, and a scheme of happiness *à quatre*, ideal on the surface, is arranged. Husbands and wives are duly devoted, and the father and daughter, who now need neither to separate nor to live wholly together, adore each other more than ever. Maggie's baby, the 'Principino', is publicly adored by everybody. Soon Charlotte and the Prince are told off as the social and effective members of the quartet, whilst the two quiet Americans, birds of a browner feather, sit at home together in contentment. The flaw in the Bowl is well covered up. Only Mrs. Assingham holds her breath, whilst her husband smokes and looks on. The Prince and Mrs. Verver are simply flung together, in the pride of youth and life and beauty. It is hardly their fault, and they begin in good faith. They are tied to their respective spouses not only by law but by gratitude.

The Ververs have dragged them out of a vagrant un-furnished life into the land of plenty and into the shining sphere that is theirs by natural right, though not, hitherto, by fortune. They are not blind to this obligation ; even the Prince, despite his ' old Roman ' notions, is alive to it. They embrace—it is to be the only time—and sacredly pledge themselves to sacrifice their love to their marriage oaths. But they are to carry out this plan *together*, and there is the weakness of it.

It put them, it kept them together, through the vain show of their separation, made the two other faces, made the whole lapse of the evening, the people, the lights, the flowers, the pretended talk, the exquisite music, a mystic golden bridge between them, strongly swaying and sometimes almost vertiginous, for that intimacy of which the sovereign law would be the vigilance of ' care ', would be never rashly to forget and never consciously to wound (p. 230).

But the Prince finds himself with his father-in-law's wife, who is also his wife's friend, a fellow guest, in April, in a country-house party of easy morals. They duly come back to their homes on the day appointed, but late in the day. They manage plausibly to account for their time by a visit to Gloucester Cathedral. (So we hear later, though at the moment we are rather led to think they have hidden the fact of their visit to Gloucester altogether.) *They* also have their happiness, their Golden Bowl, with its crack so soon to appear. Mr. Henry James has written an article on the stories of D'Annunzio ; it is the severe judgement of an intellectual artist upon an artist whose topic is sensations. But the two writers have this in common, that they try, when the lovers in their books forget the law, to hide the sword for an hour, and wave the torch—the torch that is not nuptial—and steep the scene in beauty. The method is not the same; for the Italian, ever describing and describing, harps on the taste of acridness and despair that overtakes the hour of triumph. Writing for a public less inured, Mr. James plays with its conventions, and intimates whatever he wishes; but he shuts the door upon his lovers, and is content with giving an exquisite colouring of happiness to the approaches and preparatory scenes. After Gloucester, Charlotte and the Prince are at their zenith, having now what they never had before. They have won, they have put the world under their feet. At this point the author lets us see everything through the eyes of the Prince. We see Charlotte act—she has planned the trip and even looked up 'Bradshaw'—but we are not admitted to her thoughts, except through her words and actions, and the conjectures of others. The same procedure, which continues through the book, has been noticed in *The Wings of the Dove*, and it serves to mask the difficult transition from Charlotte predominant and brilliant to Charlotte pitiful and fettered. As she fades away, we wonder if she was ever really efficient at all, but we begin to be sorry for her, even to admire her, more than in the days of her security.

VIII

For the Princess comes out. She wonders, she divines, she is invaded by moral though never by scientific certainty, the edifice of her splendid happiness is shaken, and she takes her slow revenge. In a kind of epic simile, which dissolves, as so often in this book, into a symbol, the shattering of her dream is announced. Mr. James has waited long before allowing his prose to take on these colours.

This situation had been occupying, for months and

months, the very centre of the garden of her life, but it
had reared itself there like some strange, tall tower of
ivory, or perhaps rather some wonderful, beautiful, but
outlandish pagoda, a structure plated with hard, bright
porcelain, coloured and figured and adorned, at the over-
hanging eaves, with silver bells that tinkled, ever so
charmingly, when stirred by chance airs. She had
walked round and round it—that was what she felt ;
she had carried on her existence in the space left her for
circulation, a space that sometimes seemed ample and
sometimes narrow ; looking up, all the while, at the fair
structure that spread itself so amply and rose so high,
but never quite making out, as yet, where she might
have entered had she wished. . . . The great decorated
surface had remained consistently impenetrable and inscrutable. . . . She had not, certainly, arrived at the
conception of paying with her life for anything she
might do ; but it was nevertheless quite as if she had
sounded with a tap or two one of the rare porcelain
plates. She had knocked, in short—though she could
scarce have said whether for admission or for what ; she
had applied her hand to a cool, smooth spot, and had
waited to see what would happen. Something had happened ; it was as if a sound, at her touch, after a little,
had come back to her from within ; a sound sufficiently
suggesting that her approach had been noted. . . . The
pagoda in her blooming garden figure the arrangement—
how otherwise was it to be named ?—by which, so
strikingly, she had been able to marry without breaking,
as she liked to put it, with her past.

Once awake, the Princess carries through an alarming
and patient strategy. She never breaks down ; it is long
before she breaks out, and then it is only to her husband
and to her confidant, Mrs. Assingham—to her father and
her father's wife she never breaks out. She keeps up
the game, redoubling her intimate and cordial life with
Charlotte ; goes with the culprits on the social round,
rises unexpectedly to her place as the hostess of a great

house, and says nothing.   She takes the reins and drives
the team, and carries the others off, for greater isolation,
to the country mansion, ' Fawns,' whither the Assinghams
are brought also.   In scene after scene the sense of
tension and fatality grows, Maggie's puppets living, and
smiling, and playing ' bridge ' together, whilst she moves
around them, the sense of her power half-compensating
the pain of her wrath, and her suspicions confirmed by
the docility of the evildoers.

The others respond in intricate ways, and any abstract,
or mere draughtsman's plan, of the plot, with its ori-
entally subtle ornament and sinuosity, must only be bare
and impoverished.   Charlotte has no staying power.
Her penance is to remain ignorant of how much is
known by her husband or his daughter.   She fails to
force any sign of suspicion from the Princess, even by
a kind of direct challenge.   As for the Prince, neither
does he know, for a while, how much is known.   But he
is not a person formed to suffer ; he feels that he has
met his match, and that his caresses can no longer blind
his wife.   When he knows what is in her mind, he throws
over Charlotte, to whom he never imparts his knowledge.
He, the scapegrace, has been ' furnished with the enjoyment of two beautiful women ' ; and we foresee how in
the end he will choose, since choose he must.   His position is defined by the scene in which the Golden Bowl,
by strange hap now the purchase of Maggie, is flung and
shattered on the floor by Mrs. Assingham.   The little
dealer has told her of the visit to his shop, of the strange
conversation in Italian.   The Prince is magnificent, he
never ' owns up ', or plays the wrong card ; he retreats,
however, with a new light on his wife.—And what of
Mr. Verver, whose wife has seduced his daughter's
husband ?   He is the most inscrutable of them all.   For

a long time even Maggie cannot tell what he thinks. At first she works to keep him blind; then she works 'against it having to be recognized between them that he doubts'; nor are the doubts ever put into plain words between them. But after a time we are sure that he knows, that he is terrorizing his wife by the same policy, the Verver policy of silence. In all this part of the book not a single dialogue is given between Mr. and Mrs. Verver; the author, with all his enterprise, has not faced that problem. But after a time Charlotte is seen to be prisoner, her husband's prisoner, his led animal, controlled by her fear of undisclosed knowledge. Her voice is heard obediently and mechanically celebrating the great art collection to parties of visitors at Fawns. The day is past when she could talk to her Prince of her husband as the 'poor duck', to whom, at his age, the hope was forbidden of ever seeing her the mother of his children. Even Maggie pities her, in another symbol.

The conviction . . . left Maggie's sense meanwhile open as to the sight of gilt wires and bruised wings, the spacious but suspended cage, the home of eternal unrest, of pacings, beatings, shakings, all so vain, into which the baffled consciousness helplessly resolved itself. The cage was the deluded condition, and Maggie, as having known delusion—rather!—understood the nature of cages.

Thus the position is prolonged, almost beyond the limits of the credible, without any general explosion.

But a way out must be found; and, with a wonderful and equal mixture of cruelty and self-sacrifice, Mr. Verver finds it. To punish Charlotte, and to free his daughter, even if he must lose her, he resolves to take Charlotte away to America for good. The scene in which he conveys this intention to Maggie, without ever saying too much, and pleading the claims of 'American City' as his pretext, is a solemn one. It has the sternness and grim piety we call 'puritan', though the puritans will open their eyes to find anything of themselves in *The Golden Bowl*, and it is possible that the author himself might question the epithet. The plan is made, and Charlotte dare not question or refuse it. But she regains for a moment her claim to resource and to the grand manner. She faces Maggie, and proclaims that she is carrying off her husband in order to have him all her own, undisturbed by Maggie and Maggie's filial mono- poly and *filial* jealousy. Maggie pities her, and allows her to keep up this pose, and so to save her dignity. Thus the glazed surface of the situation is still unbroken. Maggie can afford, indeed, to be generous. She and her father have lost each other, they will never see each other again. But she accepts the sacrifice, in order to be quit of the stress, and above all in order to win her husband back—which she is by no means sure that she can do, for he, too, bides his time and keeps his reserve. But she proves that she can win him. The farewells are gone through, in an atmosphere heavy with embroilment and smothered fire. To the last there is no explosion. The Ververs go, the Princess reconquers the Prince after a last scene of suspense as to what he will do, and the curtain descends. There is thus no such enigma in *The Golden Bowl* as in *The Wings of the Dove*. We know just what has happened to everybody, and how things will remain. Yet here also the close is a profound, if muffled discord, and therein resembles life more than it resembles the end of a poetic tragedy.

A discord: for the justice dealt out is not only not cheaply 'poetic', but does not satisfy any meaning of the term. No one dies; there is none of the relief and clearing of our sympathies which death, as handled by a great tragedian, affords us, and which can only be given by death. The knot is untied, only to leave us with another one. This difference of upshot is proper to the difference between poetic drama and fiction, which takes in more of life than the poetic drama and therefore has more kinds of ending. For see how fortune is allotted in *The Golden Bowl*. Who really has the best of everything? Why, the Prince, one of the contrivers of harms, who has only lost what he does not now care to keep, who has regained his beautiful wife, loving her, and who is free from every incubus. He is not at all capable of moral regrets, and his life is clear before him. Maggie, the wronged wife, the avenger, has lost her father, her other self, and has paid dear for her husband, though she has consented to do so. Her father has gone off with nothing but the satisfaction of knowing that he has saved some of her happiness. To her he is a 'great and deep and high little man'. We, however, think of him as merciless, if intelligibly merciless, as fundamentally hard and strong like his daughter. Only Charlotte suffers without compensation, though she deserves no worse than her accomplice; he has all the luck and she none. She is much overpunished. The cruel kind of cold-blooded pity felt for her by the Princess is seen in a remark made to the Prince after the departure of the others.

'And yet I think,' the Princess returned, 'that it isn't as if we had wholly done with her. How can we not always think of her? It's as if her unhappiness had been necessary to us—as if we had needed her, at her own cost, to build us up and start us.'

In the shoes of which of these four persons would the reader prefer to stand? He may say—and the book at moments will tempt him to say—that he need not answer; that the whole thing is a phantasmagoria, that the persons are excogitated shadows, and the logic is that of dreams; and that a single shout of the human voice, a single line of Shakespeare, brings back the waking world and the labours of the morning. But that retort would prove too much; for it would rule out Richardson, it would rule out Dostoieffsky, which is impossible. Yet it may help us to define more nearly the tribe of artist to which Mr. James belongs. He is one of those who show life and living things under a microscope. The life is real enough, and yet unlike the reality we know. It is unlike the reality achieved by poetic insight and poetic glamour, while partaking of it because it is also a work of the constructive imagination. The effect of this *over-reality*, if it may so be called, is a kind of bewilderment and mirage. But the art is deep and is real, and it also is founded on the watching of humanity, on the author's immersion in the fates of humanity.

LIVING IRISH LITERATURE

I

THERE was a fiction of the critics, encouraged by
Mr. Matthew Arnold, that the genius of English poetry
has been concerned above all things with the vigorous
embodiment of moral ideas, and Mr. Arnold thought that
Shakespeare was thus concerned when he wrote of the
sunrise flattering the mountain-tops.   No doubt Spenser,
Milton, and Wordsworth cared to be judged as teachers
or nothing.   Time has not altogether judged them by
that criterion, which was merely part of their doctrine;
and what remains with us of a poet is not, or need not
be, any part of his doctrine.   For Spenser, Milton, and
Wordsworth, even while they wrote, often forgot their
doctrine, and so may we while reading them.   If we give
the word *moral* a generous, intelligent meaning, we shall,
it is true, apply it as much to Milton's debates in Hell as
to the farewells of his *Samson Agonistes*, and we shall
not scruple to use it of the tragic world of Shakespeare.
Tennyson, Browning, and Mr. Arnold himself were

directly preoccupied, for much of their time, with ennoblement and with the heroic way of taking life ; and
thus, whatever their value may be as thinkers, they often
reached a high spiritual intensity, and gave it the best
words ; and in this way they were true to one great and
historic side of the English genius. On the other hand,
much of the best that they did escapes any such definition,
and bids us take care when we are affecting to define the
English genius. *Mariana*, and *The Bishop Orders his
Tomb*, and *The Forsaken Merman*, are not poems built
on a moral idea, even in a generous sense of that term,
unless indeed the term is to be emptied of meaning.
Their relation to morals can only be expressed in the
words of Shelley, who put the truth best ; ' the great
instrument of moral good is the imagination, and poetry
administers to the effect by acting on the cause.'
Spenser, too, and Shakespeare, were often moved not by
high ethical purpose, but by the passion for beauty, and
for reproducing the pageant of life and of their own
dreams under forms of beauty. There *is* a deep ethical
strain in English literature ; but there is also as deep a
counter-strain, which we must understand if we would not
ignore the medley of our stock ; a counter-strain that is
concerned with beauty first of all, or with the utterance
of wrath, ambition, curiosity, defiance, and unspiritual
love, always, however, in forms of beauty. This element
is found sometimes in poets like Spenser, whose theory
does not cover their own genius all the time, and sometimes in poets who are born to express ideas that ' lie
beyond good and evil ', although for some of their time
they express high ethical moods. It is an element found,
and ruling variously, in Marlowe and Donne, and in
Rochester and Byron, and also in poets of another order
like Dryden.

The desire, I have said elsewhere, to create forms of beauty for their own sake was the bond that consciously inspired the last great school of poets flourishing in England ; the school of which Rossetti was the chief in poetical will and intensity.   He, like his friends, thought of beauty first, and of ennoblement by the way ; although now and then, as in *The Burden of Nineveh* and *The Pilgrims*, ethical sublimity is directly attained.   But *The Stream's Secret*, and ' Love laid his weary head ', and the prefaces to *The Earthly Paradise*, and Burne-Jones's *Days of Creation* are the characteristic productions of the group.   The ' English genius ', it seems, is more comprehensive than ever, when it has to explain the associated work of an Englishman, a Welshman, a Borderer, and an Italian.

In England there has been no school of successors. The poetry recently written has neither the virtues of the Victorian ancients, with their expression, sometimes triumphant, of ennobling ideas, nor yet the virtues of Rossetti and his friends, with their animating cult of beauty, and the novelty of consummate form they accomplished.   There are long poems, narrative or dramatic, of high intention and casual excellence, but without real plastic power.   The most genuine long poem of the last ten years is *The Dynasts* of Mr. Thomas Hardy ; an ironical epic in dramatic and choric form, a backward vision over a great historic horizon, a piece of poetic brainwork, unpopular and unrecognized.   It could only be in verse ; and yet who does not feel that the verse, straining as it does at new rhythms and at discords that echo the discord of the author's philosophy, is written, after all, with his left hand ?   But most of the new poems of any note are short ones, and their common doom is to reach high finish without any poetic brainwork behind, without any sustenance of vital ideas. There is little of which we can be sure that it will last as long as *The Blessed Damozel* and *The Garden of Proserpine* have lasted already. There is much that sounds well at first, but turns out, like the better verse of Mr. Stephen Phillips, to be a medley of echoes from the Victorian ancients. Mr. William Watson has the high and humane emotions, the keen ethical enthusiasm on which one kind of English poetry is so ready to rest; but his music, too, is studious rather than his own, and his style is faint and elegant, and his ideas are in very low relief. Others produce new Hellenics, and tragedies after the antique, thinking that it makes for nobility to sacrifice romantic life and colour, and only winning a kind of pallor that makes us feel we are in a gallery of inferior plaster casts. Pallor and low relief are certainly not the faults of Mr. Kipling's verses: he is too much of a man for that, and has too good an eye for common humanity. But he thinks that he can carry the kingdom of poetry, as his heroes conquer the barbarians, by cunning and violence; and poetry takes her revenge when he falls into affected, strained, and impure expression, the result of violence. We not only live by poetry, we want also to live with it; and we cannot live with a brass band, pounding away with terrific energy, and not always in tune. Still, Mr. Kipling is a rebel against the rule of little, sterile finish.

II

While this is so, and even if it were not so, we should not fail, in our search for a living poetry, for a poetry produced in a unison of spirit and effort, to keep watch upon Ireland. There, in any case, we shall not find the artistic vices of a deep, old, settled culture in its interval of exhaustion, such as we find in England. We shall

rather find the opposite hindrance to art, of passionate
and vital feeling only struggling into form, of ideas that
are so deep in the spirit of the nation that they find it
all the harder to express themselves. But that is not
exhaustion, it is immaturity. Form and expression may
come through training, if once the poetic substance is
there; but ideas and feeling can never come through
training, if the poetic substance is not there; and true
form, as distinct from accomplishment, cannot in that
case come either. England has little to say in poetry
at the present moment, and says it with considerable
scholarship. Ireland has much to say, but is only
beginning to see how to say it. Already the better
instinct among Irish writers is towards training. This
Ireland must have, if she is to realize what has so long
been locked away in high, pathetic, half-expression.
Under every Irish problem, intellectual as well as material,
lies that of education, of finding the keys of knowledge.
Now one part of education is instruction; and half of
Ireland, the half whence most of the new writers come,
the unprosperous, rebellious-minded half, has never had
enough chance of instruction or of the artistic training
that instruction may be made to serve. The public that
exists, or might exist, in intelligent sympathy with those
writers has been distracted by trouble and politics, and
has had still less instruction. It is no inborn weakness,
as the Anglo-Saxon thinks, it is this want of sufficient
training in the artists and their audience, that has been
the chief obstacle to the free flowering of the Irish
imagination. That is evident, if we look back over a
century, and read that patient and affectionate anthology,
the *Treasury of Irish Poetry in the English Tongue*,[130] put
together by Mr. Stopford Brooke and Mr. Rolleston. The
value of their collection is just that it does not contain,

and is not meant to contain, only what is good, though it does contain all that is best. At first it is sad reading ; so brave, so passionate, so ineffectual seem nine-tenths of the verses in it. We feel inclined to say to the Irish poets, in their endeavour to interpret the soul of their country, ' There is much music, excellent voice, in this little organ, yet cannot you make it speak.' And yet, looking closer, the effect is happy and invigorating. There is plenty of poetry scattered in the book, though there are not many perfect pieces ; there is the poetry of defiant and never-crushed sorrow, the poetry of nature and of home, the poetry of roguish and boisterous humour. There is more that is good at the end of the nineteenth century than at the beginning : indeed, with many pauses and relapses, there is something like a ' progress of poesy ', and there is certainly a progress in the craft of poesy. ' It is only quite lately,' says Mr. Stopford Brooke, in his *Introduction*, a delicate piece of historical tracery, ' that modern Irish poetry can claim to be a fine art.'

The first united impulse came in 1842 from the writers in *The Nation*, from Thomas Davis, Gavan Duffy, and many more ; with their forerunners like Callanan, and their successors like Kickham the Fenian. They made a freer air, which they did not live to breathe. They sometimes wrote well, though rarely for long at a time, and they made art more possible. They left a mass of verse that is only respected, and therefore hardly remembered ; it remains the prey of historians, who use it as a basis for generalities. Their line was action, and they fought a losing battle which was necessary to the victories of the far future. This, indeed, was true both of their verse and of their politics. Noble, appealing figures, like those of knights upon the tombs, they command our love and admiration for their sacrifices.

It was hard work for them to summon up the poetry of hope or delight, and they were torn between the rhetoric of their patriot cry and the rhetoric of English models. Many of them drifted into an alternation of wail and hatred, whose monotony is reflected in that of the keening, interminable, weary-footed tunes. It was so easy to pervert passion into fever, and style into a bastard, angry, oratorical movement! A little apart from them, and more widely cultured than most of them, stood the truest Irish poet of his time, one of the truest of any time, James Clarence Mangan. He was ' kept out of public life ', so we hear, ' by a passion for opium and rum'; but his spirit, through the fray, seems to stand at watch over the battlefield like a fiery and a troubled star. Even Mangan found little respite for creating a sure and personal style. The spirit of dreadful hours was oftener with him than the spirit of delight. He made some lines of a clear and vestal perfection, as when he sang to his *Dark Rosaleen,* who is Ireland:—

> Over dews, over sands,
>   Will I fly for your weal:
> Your holy, delicate, white hands
>   Shall girdle me with steel!

Mangan makes us feel that on the whole the sorrows of Ireland have hurt her poetry hitherto, and that the newer writers have done better to break with them for a time. Yet surely, unless Ireland become happy unexpectedly, the poets, once assured of their art, must return to her sorrows some day and sing them afresh and aright. Italy, until she attained her unity and freedom, was never silent on her own sorrows. *Her* poets, Dante, Guidiccioni, Leopardi, having great movements of culture—mediaeval, renaissance, romantic —behind them, and having also behind them a great technique, gave to their patriotic wrath and melancholy, at intervals and over many centuries, a classic form, which no one has ever given to the sorrows of Ireland for more than a few verses at a time.   That form, whenever it arrives, and whether it prove to be elegiac or triumphal, must surely also break with the past; it will have to be something fresh in movement and in tone, the musical vesture of a mood and circumstance as yet unforeseen. In one little symbolic play, or rather scene, a morality with a humorous and homely groundwork, *Cathleen ni Houlihan*, written by Mr. W. B. Yeats, there is a tender renewal of the old patriotic theme.   Cathleen, the wandering old woman, who has lost her four green fields, while many men have died for the love of her, is one of Ireland's traditional poetic names; and at her call the young cottager leaves home and bride, for the French have landed in Killala Bay, and he is moved to join them against the oppressor.   He knows, and the Irish hearers of the play know, who Cathleen, the daughter of Houlihan, is.   They respond like devotees to every long-accustomed touch, and enjoy as much through realized expectancy as through the renewal of surprise, when they hear the prophecy :—

They that had red cheeks will have pale cheeks for my sake ; and for all that, they will think they are well paid.

Or the conclusion :—

Peter (*to Patrick, laying a hand on his arm*): Did you see an old woman going down the path ?

Patrick : I did not, but I saw a young girl, and she had the walk of a queen.

But the talent of Mr. Yeats, and of other living Irish writers, has moved away from these direct appeals to the passion for freedom.   It has moved along three lines of interest, which are separate, but which ever cross and

mingle. These are the legendary, the popular, and the
mystical. The first of these interests, which centres on
Old Irish cycle and story, has already expressed itself in
a small literature of translation, of lyric, and of narrative
verse. The second of them, the interest in the real and
contemporary but primitive nature of the people, speaks
already to some slight extent in fiction, but much more
upon the stage—in a living, though still nascent, drama
that is prose in form but often poetic in strain. The third,
the mystical impulse, speaks chiefly through lyric or
lyrical prose, and has also attempted to reclothe some of
the legendary tales and poems with its own spirit. This
is the newest, the most exotic, the least traditional
interest of all the three ; but it is not the least powerful ;
it is not exhausted, and perhaps it is only beginning.
But the first two sources of inspiration are older. The
second derives from the native school of Irish novelists,
Carleton and Banim, who until lately were little known
in England. The first is rooted just as deep, for the
use of native heroic legend in Anglo-Irish verse began
before living memory, unless it be the memory of quite
old men ; for it began with Mangan, and was powerfully
continued by Sir Samuel Ferguson, and since his time it
has never ceased : nor can it well cease, partly because of
its own profound attraction, and also because it is now
one of the great labours of learning and culture to reveal
old Irish literature—'the matter of Ireland'—not to
Ireland only, but to all men ; and this kind of revelation
has always ended in nourishing art.

III

As with the world of Icelandic saga and German and
southern romance, so also with Irish ; behind the work
of the poet lies the work of the scholar ; and the poet is

surely grateful. If he were not, he would deserve to
listen to bad verses for a hundred years in purgatory; or
to be tantalized there by hearing the shade of some far
forerunner chanting, in the ancient tongue he does not
know, undiscovered tales of Deirdre and Cuchullin. Such,
indeed, but for the devotion of scholars, would even now
be his plight. But there is no danger of such ingratitude.
The old heroic and lyrical material has been opened up
during the last twenty years by German, English, Irish,
and French students. They tell us that there is still
a wealth of manuscripts untouched. A trainband of
younger decipherers and translators is arising from the
School of Irish Studies founded in Dublin by Dr. Kuno
Meyer, whose own English versions are all the more
exquisite for their faintly un-English touch. His *Songs
of Summer and Winter* include this brief poem:—

> My tidings for you:—the stag bells,
> Winter snows, summer is gone.
>
> Wind high and cold, low the sun,
> Short his course, sea running high.
>
> Deep-red the bracken, shapes are hidden,
> The wild-goose has raised his wonted cry.
>
> Cold has caught the wings of birds:
> Season of ice—these are my tidings.

When will the modern Irish poets give us, with such joy
and freshness, the sensation of nature herself, unbrushed
by the shadow of their own dreams and desires, that this
unknown countryman of theirs gave long ago? But it
is in story rather than in song—though the stories themselves contain many songs, which come dramatically
enough in place, like the songs in the Old Testament or
in the plays of Shakespeare and Fletcher—it is in story
above all that the riches of the Old Irish are now
disclosed. The labours of Dr. Whitley Stokes, and of

Mr. Standish Hayes O'Grady in his *Silva Gadelica,* and of many more in the *Revue Celtique* and elsewhere, have brought this about.   Dr. Douglas Hyde, another leader of Irish culture, has chronicled the stories, and enumerated a long list of the translations, in his invaluable *Literary History of Ireland* (1899).   But the layman has still to search for these in rare books and learned journals.   For him, nay, for the poets themselves, who have by no means kept pace with this mass of artistic material, it is imperative that there should be some uniform series of the best translations, issued under authority, and as easy to buy as those of the Norse classics.   This is the next great gift that the Celtic scholars can offer to the Celtic artists and to the world at large.   It is the more required because no great number of persons will ever master the old Irish language, which is one of the hardest, we hear, in Europe, and is only now being mastered by the scholars themselves.   Its standard lexicon is still being written, and it is the most important field yet remaining to be fully tilled by mediaevalists.

Speaking in 1893 to the Irish Literary Society,[131] Mr. Stopford Brooke, with signal accuracy, named the three tasks, apart from the exact translation of the old literature, that await the interpreters of Ireland.   One was the elaboration, ' by some Irishman of formative genius,' of the old heroic writings into separate epical works having unity of style and structure, and written in prose ; the labour, in fact, of an Irish Malory. Another was the free poetic treatment in verse of the greater episodes in the same heroic writings.   Lastly, there was the harvesting of the mass of native folk-story, especially that founded on supernatural motive, which is still alive amongst the people.   To this we may add a fourth task, the artistic reproduction of popular life and of the native Irish soul as it now is. On these four lines the work has already begun to advance, though with different degrees of success and of energy.

There is no Irish Malory yet. Perhaps it is too late in the day for him to arise ; for Malory came just in time to catch the living harmonies of heroic romance, of the age of faith and chivalry. He was not parted from that age, like modern writers, by four centuries of Renaissance literature. The style of the French stories that he adopted when he founded a pattern of English prose was not a dead style or a far-off classical antique. But our translators, who try to seize the note of Old Norse or Irish prose, are reaching out hands to a distant shore, in love rather than in hope. They are distracted by all the intervening models of prose, rhetorical, romantic, or archaic. There is no reason why this obstacle should not be surmounted by genius. Supreme constructive tact, reverence for the classics themselves, perception of their endless varieties of tone, as well as an adequate gift of words, are all required. The originals are national monuments, and must not be lightly patched and pieced. Otherwise, we shall simply get work of the order of Kingsley's *Heroes*, admirable in its way, but merely preliminary and secondary, which will never satisfy the national hunger to know the essence of the Irish classics. In this direction something has been already done which calls for gratitude. Mr. Standish O'Grady (whom the English reader must not confound with Mr. Standish Hayes O'Grady, of *Silva Gadelica*) was a pioneer in the work of fusing the stories in a modern narrative. Of late a steady effort has been made for what Mr. Stopford Brooke calls the ' floating of Irish story in the world' by the books of Lady Gregory, *Cuculain of Muirthemne* and *Gods and Fighting Men*.

On her choice of version and detail and on her handling some grave criticism has been passed by an expert ;[132] and on the other hand she has been praised lyrically in the prose of Mr. W. B. Yeats. But if we look on her work as having the same kind of interest and attraction, not as Malory's *Morte d'Arthur*, but as Kingsley's *Heroes*—with the difference that she is opening fresher fields, and 'floating', with whatever deflection from the manner of the originals, some of the best stories in the world—her service will be honourably recognized. In level and delicate narrative her style is happy, and in lyrical prose elegy it is more than that, it is free and noble. Her work has a distinct niche of its own, although it may have to be done over again, for the sake of letters and not merely of scholarship, in a different and stricter spirit ; since, after all, the old Irish tales are classics, and we must have them, or the best of them, reproduced, by some one with a competent knowledge of the old language and with a genius for style, in a style that will recall their own. One great advantage of Lady Gregory's diction is that it is free from the penetrating blight of Macpherson's ' Ossian ', on which so many of those have foundered who affected to renew the ' Celtic spirit '. Another and even greater advantage of her diction is that it is tinted with an idiom which she knows intimately, the idiom of the humble Anglo-Irish speakers, with its turns that seem at once homelike and far away. How well she knows it may be seen from her *Poets and Dreamers*, a book of value, the best book she has written, which tells us, better than many elaborate histories, of the indwelling fancy of the Irish folk, of their faculty for dreams and their power to see the fairies, and also of their natural turn for ballad and satire. The literary poets, Mr. Yeats and his friends, seem to have lost one of the gifts of Raftery, the renowned blind wandering singer, who is so well chronicled by Lady Gregory ; and yet satire is one of the oldest pursuits of the Irish race. In two chapters of *Poets and Dreamers* we come very close to the people ; in ' Workhouse Dreams ', taken down from ' old men sitting on a bench against the white-washed wall of a shed, in their rough frieze clothes and round grey caps'; and in 'West Irish Ballads', which, says Lady Gregory, are ' sung and composed by the people, and, so far as I know, not hitherto translated'.

Another song I have heard was a lament over a boy and girl who had run away to America, and on the way the ship went down. And when they were going down they began to be sorry they were not married ; and to say that if the priest had been at home when they went away, they would have been married ; but they hoped that when they were drowned it would be the same with them as if they were married. And I heard another lament that had been made for three boys that had lately been drowned in Galway Bay. It is the mother who is making it ; and she tells how she lost her husband, the father of her three boys. And then she married again, and they went to sea and were drowned ; and she wouldn't mind about the others so much, but it is Peter, the eldest boy, she is grieving for. And I have heard one song that had a great many verses, and was about ' a poet that is dying, and he confessing his sins '.

The same book, moreover, introduces English readers to Dr. Douglas Hyde's Irish poems, which are sung over the country ; but, as we see from Dr. Hyde's *Love Songs of Connacht*, the full beauty of this kind of work is not for those ignorant of the Gaelic. It is clear that a deep inexhaustible vein in the rock, the vein of folklore and of folk-feeling, has now been struck ; and on this must Anglo-Irish literature have its roots fed and watered.

IV

The seizure by living poets, after the manner Ferguson initiated, of tales and motives from the old Irish, does not resemble the dealings of Coleridge or Keats with the British ballad. The nearest parallel is the handling by William Morris of northern subjects in his own poetry. There is the same use of the old story and its facts; and there is an infusion, too, of wholly modern feeling, which the poet wagers that he will somehow reconcile with that more primitive matter. Morris infused, as we have seen, a temper towards beauty which belonged to his group and is not found in the northern stories at all; and something of the same temper, with a difference, with a greater strangeness and remoteness, is infused by Mr. Yeats into all of his verse that is based on legend, from the *Wanderings of Oisin* (1889), which first signalized clearly the new impulse, onwards until now. There is no trace of this modern temper in such work as Dr. Todhunter's *Three Sons of Turann* (1896), which is, therefore, truer to the original spirit; and his short, rhymeless cadences, as of biblical prose trembling into metre, are a perilous but successful experiment. The same poet's fierce, haunting ballad, *Aghadoe*, in another kind, is well remembered.

Many impulses of living Irish verse centre in Mr. Yeats. Into the old tales he has brought two things he did not find there. One is the fruit of a transcendental theory, drawn from his own nature, and also much coloured by Blake's theory; it is a certain view of beauty, of the visible world, of values; and this theory he has also set forth in prose that ranks with the best of any poet's prose in our day. It answers to nothing that is present, or even latent, in his old Irish originals. And it has, secondly, found expression in his form for good and ill. For ill, since there are times when his words are barely held together save by the tune, and he crosses even the line Shelley drew for himself in this regard, and is not incapable of confounding, in practice, 'obscurity of expression with the expression of obscurity.' But for good in the main; for he gives us a new poetry, moving safely among viewless things, and hitherto unexpressed desires, and the half-human regrets of disembodied souls. His is not the phantasmal theatre of Shelley, where Love and Life and Demogorgon, in shapes less than half-mortal, people a world of naked but glorious elements. It is not the best verses of Mr. Yeats that are touched with his doctrines of 'magic' and the transcendental, or which he covers with the bright mist of his own poetic mythology and symbol—the 'Secret Rose', the 'demons', the 'elemental ones';—all that reminds us too much of Bulwer Lytton. Or it may be that such notions are too deeply part of himself ever yet to have found adequate words, since the deepest things within us are the last to find words. But his writing is at its best whenever it calls up the crowd of listening faces and a speaker's voice, or where it is full of sparks from the turf-fire and the ingle, and where it is agreeable to any doctrine known in history, and calls for no initiation but a sense for poetry; as in the lines chanted by the Little People over the bridal Cromlech of Grania and Diarmuid :—

> Give to these children, new from the world,
>   Rest far from men.
> Is anything better, anything better?
>   Tell us it then!

The fairies who sing thus may be very old, but they understand the human need for that rest which is the consolation of mortals and is denied to themselves ; and

their song is a new fairy song in literature—as far from
that of Allingham and his stately models as it is from
that of Thomas the Rhymer or the ballads of the
northern underworld.

Mr. Yeats's purpose to found an Irish poetic drama
still quickens, under the influence of the theatre. He
has rewritten much in the three plays, which are now reprinted in his volume of *Poems*, 1895–1905. They are
all better composed than at first ; there is what the author
calls ' an addition to the masculine element, an increase
of strength in the bony structure '. Still, only one of
them is highly dramatic in motive, namely, *On Baile's
Strand*, where Cuculain slays his own son unwittingly in
fulfilment of a curse, as Oedipus did his father, and dies
fighting the sea-waves—an episode here inwoven from
another part of the story. This is one of the most
dramatic tales ever conceived. The passionate side of it
is firmly and nobly brought out, while it may be suggested
that Mr. Yeats would lose no originality were he to study
further the Greek methods of suspense and discovery.
How the audience of Sophocles hangs on every unwitting
fatal premonitory word of the parricide, which he does
not know is a sword turned against his own heart ! The
old Irish tales may have to be carefully searched before
they will yield many such dramatic situations as those of
the dying Cuculain or the tale of Midhir and Etain. In
The King's Threshold the poet Seanchan will starve
sooner than yield the precedence at the King's table
that is the due of the poet. The drama here is too slight,
save in so far as the tale is a symbol of the claims of
poetry. *The Shadowy Waters*, even as recast, is less
a play than a high lyrical dialogue with poetic scenery.
The motive is love, but love of a super-terrestrial kind,
hardly love at all, except as contrasted with the

commoner and ruddier affections of earth. The difficulty is to make an audience of men and women sympathize with such bodiless love; and though Mr. Yeats has inserted passages of pure humanity, and has cleared and recomposed the story, it is only to enforce more strongly his original theme.

The final impression left by these two latter plays remains, in spite of all changes, lyrical and musical rather than dramatic. When he wrote them, Mr. Yeats was moving slowly, if consciously, in his patriotic purpose, towards real drama. Tragedy, however, is more than a series of lyrical moments, and for tragedy there must be a reserve of central fire, and the poet must be its master. Passion that comes and goes, as the wind lives and dies, in quick little interrupted gusts, is not enough—that is the passion of youth. A fuller and a stronger-headed sense for tragedy is the real consolation of middle age.

V

Mr. Yeats's *Deirdre*, recently printed, is a versified play on the most famous and glorious of all Irish romances, often before courted by sagamen and poets, but hitherto rather for the narrative than for the dramatic purpose. Mr. Yeats has woven the catastrophic scenes into one long act, lasting an hour and with a single climax. He has arranged them with a certain measure of Greek convention, well fitted to the small stage of the Abbey Theatre in Dublin, and also to the story and its needs. On the left, facing the audience, are grouped three strolling musicians, women, who have been in Conchubar's royal house and learnt of a mischief that they dare only impart covertly—a mischief threatening Deirdre and her lover Naisi, who are arriving, upon the treacherous invitation of the King, to share his banquet.

The musicians also prologuize, and briefly tell the beginning of the tale—how the King, now old, had found a child of unknown parentage on the hillside and reared her up :—

> He went up thither daily, till at last
> She put on womanhood, and he lost peace,
> And Deirdre's tale began. The King was old.
> A month or so before the marriage-day,
> A young man, in the laughing scorn of his youth,
> Naisi, the son of Usnach, climbed up there,
> And, having wooed, or, as some say, being wooed,
> Carried her off.

The musicians suspect the King, and try to warn Prince Fergus, who is in good faith escorting the lovers. They play the chorus—the benevolent, non-committal onlooker of all ages. Only Deirdre takes the warning. Her mind misgives her, for no King or retinue is there to greet them. Perhaps of only half-mortal birth, she is 'fey', and, like Juliet, foresees a doom. Her mind is sharpened by the hint of the chorus :—

> Ah ! now I catch your meaning, that this King
> Will murder Naisi, and keep me alive.

But Naisi, when he enters, proves to be a brave, lover-like fool whom the King's promise has deceived. He is as credulous as Fergus, and neither can read the plainest warning. He is a man who is bound to run into a snare, and he does so. The construction is not so good at this point, or the movement so swift, as it becomes later. The action halts, while Fergus and Naisi are blind to the apparent. Brown-faced armed Libyans have been silently passing by, and the Musician has given the broadest hint of their intentions. Yet the two men rebuke Deirdre's foresight as cowardice. The poet, in fact, has to account for the lovers' running into peril.

But he need not have laboured the point, for they are already entrapped. The question of the King's sincerity might have been settled for them before the play began. They might have come upon the stage almost undeceived ; and though to arrange thus would have sacrificed some of the pretty play that is made with presentiments, it would have strengthened the story and would have shortened the act, which lasts a whole hour. As it is, we wait with some impatience until Naisi shall open his eyes. Now the suspense truly begins. Henceforward the play is as tightly spun as the African net into which Naisi is too easily allured. The nature of Deirdre is unfolded to us by events, not by description. She is the most distinct character that Mr. Yeats has hitherto invented. She has had little joy of love, though she has wandered with Naisi 'half a dozen years'. She has apprehensions and foresight of evil, but no fear ; her passionate essence is a resourceful courage and a power, again like Juliet's, to dissemble and die :—

> I have found life obscure and violent,
> And think it ever so.

Also she has the deepest of reasons, apart from her love for Naisi, for never yielding, in the fear that magical spells may, after all, win her mind to Conchubar ; for stones of love-charming potency have been sewn, so it is rumoured, into the embroideries of the bridal bed. Hearing this, she prays :—

> O Mover of the stars,
> That made this delicate house of ivory
> And made my soul its mistress, keep it safe!

Deirdre, therefore, though tied in life and death to her lover, is solitary-minded. She even thinks of defacing the beauty which is the cause of all the misery. Naisi is at last, over-suddenly, convinced, and events thicken, or rather begin.   The messenger enters and bids Fergus and Deirdre to the feast, ' but not the traitor that bore off the Queen.'   But Conchubar is a traitor too, for he has broken his pledge of safe-conduct.   Naisi finds the place beset.   While the musicians sing, they play chess, like the king and queen in a famous old story ; calmly at first, but in the end Deirdre cries :—

> Bend and kiss me now,
> For it may be the last before our death.
> And when that 's over we'll be different ;
> Imperishable things, a cloud or a fire.
> And I know nothing but this body, nothing
> But that old vehement, bewildering kiss.

At this moment Conchubar spies in, retires, and Naisi rushes out, taunting him, only to be netted by the Libyans and brought back.   Meanwhile Deirdre commits her story and the care of her name to the chief musician, who lets her take a knife :—

> There are times
> When such a thing is all the friend one has.

Now at last comes the drama.   The King offers Naisi freedom to escape if Deirdre will enter the house publicly, of her own will, as Queen, to show that Conchubar has ' not taken her by force or guile '.   At this point, to hold the spiritual balance and to end the story with the right, inextricable, tragic clash of sympathies, it is necessary to dignify Conchubar as well as the lovers, and not to leave him merely a vindictive and deceived elderly husband. He does right to make the offer which they do right to refuse.   Both parties, in Hegel's phrase, are *justified*. Deirdre implores Naisi to accept the chance ; she seems to try and make him understand that she will wait till he is free, and then will slay herself in good time.   But Naisi refuses : —

X

> O eagle! if you were to do this thing,
> And buy my life of Conchubar with your body,
> Love's law being broken, I would stand alone
> Upon the eternal summits, and call out,
> And you could never come there, being banished.

Deirdre then kneels to the King, who, unseen by her, signs for Naisi to be led behind the curtain. While he is being done to death, in the Greek manner, off the scene, she pleads vehemently for his life, taking the blame on herself, and praising the value of Naisi in council. Then she turns and discovers—the executioner has come out with his sword bloody. Her one aim now is to die with Naisi after touching him once more and laying out his body. To reach this aim she suddenly turns actress; she must cajole permission out of the King to perform the last offices to Naisi. The culminant scene that follows is the best written in the play, and the hardest to represent on the stage. Deirdre feigns to be fascinated by her new master :—

> Although we are so delicately made,
> There's something brutal in us, and we are won
> By those who can shed blood.

She even pleads that it is best she should be suffered to see Naisi bloodstained and his beauty gone ; for this will bring her the nearer to Conchubar, since it is better, when she is beside *him*,

> That the mind's eye should call up the soiled body,
> And not the shape I loved.

The King doubts her motive, and only yields to her taunt that he is afraid of the dead. She may, he says, have a knife concealed ; she offers to be searched. The King lets her go, convinced. It sustains his dignity that he has been convinced, and that he did not have her searched. The musicians fill the interval with fateful exclamations.   The curtain is drawn back, the lovers are seen lying dead, the King is baffled, and the threatening clamour of Fergus's men is heard.   He turns unarmed to face them :—

> There's not a traitor that dare stop my way.
> Howl, if you will; but I, being king, did right
> In choosing her most fitting to be queen,
> And letting no boy lover take the sway.

Deirdre is the best play Mr. Yeats has written, not so much in poetic beauty as in construction and the logic of feeling.   He has worked to keep his lyrical instincts from smothering the drama.   He has painted one distinct character, and dimly pencilled the others.   As the climax draws on, the texture of the plot is firmer.   *Deirdre* is an actable play, written in verse, upon a heroic subject. It should rather be called the end of a play than a play. The expository prologue has in it the matter of a whole act.   But the Greek devices that are used are never intrusive and add to the reticent beauty of the whole.

VI

There is much lonely poetry now being written in Ireland, as we shall see, in the form of a lyrical self-communing, which the poet utters to himself and forgets that he is uttering aloud.   He is in no special situation ; he is alone in the world, and his disembodied spirit is speaking.   This element is fading out of the plays of Mr. Yeats, who in *Deirdre* has forced himself to think of situation ; the remoteness of spirit in Deirdre's speeches is dramatic, it is all in character.   It will take some time before players can be trained to interpret a poetic drama of this kind, and to speak blank verse.   The company at the Abbey Theatre speak their prose so well that this

defect may almost be forgiven them ; indeed, the Abbey
Theatre is the heart and focus at present of the Irish
prose drama. No one can understand the movement of
the native literature without seeing and hearing them.
The plays are written for them, and they are born and
trained to act the plays. There is nothing like it in
Britain. The pieces that are now being made for the
Irish Theatre Society, and acted by its company, have
a purity of inspiration, a freshness as of wild fruits, and
a beauty in presentation, that revive the soul of the
playgoer, long used to find his best satisfaction in the
town irony of Mr. Pinero and the hard, corrosive satire
of French and German dramatists. There is a freedom
from ' petrifaction of feeling ', and a piety and pathos
that spring straight from the people. Even the stormy
irony of Mr. J. M. Synge, drawn from just the same
fountain, is exhilarating ; it has none of the *cassant*
effect that is left by Sudermann's *Die Ehre* or by *The
Gay Lord Quex*. The two chief writers of comedy are
Mr. Synge and Lady Gregory. The prose of Lady
Gregory is mostly humorous ; that of Mr. Synge is
poetic and sardonic. The actors speak both kinds of
prose to perfection, and this is high praise. To English
ears the rhythms of the language assigned by Mr. Synge
to peasants and vagrants are difficult and eloquent ; they
are so strange that we require the repeated assurance of
those who know Ireland that they represent real diction
and natural rhythm. The actors can reproduce these
effects not only because they are Irish-born themselves,
but because they are carefully trained against the peril of
forgetting the cadences of familiar life and adopting the
outworn ones of the official stage. In the love scene of
The Playboy of the Western World, which was mobbed
for its satiric veracity, we read :—

CHRISTY (with rapture): If the mitred bishops seen you that time, they'd be the like of the holy prophets, I'm thinking, do be straining the bars of Paradise to lay eyes on the Lady Helen of Troy, and she abroad, pacing back and forward, with a nosegay in her golden shawl.

Such melodious and passionate extravagance is an ancient feature of Irish style. The more piercing and plaintive cadence is doubtless commoner, and falls from the lips of these players with a noticeable lack of effort. In Mr. Synge's *Riders to the Sea* the son is talking to his mother about the lost body of his drowned brother. The dead wandering under the ' humming water ' or the ' whelming tide '—that is a theme that Shakespeare and Milton have set for the organ. It is here transposed, as if for some keen and wailing instrument:—

BARTLEY: How would it be washed up, and we after looking each day for nine days, and a strong wind blowing awhile back from the west and south?

MAURYA: If it isn't found itself, that wind is raising the sea, and there was a star up against the moon, and it rising in the night. If it was a hundred horses, or a thousand horses you had itself, what is the price of a thousand horses against a son where there is one son only?

These words, as uttered by the performer, sounded, what they really are, natural and instinctive and not a scholar's fancy ; and the whole piece brought out that accord between author, audience, and actors, which is the reason for a theatre existing.

Some clue to the talent of Mr. Synge, to the life he portrays and so to the primary sources of his power, may be found in his book on *The Aran Islands* (1907). There could be no more persuasive defence of his art. Some of the tales and suggestions for his plays are there to be seen ; and there also, reported from the lips of the fishers and kelp-burners, is some of the language of *The Playboy* and *In the Shadow of the Glen*, which at first seems too good to be real. The topic of the latter play is ready-made. An old man tells how he was walking in hard rain, and wanted shelter, and looked in at a lighted window.

I saw a dead man laid on a table, and candles lighted, and a woman watching him. I was frightened when I saw him, but it was raining hard, and I said to myself, if he was dead he couldn't hurt me. Then I knocked on the door and the woman came and opened it.

He is bidden, receives a cup of tea and a fine new pipe, and is left to watch the dead man while the wife goes out to tell the neighbours, locking the door. The visitor smokes his pipe :—

I was smoking it with my hand on the back of my chair—the way you are yourself this minute, God bless you—and I looking on the dead man, when he opened his eyes as wide as myself and looked at me.

‘ Don't be afeard, stranger,’ said the dead man, ‘ I'm not dead at all in the world. Come here and help me up and I'll tell you all about it.’

Well, I went up and took the sheet off of him, and I saw that he had a fine clean shirt on his body, and fine flannel drawers.

He sat up then, and says he—

‘ I've got a bad wife, stranger, and I let on to be dead the way I'd catch her goings on.’

The wife comes in with a young man, and retires with him. The dead man gets up and uses the stick on the young man ‘so that the blood out of him leapt up and hit the gallery’. ‘That,’ says the old sagaman, ‘is my story.’

The sea is the livelihood and the death of these people, and they reflect its moods of ferocity and peacefulness. When it takes their young men, as it continually does, it is odds if the bodies are found, or, when found, if they will be recognized. A man is washed ashore in Donegal, with his purse or bits of his dress remaining, and the people on the islands try 'for three days' to fix his identity. The mother is seen, 'still weeping and looking out on the sea.' The married sister of the dead man comes and puts together the information, and concludes that 'it's Mike sure enough'.

Then she began to keen slowly to herself. She had loose yellow hair plastered round her head with the rain, and as she sat by the door suckling her infant, she seemed like a type of the women's life upon the islands.

Here is the germ of *Riders to the Sea*. The land is full of the fairies, and of tales of human beings who are away with them. Songs are known and chanted in the Irish, including some of the Love Songs of Connacht, Dr. Hyde's treasury. When the dead are found, the funeral is in keeping. Mr. Synge describes one such occasion, with its procession of red-dressed women, its magnificent gesticulation and loud lament, and some grim accessories. The grave has to be cleared of an old coffin and its contents.

A skull was lifted out, and placed upon a gravestone. Immediately an old woman, the mother of the dead man, took it up in her hands, and carried it away by herself. Then she sat down and put it in her lap—it was the skull of her own mother—and began keening and shrieking over it with the wildest lamentation (p. 122). . . . In this cry of pain the inner consciousness of the people seems to lay itself bare for an instant, and to reveal the mood of beings who feel their isolation in the face of a universe that wars on them with winds and sea (p. 40).

'There is no distinction between the natural and the supernatural.' No one, spending any time in such a place, can help the mystical moods which at once unite him with the people and take him mentally far away from them. The sea and the colours breed dreams, and through them courses the music habitual in the island cottages. Yet there is no vagueness about the impression, the sharpness and definition of every scene are wonderful ; and this quality has passed into the art—as yet short of its full maturity—of Mr. Synge. His book shows a new piece of human life, and therefore new material for art. This is the hope of the literary movement in Ireland; the subjects are infinite and fresh. There is room for many new writers, and they would not elbow each other : there is room for novelists as well as for playwrights. Indeed, much of the life of which we have glimpses could only be told in a novel, for it is beautiful and expressive without being dramatic at all.

VII

Another side of the same life is seen in the plays of Lady Gregory, who writes easily, has the theatrical sense, and does not let the old sagas, or any literary sentiment, get between her and the people. She, too, writes for the actors—for a first-rate comedian, Mr. W. G. Fay, and his brother, Mr. Frank Fay, and for Miss Maire O'Neill, and Miss Sarah Allgood, and their companions. Most dramatists write for a single actor, not for a whole cast. Lady Gregory's favourite line is merry comedy ; tending, I should add, to farce, except that farce implies avowedly overdrawn humours, whilst Lady Gregory's skill lies in her light naturalness. It is not possible to separate her writing from the performance of Mr. William Fay. He is a small, dark man, with an infectious enjoyment of his own performance, and a voice of remarkable gusto, boisterous or rasping or cajoling as occasion may need. In *The Rising of the*

Moon he is a 'ballad-singer', really a runaway, who flatters and scares the constable into letting him escape. When, by a sudden 'trick change', he throws aside the hat and coat, and therewith the cringe, of the ballad-monger, and becomes a fine young fellow squaring up to justice, he shows the born actor's power to give the illusion of varying size and stature—to appear, like Milton's angels, 'dilated or condensed' at will. In another piece, *The Jackdaw*, he is Michael Cooney, 'one of seven generations of Cooneys, who never trusted any man, living or dead'. He is Suspicion in the flesh, with a hard eye that looks askance. His brother, Mr. Frank Fay, acts the title-part in the best of Lady Gregory's comedies, *Hyacinth Halvey*, the young ne'er-do-weel, who finds himself invested with a reputation for virtue which clings to him like some magic shirt, and which he has grace enough to resent wearing but not enough force of character to strip off. It is in vain that he steals a sheep from a wall and silver from a church poor-box ; his reputation is too strong for him. Mr. Frank Fay's aspect as Hyacinth can only be described *penaud* ; he has a genius for looking foolish. Hyacinth, to his disgust, is at last shouldered by the populace as a hero and borne off to be chairman of a sober meeting.

One of these trifles, translated by Lady Gregory from the Irish of Dr. Hyde, *The Poorhouse*, is of a lighter sort. Two old fellows, Colum and Paudeen, are lying on their beds near one another, with their heads propped on pillows and their feet towards the audience. Old inhabitants of the poorhouse, they snap and wrangle, and the pillows fly, whilst other inmates grin by the fire. An ancient sister of Colum enters and offers to take him to her home. He timidly suggests that she shall also take

Paudeen, his inseparable and intimate enemy. She will not, and Colum prefers to stay. She leaves coldly, and bad words and pillows fly once more between the beds. It is nothing; but it is far from the vulgar conventions of the English popular farces that make their writers' fortunes.

It is uncertain whether Lady Gregory will construct a drama. She has, however, shown her power to write a scene that is not humorous. The *Gaol Gate* is in a curious, effective, but dangerous rhythm between verse and prose. It expresses a single note of desolate angry sorrow, and represents two or three moments of changing pain. A youth has been imprisoned on the charge of a moonlight murder; he is innocent, but refuses to inform upon the culprit. His mother, Mary Cahel, and his wife, Mary Cushin, have trudged, after many delays, to the jail gate, which they reach in the early morning. The jailer looks out, and they learn gradually, first that the youth has died, and then that he has been hanged, whereon the widow exclaims in agony: *It was they that took him, and not the great God at all!* She curses the companions who had escaped and refused to save him. A scanty bundle of his clothes is flung out, and the door shut. Mother and widow lament the dead. Excepting for the brief space when they know of his death but do not know the manner of it, there is no drama here. But there is pathos, the feminine counterpart of drama; and such pathos is strong enough, if sustained, to help out a longer play with a more vital action, in which pathos is overruled by tragedy, or the spirit of *intermezzi* by a comic plot.

VIII

At the other pole are the mystical poets, who are only in superficial contact with Mr. Yeats, though sometimes in his debt for stray turns of cadence, and akin to him in spiritual tenets which they take more doctrinally and gravely than he does. They too keep politics out of their verse, though they spring from the rebel camp. They too have escaped academic drill, to the good of their mental freedom if not of their craft ; for if drill may deaden power, it may also save a wasteful and solitary struggle with the alphabet. They show little sign of that assured attitude towards words which may come from a wide poetical reading. For the same reason they do not fall into the sterile echo and reminiscence of English models. Their production so far is scant enough, though its slightness may be only that of undevelopment ; and with one or two exceptions it is marked by a hardly distinguishable likeness of note.

Their creed, or attitude, allies them with our seventeenth-century visionaries, Lord Herbert of Cherbury or Henry Vaughan ; the creed that the poet must be wisely passive, and that truth is revealed while the will is asleep.

> I am contented, for I know that Quiet
> Wanders laughing and eating her wild heart
> Among pigeons and bees.

The suppression of ' will ', of the active devouring assertive element in us, may fairly be called a tenet of these poets. The general soul, or ' memory of the world', or the 'ancestral self', or the 'Quiet' (which, or who, recalls, in name only, the god of Browning's Caliban) will flow into us, and let us speak, if we only wait and do not strive or cry. The student of historic mysticism will recognize this temper at once, and know it for a potent source both of poetry, as in Scheffler or Traherne, and of a prose essentially poetic, as in Henry More. He will also be ready to fear lest the ' generation of a mystic be the corruption of a poet ', and lest the effort to express the

wordless Absolute be not only itself defeated, but lead to
the defeat of words, of style, themselves. The mystical
system-weaver wisely stops with a formula, but the
mystical poet has his wings burnt long before he has
flown into the sun. Yet the effort is eternally recurrent,
so that the high-hearted experiments of ' A. E.' and his
friends at once command our sympathy.

Two poets first call for mention who are more strictly
scholarly in form than their companions. One is the
late Mr. Lionel Johnson, a critic of wide and deep
reading, a Roman Catholic, and a patriot, who died sadly
and before his time, and whose book on Mr. Thomas
Hardy showed a severe and sensitive mind. His verse,
of which a small selection is published, has a studious
subtlety and occasional glory of phrase that increase our
regret. Another young writer, Mr. Charles Weekes,
published in 1893, but at once withdrew, a volume called
Reflections and Refractions. Some of this verse ought
to reappear ; it has a fine edge, and its nascent but real
power over the horrible, as in the poem *Louis Verger,
being some Sensations of an Assassin,* should not be
ignored. So, too, in the verses called *Phthisical,* there
is power and finish :—

> So Patroklus died ;
>   And, as fast
>   His avenger lies asleep.
>   Will you weep
>   When you know that I have found
>   Sleep at last ?

' A. E.', the literary name, as is well known, of
Mr. George Russell, has published *The Earth-Breath*
(1897), *The Divine Vision* (1904), and other pieces. But
some of his truest work is in his earlier *Homeward Songs
by the Way.* He now has a smoother, less peccable

technique, a more accurate rhythm and diction. But there is some fading of the half-articulate power to express inward and hidden things ; and A. E. is prone, like all mystics in their weaker hour, to fall back on key-words and fixed language. The significant harping on the word 'ancestral', to express, one may suppose, that inherited shadow-consciousness which feeds our own ; and many references to the 'Sacred Hazels', which in the old tale hung and blossomed purple over the wells of know-ledge, are instances. This complaint, or warning, uttered, we owe honour to A. E., who is coming to be better known in England as one of the few poets alive who, when at his best, can seize the elusive and vanishing essence of human words in the service of mystical expression.

We must pass like smoke or live within the spirit's fire ;
 For we can no more than smoke unto the flame return ;
If our thought has changed to dream, our will unto
  desire,
 As smoke we vanish though the fire may burn.

Lights of infinite pity star the grey dusk of our days :
 Surely here is Soul : with it we have eternal breath :
In the fire of love we live, or pass by many ways,
 By unnumbered ways of dream to death.

Here, certainly, is a successor to the old poets of Bemerton, George Herbert, and Norris—to their want of long-upheld perfection and to their recompensing splendours and flashes. *The Fountain of Shadowy Beauty* is a dream of more sustained length. The Platonism of that elder age sounds again in the repeated utterance of a love that becomes its own negation :—

  O beauty, as thy heart o'erflows
   In tender yielding unto me,
  A vast desire awakes and grows
   Unto forgetfulness of thee.

A pleasant earthly retort might and should be written by the mortal mistress to this announcement ; but that would call out another side of the Irish character. The same tones are heard in the following :—

> Away ! the great life calls ; I leave
> For Beauty, Beauty's rarest flower ;
> For Truth, the lips that ne'er deceive ;
> For Love, I leave Love's haunted bower.

Perhaps the poet will come back in fancy from such a sojourn, and write the better for his absence. As so often, the mystic mood co-exists with practical ability in A. E., who is known to be an admirable promoter of the industrial and agricultural movement in Ireland ; but it is natural, in the pauses of such a life, to write :—

> What of all the will to do?
> It has vanished long ago,
> For a dream-shaft pierced it through
> From the Unknown Archer's bow.

It is just the life of affairs that produces such words, in revulsion against itself. Behind the verse of A. E. we feel a genuine religious passion and internal self-discipline. His desire to re-enter those purged ethereal moods, where he seems to find his real self, is not always a help to art, which is ever distracted by the merely self-mining instinct ; but A. E. is imperfectly expressing deep things which no one in England is now expressing at all. He only writes from experience, and the experience that he puts into verse is inward and far-withdrawn. Working in a land of failures, and retaining his faith in it nevertheless, he will be remembered, whatever his art may finally come to, for his effort to clear some ground and build some habitation where young, serious, and inward spirits can feel that they may breathe and that they are not alone.

The eight friends of A. E., whose verses are edited by him in the fifty-six pages of *New Songs*,[134] do not write derivatively.   But the best of their verse is symbolic, or introverted, or a little abstract.   There is a good deal of variety in the note.   Only two short poems, by different authors, need be quoted here.   If traces of Mr. Yeats or Mr. Russell be found in either case, it does not matter ; the rhythms are beautiful, they are not imitations, and there are lines in each that any one might wish to have written.   The first piece is signed ' Seumas O'Sullivan '. I suppose the *Twilight People* are the ancient fairies, or the under dwellers, the ' Sidhe ' of legend.   The poem calls for musical setting.

It is a whisper among the hazel bushes ;
  It is a long, low, whispering voice that fills
With a sad music the bending and swaying rushes ;
  It is a heart-beat deep in the quiet hills.
Twilight people, why will you still be crying,
  Crying and calling to me out of the trees ?
For under the quiet grass the wise are lying,
  And all the strong ones are gone over the seas.
And I am old, and in my heart at your calling
  Only the old dead dreams a-fluttering go,
As the wind, the forest wind, in its falling
  Sets the withered leaves fluttering to and fro.

Miss Susan Mitchell, the writer of the second piece, should explore further the cadences of the heroic couplet, which is now, since Keats and Morris, so seldom heroic. Here the metre has some of the Jacobean clang and colour ; the title is *The Living Chalice.*

The Mother sent me on the Holy Quest
Timid and proud, and curiously drest,
In vestures by her hand wrought wondrously ;
An eager, burning heart she gave to me.
The Bridegroom's feast was set and I drew nigh.
—Master of Life, thy Cup has passed me by.

Before, new drest, I from the Mother came,
In dreams I saw the dazzling Cup of flame;
Ah, divine chalice, how my heart drank deep :
Waking, I sought the love I knew asleep.
The Feast of Life was set and I drew nigh.
—Master of Life, thy Cup has passed me by.

Eyes of the Soul, awake, awake and see
Growing within the ruby-radiant tree ;
Sharp pain has wrung the clusters of my Vine :
My heart is rose-red with its brimmed Wine.
Thou hast new-set the feast, and I draw nigh :
—Master of Life, take me, thy Cup am I.

The sense of this noble and adequate Grail-poem needs
no expounding to those at all versed in such imagery.
The Rossettis, one may think, would have hailed it. Good
work like this is born in solitude, but is also born of a
society and of its ' impact of hot thought on hot thought '.
Irishmen properly repel advice as to their own concerns,
but they do not resent the expression of a hope founded
upon sympathy. Let them remain mystical, and makers
of twilight landscape-verses, but let them also widen their
scope ; let them write, as their tradition bids them (and
as they could), on simple or stately human things as well ;
tales, war-songs, epithalamies, satires ! And let them
be much sterner (as they can be) in their heed for style,
if they would found the national and enduring poetry of
their dreams.

NOTES

[1] The tale has been repeatedly told; by, amongst others, D. Berti in his standard *Vita di Giordano Bruno* (last ed., 1889), which includes the documents of the trial; by Miss I. Frith (Mrs. Oppenheim) in her *Life of Giordano Bruno the Nolan*, 1887; by Mr. John Owen, *Skeptics of the Italian Renaissance*, 1893, ch. iv, pp. 271-6. But more accurate accounts are found in J. A. Symonds, *Renaissance in Italy* (*The Catholic Reaction*, part II, ch. ix, pp. 50-5); and in Mr. J. Lewis McIntyre's *Giordano Bruno*, 1903, pp. 21-47—the best and fullest narrative. Mr. McIntyre's book appeared after the article that is here reprinted and revised, and I have borrowed a few points from his exposition, which enters into somewhat different detail and has another purpose. For a brief but accurate sketch of the visit, and a luminous treatment of Bruno's importance, see R. Adamson, *Development of Modern Philosophy*, 1902, vol. ii, pp. 23-44. See note 46 *post*.

[2] *Mémoires* in Petitot, *Collection*, series I, vol. xxxiii.

[3] Pennant, *London*, ed. 1805, vol. iii, pp. 111, 160.

[4] Berti, *Doc.*, ix, appended to *Vita*.

[5] Dedication to *De l'Infinito*: in *Opere italiane*, ed. Lagarde, Göttingen, 1888, p. 305; cited here as 'L.'

[6] Lagarde, pp. 263-5.

[7] Not in *Opere latine*, ed. F. Fiorentino, Naples, 1879.

[8] For Toby Matthew and Culpeper, see L., p. 220. For Bruno's whole account of the Oxford incident, L., p. 176 foll. For the visit of Alasco, Camden, *Annales*, part III, *sub anno* 1583; and Wood, *Ath. Ox.*, s.v. 'Alaskie'.

[9] Works of Samuel Daniel, ed. Grosart, vol. iv, p. 7. This reference is indicated by Mr. Lewis Einstein (*The Italian Renaissance in England*, 1902, p. 356), who, however, does not cite the allusion to the Schools. For Dicson's *De Umbra Rationis*, 1583, and its relation to Bruno see McIntyre (p. 36), who remarks: 'The poet Thomas Watson has also connected Bruno with Dicson

in his *Compendium Memoriae Localis* (1585 or 1586); ... Watson had been in Paris in 1581, when he met Walsingham, and he may of course have met Bruno also.'

[10] L., p. 176.   [11] *Ib.*, p. 217.   [12] *Ib.*, p. 136.

[13] In the article on M. Gwinne in the *Dict. Nat. Biog.* occurs the curious error that Bruno and his friends had supper at Lord Buckhurst's before proceeding to the disputation.

[14] Berti, *Doc.*, xiii.   [15] L., p. 136.   [16] *Ib.*, p. 144.

[17] *Ib.*, p. 148.   [18] *Ib.*, p. 173.   [19] Berti, *Doc.*, xi.

[20] The original suggestion (see Ames, *Typographical Antiquities*, 1749, p. 352) is found in Baker, who appears to have based it, if on anything, on Vautrollier's letter to T. Randolph in L'Espine's *Treatise of Apostasy*, 1587, which Vautrollier printed in London. But the letter says nothing of Bruno. See McIntyre, pp. 35 and 358: 'Vautrollier traded in Scotland as early as 1580 as a bookseller; he had already enjoyed the patronage of King James, and was even encouraged to return with a printing press, which he did in 1584. Thereafter he published in both Edinburgh and London till 1587. On the other hand, some of Bruno's works were printed in 1585, so that the theory of Vautrollier's flight to Scotland, owing to his being the printer of Bruno's works, falls through.' See Dickson and Edmund, *Annals of Scottish Printing*, 1890, p. 381. Apart from this, I was told by the late Mr. Proctor, of the British Museum, who searched into the matter, that the Italian books of Bruno were certainly not from Vautrollier's press, though they were from some English press. The tradition is named in *Dict. Nat. Biog.*, s.v. 'Vautrollier', where 'Bruno's "Last Tromp"' is alluded to. This must be an erroneous description of the *Spaccio*.

[21] L., p. 115.

[22] On *Essay on Man*, iv. 103, 'See Sidney bleed'. Warton also names the *Spaccio*, and gives Toland (*General Dictionary*) as authority for its being printed in London. T. Zouch, *Memoirs of Sir P. Sidney* (1808), embroiders (p. 337), adding that Bruno was 'well known to the queen and much beloved by her courtiers. Sir Philip Sidney and Sir Fulke Greville were his most intimate friends. With them and some others he was frequently assembled. Philosophical and metaphysical subjects, &c.' All this mythology has passed into more than one account of Sidney.

[2] Berti, *Vita*, cap. ix; Frith, *Life*, p. 128; Owen, *Skeptics of*

Ital. Ren., l.c.; and many other English writers. The whole story is hideously muddled in G. Stiavelli, *Vita di G. B.*, 1888, and in D. Levy, *G. B.*, 1887, p. 137, &c. The remarks in Höffding, *op. cit.*, Eng. trans., 1900, vol. i, pp. 114–18, are of course reliable.

[24] L., p. 404.   [25] *Ib.*, pp. 747–54.

[26] *Opere latine*, ed. Fiorentino, vol. ii, p. 317.

[27] L., pp. 1–13.   [28] Berti, *Doc.*, xiii.   [29] L., p. 746.

[30] *Opere latine*, vol. i, pt. i, p. 217 (in prose).

[31] *Ib.*, vol. i, pt. ii, p. 227.

[32] B. Tschischwitz, *Shakspere-Forschungen*; and W. König, in *Sh.-Jahrbuch*, xi. 27. The refutation is in R. Beyersdorff's *G. B. und Sh.*, Oldenburg, 1888. See, too, G. Brandes, *William Shakespeare*, Eng. tr. (1902), pp. 349–51. Brandes refers to Brunnhofer (*G. B.'s Weltanschauung und Verhängniss*, Leipz., 1882, p. 33), who failed to hear of any work in the Bodleian throwing light on Bruno's visit to England (H. Nettleship quoted as authority).

[33] L., pp. 181, 342.

[34] L., p. 128: 'Habbiamo dottrina di non cercar la divinità rimossa da noi; se l'habbiamo appresso, anzi di dentro più che noi medesmi siamo dentro a noi'. Cp. *De la Causa*, Dial. ii. (L., p. 242), where Bruno says that the soul of the world is diffused 'come una voce, la quale è tutta in tutta una stanza, et in ogni parte di quella ; perchè da per tutto s'intende tutta'.

[35] H. Benivieni's *Hymn of Heavenly Love* is discussed both by himself and by Pico della Mirandula (*Commento*, 1519, tr. by T. Stanley, 1651). Cp. Ficino, *Sopra lo Amore o ver' Convito di Platone*, Flor., 1543. These are the bases for the study of Italian, and so for the origins of English, neo-Platonism ; together with the well-known passages in Castiglione's *Courtier* (tr. Hoby, ed. Raleigh, *Tudor Translations*). There are also Bembo, *Gli Asolani* ; and Equicola, *Libro di Natura d'Amore*, Venice, 1525.

[36] L., p. 642.   [37] L., p. 681.   [38] L., p. 724.

[39] By Mr. T. Whittaker, *Essays and Notices*, 1895, who remarks : 'A definite influence from Bruno I am inclined to think may be traced at least in Spenser's Cantos on Mutability.' The present writer, ignorant of this hint, struck later on the same parallel; see *Quart. Rev.*, Oct., 1902, for the original article here reprinted (and revised).

[40] *Life and Works of John Toland*, 1726, ii. 383 ; letter of Leibniz to Toland.

[41] L., p. 422.   [42] L., p. 550.   [43] L., p. 553.   [44] Cp. L., p. 226.

[45] Bacon, *Hist. Nat. et Experim.* (Ellis and Spedding's ed. of *Works*, ii. 13), groups 'Brunus' with Patricius, Telesius, Campanella, and other modern thinkers who have come on their stage with their systems, 'et novas fabulas egerunt, nec plausu celebres nec argumento elegantes.'

[46] s.v. 'Carew', *Encyc. Brit.*, ed. IX, vol. v, p. 101. The authorship of the article is noted in the posthumous *Development of Modern Philosophy*, by R. Adamson, 1903, p. 39 note, and the imitation by Carew is also mentioned by Adamson in his lecture on Bruno. See note 1, *supra*.

[47] *Anatomy of Melancholy* (ed. Shilleto, 1893); in vol. i, p. 10 ('Democritus Junior to the Reader') Bruno is linked with Copernicus as holding the 'prodigious tenent, or paradox, of the earth's motion'; in vol. ii, pp. 47, 57, 62–3 ('Digression of Air'), with Campanella as arguing for the infinity of worlds; 'Kepler will by no means admit of Brunus' infinite worlds'. In vol. iii, p. 445 ('Religious Melancholy in Defect') Bruno is an atheist: 'Averroes oppugns all spirits and supreme powers; of late Brunus (*infelix Brunus*, Kepler calls him), Machiavel, Caesar Vaninus, lately burned at Toulouse in France, and Pet. Aretine, have publicly maintained such atheistical paradoxes.'

[48] J.-P. Niceron, *Mémoires pour servir . . . hommes illustres . . . avec un catalogue de leurs ouvrages*, 1729–45, vol. xvii, p. 210.

[49] *Spectator*, No. 389, May 27, 1712; the prices are given in a note.

[50] *Remarks* on *The Grumbling Hive*, l. 321.

[51] *Life and Works of J. Toland*, 1726, vol. ii, pp. 376, 383, 400.

[52] See *A Collection of Several Pieces of Mr. J. Toland*, 1726, for Scioppius's letter and the notes on *De la Causa* and *De l'Infinito*.

[53] See note 67.

[54] North's very accurate English for Plutarch, *Numa*, ch. xxii. See Thuc. ii. 44–6; and for the lyrical references, on the Dead at Thermopylae (No. 4, Bergk); 99 (ἄσβεστον κλέος οἵδε); 100 (εἰ τὸ καλῶς θνήσκειν). Theognis, ll. 237 foll.

[55] *Pyth.* i. 99; *ib.*, xi. 56; *Isth.* iii. [iv.] 58. See too *Ol.* x. [xi.] 4, xi. [x.] 91–6, *Nem.* vi. 31.

[56] *Odes*, iii. 30 ('exegi monumentum'); Ovid, *Met.* xv. 871; Propertius, *Eleg.* iii. [iv.] 2. 17–24.

[57] See the Ovidian and Horatian passages just cited; the 'vive,

precor' of Statius, *Thebais*, xii. 816; Catull. i. 10; the 'fortunati ambo' of *Aen.* ix. 446. See Martial, *Epig.* i. 1, iii. 95, v. 15, v. 60, &c.

[58] See *Opera* (Bâle), 1554, vol. ii, p. 1274 a. *Africa*, bk. I. *ad init.* [to his patron] :—

'... quantum tua clara favori
Fama meo conferre potest, modo mitis in umbra
Nominis ista tui dirum spretura venenum
Invidiae latuisse velis, ubi nulla vetustas
Interea et nulli rodent mea nomina vermes.'

Bk. viii, p. 1322 a:—

'Credite, cunctarum longe blandissima rerum est
Gloria, nec levibus stimulis agit insita ; fortes
Egregiosque animos generosaque pectora pulsat.'

[59] See Zeller, *Stoics and Epicureans*, Eng. tr., p. 284 ; fame was at best admitted, it seems, to be a προηγμένον, or derivative good. Cic. *de Fin.* iii. 17, implies this, and rejects *gloria*, while accepting *bona fama* for its uses.

[60] *De Off.* ii. 9-14. 'Vera gloria radices agit atque etiam propagatur, ficta omnia celeriter tamquam flosculi decidunt, nec simulatum potest quicquam esse diuturnum.'

[61] The aim of contrasting real with hollow fame runs through the passages in the *Tusculans*, and is seen not only in the well-known one, 'Etsi enim nihil habet in se gloria cur expetatur, tamen virtutem tanquam umbra sequitur' (i. 45, 109), but also in iii. 2, 3 : 'Est enim gloria solida res quaedam et expressa, non adumbrata ; ea est consentiens laus bonorum, incorrupta vox bene iudicantium de excellente virtute; ea virtuti resonat tanquam imago. Quae quia recte factorum plerumque comes est, non est bonis viris repudianda.' Cp. *Pro Marc.* viii : 'est illustris ac pervagata mul· torum et magnorum vel in suos vel in patriam vel in omne genus hominum fama meritorum.'

[62] Leopardi's Ode (1820) to Angelo Mai on this occasion shows a temper other than that of the humanist. *Opere*, ed. Ranieri, 1882, ii. 45. But see his *Parini* for his view of fame.

[63] 'Quibus amputatis cernis profecto quantis in angustiis vestra gloria se dilatari velit ... Quid autem interest ab iis qui postea nascentur sermonem fore de te, quum ab iis nullus fuerit qui ante nati sunt ? ... quum praesertim apud eos ipsos quibus audiri nomen nostrum potest, nemo unius anni memoriam consequi potest?' (vi. 21, 23).

⁶⁴ vi. 23, 25. Cp. the satiric and pessimistic handling in Juv. *Sat.* x. 114 foll.

⁶⁵ 'Nomen Attici perire Ciceronis epistolae non sinunt.... Profunda super nos altitudo temporis veniet, pauca ingenia caput exerent et in idem quandoque silentium abitura oblivioni resistent ac se diu vindicabunt. Quod Epicurus amico suo potuit promittere, hoc tibi promitto, Lucili: habebo apud posteros gratiam, possum mecum duratura nomina educere (*Ep.* 21. 6).... Gloria multorum iudiciis constat, claritas bonorum.'

⁶⁶ 'Quamdiu videbatur furere Democritus! vix recepit Socratem fama. Quamdiu Catonem civitas ignoravit! respuit nec intellexit, nisi cum perdidit... paucis natus est, qui populum aetatis suae cogitat; multa annorum milia, multa populorum supervenient; ad illa respice. Etiamsi omnibus tecum viventibus silentium livor indixerit, venient, qui sine offensa, sine gratia iudicent. Si quod est pretium virtutis ex fama, nec hoc interit. Ad nos quidem nihil pertinebit posterorum sermo; tamen etiam non sentientes colet ac frequentabit' (*Ep.* 79. 14).

⁶⁷ *Ep.* 102. 18. I can find no more searching modern scrutiny of the worth of fame than Schopenhauer's (*Parerga und Paralipomena*, vol. i, pp 437 foll., in Grisebach's Leipzig edition; *Aphorismen zur Lebensweisheit: Von Dem, was Einer vorstellt*; also in vol. ii, pp. 487 foll., *Von Urtheil, Kritik, Beifall und Ruhm*, § 242). Is Seneca modern, or is Schopenhauer antique in spirit? Or do not both speak for human nature at all seasons? The Stoic is quoted with approval by the German, whose analysis, though closer, follows on the same lines. Schopenhauer's angry sense of being slighted by his time and land leads him to dwell fiercely on the *livor silentii* and on the theme that the really great man seeks and has only posthumous applause; but he works these ideas out in the noblest style. His view is nearly the same as the more easy version of Stoicism, that fame, if not strictly a good, is desirable, and follows upon true desert. His own view of art as producing the only permanent things and giving the only valid satisfaction causes him, however, to give a more nearly absolute value than Seneca to true posthumous fame, when it is bestowed on works of art, and is approved alike by the seal of time and the scorn of contemporaries. Rank and Honour form the other sections of 'was Einer vorstellt' as goods; Fame (*Ruhm*) is higher and sounder than these. There is a curious likeness to the tone of

Spenser and other Elizabethans in his attacks upon the destructive principle of calumny, *Der Neid*, the Blatant Beast. One other expressive passage may be quoted (see note 53) from the same chapter:—

'Jedoch auch, wenn man seinen Blick weiter ausdehnt und das Lob der Zeitgenossen aller Zeiten überhaupt ins Auge fasst, wird man finden, dass dasselbe eigentlich immer eine Hure ist, pro-stituirt und besudelt durch tausend Unwürdige, denen es zu Theil geworden. ... Hingegen ist der Ruhm bei der Nachwelt eine stolze, spröde Schöne, die sich nur dem Würdigen, dem Sieger, dem seltenen Helden hingiebt....'

This profound sentence identifies the love of fame, in its ground-principle, with the love of begetting, as noted in text *supra*, p. 38, though a different turn is given; Fame is the bride who surrenders to the patient conqueror. Compare the parallel from Plato quoted in the text, p. 39.

[68] 'Intra unius gentis terminos praeclara illa famae immortalitas coarctabitur...' (*De Cons.* ii. 7). A curious parallel recurs in that necessary document of the Renaissance mind, Jerome Cardan's *De proprii vita liber* (died 1576). The great physician diagnoses the love of fame as a kind of disease ; but he is more savage than the Stoic, and heralds the disgust of the modern pessimist of Leopardi's type, and the general indifference of the later modern intellect, when philosophizing, to posthumous glory. Our in-creased sense of the fugitiveness of the material universe, books included, may help to answer for this.

'Scribes, inquam, quomodo legenda : Et de qua re praeclara, et adeo tibi nota, ut desiderare legentes possint? quo stylo, qua sermonis elegantia ut legere sustineant ? sit ut legant, nonne aevo praeterlabente in singulos dies fiet auctio, ut prius scripta con-temnantur, nedum negligantur? At durabunt aliquot annis ? quot ? centum ? mille ? decies mille ? ... Atque omnino cum desitura sint, etiam si per reditus Mundus renovaretur, ut Academici volunt, non minus quam si ut initium habet, et finem accepturus est, nil interest an post decimam diem, an decem millia myriadum anno-rum? Nihil utrumque, et ex aequo ad aeternitatis spatium. Interim tu discruciaberis spe, metu torqueberis, laboribus enerva-beris ? quicquid vitae est reliquum suavis amittas ? O egregium inventum !' (cap. ix, *Cogitatio de nomine perpetuando*).

[69] Boethius, *De Cons. Philosophiae*, bk. II, prose 7.

[70] Cp. Dante, *Inf.* v ; Petrarch, *Trionfo della Fama* ; Boccaccio, *Amorosa Visione.* Compare, too, the later catalogue of Skelton in his *Crown of Laurel,* a poem adapted freely from Chaucer's. These lists are instructive in the history of the reputation of the classics.

[71] *Civilization of the Renaissance in Italy* (tr. Middlemore, 1898), pt. II, ch. iii, pp. 139–53. Burckhardt speaks chiefly of Italy in the fourteenth century.

[72] The chief passage in point is in *De Monarchia,* i. 1 : 'Omnium hominum in quos amorem veritatis natura superior impressit, hoc maxime interesse videtur, ut quemadmodum de labore antiquorum ditati sunt, ita et ipsi posteris prolaborent, quatenus ab eis posteritas habeat quo ditetur. . . . In proposito est, hanc [Monarchiae notitiam] de suis enucleare latibulis, tum ut utiliter mundo pervigilem, tum etiam ut palmam tanti bravii primus in meam gloriam adipiscar.'

[73] *Par.* vi. 112 ; *Purg.* xi. 85–117.

[74] *Storia letteraria d'Italia: Il Trecento* (Milan, n.d.), p. 14. Cp. G. Körting, *Petrarca's Leben und Werke,* Leipz., 1878, p. 647, &c.

[75] See *Opera,* ed. 1554, vol. i, *De Origine,* &c. *ad. init.*

[76] *De Remediis Utriusque Fortunae,* bk. I. dial. 117. See also 44, *De scriptorum fama* ; I. 92, *De gloria* ; II. 25, *De infamia* ; II. 88, *De celebritate nominis importuna* ; and II. 130, *De studio famae anxio in morte.* On the lost *De Gloria* see *Epp. Senil.* xv. 1, pp. 1049–50 ; and the unconvincing doubts of P. de Nolhac, *Pétrarque et l'Humanisme* (ed. 2, 1907). I owe this reference to the kindness of the Rev. E. H. R. Tatham.

[77] See *Conf.* x. 37–8.

[78] *Dial.* iii. pp. 410–15, &c. On all this see a careful study by E. Segrè, *Studj Petrarcheschi,* Florence, 1903, especially pp. 3–137 : ' Il *Secretum* di Petrarca e le *Confessioni* di Sant' Agostino '.

[79] See on this the chapter on ' The Italian Influence in France ' by the late M. Joseph Texte in his *Études de littérature européenne,* 1898, pp. 39–44.

[80] On the aims of the Pléiade see Lanson, *Hist. de la litt. franç.,* 1895, p. 273, who quotes the verses ascribed to Charles IX :—

Tous deux également nous portons des couronnes,

Mais, roy, je la reçus ; poète, tu la donnes.

[81] *Odes,* i. 8, Epode 3. Cp. *Odes,* i. 3, str. 3 ; i. 16 (with echo of ' carent quia vate sacro ') ; ii. 2 (to Calliope) ; iii. 4 (to the daughters

of Henry II) ; v. 2 (to Margaret of Savoy). So *Poèmes*, bk. I : to Jean de la Peruse ; and *Hymnes*, ii. 9 (*de la Mort*). Here Ronsard asserts his intention to quit the exhausted water of Helicon and seek a fresh spring :—

> quelque chanson nouvelle
> Dont les accords seront peut-estre si tresdous
> Que les siecles voudront les redire apres nous :
> Et suivant mon esprit, à nul des vieux cantiques
> Larron ie ne devray mes chansons poétiques.

[82] *Odes*, i. 11, antist. 2.

[83] *Odes*, v. 17. For next quotation see *Élégies*, ii.

[84] *Défense*, pt. II, ch. vi.

[85] For this and the next quotations see : Sonnet, ' Heureux de qui la mort ' ; Sonnet, ' Ne te fasche, Ronsard ' ; also ' Que n'ay-je encor la harpe ' ; and ' Espérez-vous que la postérité . . .'.

[86] See *Astr. and Stella*, No. 90.

[87] These originally spring, not from *Trionfi*, but the Canzone ' Standomi un giorno '.

> A hasty longe rynnyng awaye of the tyme
> Is a poyson to fame to cause it to declyne
> Our Tryumphes shall passe our pompes shall decay
> Our lordshyppes our kyngdomes shall all awaye
> And al thyng also that we accompt mortall
> Tyme at the lengthe shall clene deface it al. . .
> . . . Al the hye fame where to that man pretende
> Even as the smoke doth vanysshe awaye
> So at the last al thynges do playne decaye.

These unshod lines tumbling over a stony metre are from Henry Parker, Lord Morley's (died 1556) little-remembered version of *Trionfi*, as republished by the Roxburghe Club. It is only of interest as being the first and one of the few versifications in English of that influential book.

[88] O cursed Eld ! the cankerworm of wits,
> How may these rimes, so rude as doth appeare,
> Hope to endure, sith workes of heavenly wits
> Are quite devourd and brought to nought by little bits ?

> (iv. 2. 33).

Cp. ii. 9. 21 ; ii. 10. 1-4 ; iv. 1. 21-2.

[89] *Poems of Shakespeare*, 1898, p. cv.

[90] *Lines to Shakespeare*; and *Epistle* to the Countess of Rutland *Forest*, No. 12.

[91] No. 44, ed. 1605. See the present writer's *Michael Drayton*, 1906.

[92] *Au roy*, No. 93: Cp. Corneille's lines to Mlle du Parc: *Œuvres*, p. 262 (in *Grands Écrivains de France*). I owe these two references to my colleague Dr. Charles Bonnier.

[92a] *Hesperides*, No. 211. Cp. the 'Sculpte, lime, cisèle' of Gautier.

[93] *In Quintum Novembris*, ll. 172-3, 192-6 : Fama, bonum quo non aliud veracius ullum, Nobis digna cani.

[94] The unprofessional reader, acquainted with German, may not dislike to hear the titles of a few of these works, which are all necessary implements of scholarship :—W. Franz, *Shakespeare-Grammatik*, Halle (Niemeyer), 1900 ; and the useful abridgement, *Die Grundzüge der Sprache Shakespeares*, Berlin (Felber), 1902. These works supersede much of Abbott's *Shakespearian Grammar*, which, however, still does good service. See, too, A. Schmidt, *Shakespeare-Lexicon*, 2 vols., Eng. tr. of 3rd edition (revised by Sarrazin), 1902, Berlin ; Goswin König, *Der Vers in Shakspere's Dramen*, Strassburg, 1888 (in the series *Quellen und Forschungen*, No. lxi) ; *Jahrbuch der Deutschen Shakespeare-Gesellschaft*, von Alois Brandl und Wolfgang Keller, Berlin, 1901-6, vols. xxxvii-xlii ; and *Shakespeare Phonology*, by Dr. Viëtor of Marburg. The essays by various hands in the *Stratford Shakespeare* (Bullen) should also be mentioned.

[95] Among these may be named M. J. J. Jusserand's *Histoire littéraire du peuple anglais de la Renaissance à la Guerre Civile*, vol. ii, Paris (Firmin-Didot), 1904 ; this is a history less of letters than of the social and commercial conditions—of the *habitat* of writers. It is wonderfully full and learned. Mr. Sidney Lee's *Great Englishmen of the Sixteenth Century* (Constable), 1904, is not always so strong in the presentation of Renaissance ethics as in the skilled sifting of positive evidence. Mr. Lee's picture of Bacon's intellectual importance and frontiers rests on much concealed labour of this kind. Reference should also be made to the same author's *Shakespeare and the Modern Stage*, and Mr. Morton Luce's *Handbook to the Works of W. Shakespeare* (2nd ed. 1907).

[96] The book occupies fascicles 55 to 65 of the *Folkeudgave*, or popular edition, of Brandes's collected works (*Samlede Skrifter*,

Copenhagen, Gyldendalske Boghandels Forlag, 1901). For
English translation cp. note 32 *supra*.

[97] N. J. Halpin, *Oberon's Vision in the M. N. D.*, *illustrated by
comparison with Lylie's Endymion*, 1843 (Shakespeare Soc.).
See R. Warwick Bond, *Works of John Lyly*, Oxf., 1902, vol. iii,
pp. 81–103 : *On the Allegory in Endimion*.

[98] See note 32 *supra*.

[99] J. Churton Collins, *Studies in Shakespeare* (Constable), 1904,
pp. 288–91.

[100] *Ethices* Pars III, prop. xxxv. schol. The description is of the
greater hatred which the 'zelotypus' will feel, in proportion to his
love for the loved object : ' quod rei amatae imaginem imagini eius,
quem odit, iungere cogitur, quae ratio plerumque locum habet in
amore erga feminam. Qui enim imaginatur mulierem, quem amat,
alteri sese prostituere, non solum ex eo, quod ipsius appetitus
coercetur, contristabitur, sed etiam quia rei amatae imaginem
pudendis et excrementis alterius iungere cogitur, eandem aversatur.'

[101] See the introductions by C. H. Herford to his edition of *The
Works of Shakespeare*, 10 vols., 1901 (Macmillan, Eversley
Edition).

[102] See Prof. Bradley's paper in *Hibbert Journal* for July, 1904,
on 'Hegel's Theory of Tragedy'. The original material is in
Hegel's *Aesthetik*, in *Werke* (1838), vol. x, part III, pp. 319–575.
This contains the most striking, profound, and philosophic theory of
poetry and the drama conceived since the time of Aristotle; and
although Hegel, starting with the preconception of Greek tragedy
as an ideal type, is never quite just to any other kind, his whole
treatment is full of light and of large sayings.

[103] *Studies in Shakespeare* (see note 99), pp. 127–79.

[104] 'English Men of Letters' Series, 1907.

[105] *Nouveaux Lundis*, vol. iii (May 30, 1864).

[106] *Naturalismus in England*. This is part of the larger work,
Main Currents of Nineteenth-Century Literature, the whole of
which is now in English (London, 1901–5), and has long been
known in German as *Hauptströmungen in der Literatur des
neunzehnten Jahrhunderts*.

[106a] (Addendum to p. 135). A word should be given to the valuable *Zeitschrift für vergleichende Litteraturgeschichte*, edited by
Dr. Max Koch : Berlin, vol. i, 1887 ; vol. vii (next series, vol. i),
1892 ; new series, ed. Drs. Wetz and Collin.

[107] Vol. i, 1895; vol. ii, 1897; vol. iii, 1903; vol. iv, 1903; vol. v, 1905. Not to lengthen the text, the last two volumes are not included in this review; but in the last of them Dr. Courthope is on his own ground, the eighteenth century, and speaks in fuller sympathy, perhaps, than with some earlier periods.

[108] Flaubert, *Correspondance* (*sub anno* 1860), vol. iii, p. 196.

[109] John Smith, *Select Discourses*, Discourse I, ed. 1673. This phrase is given as a rendering of Plotinus's κέντρον κέντρῳ συνάψας.

[110] The Gifford Lectures, 1901-2 (London, 1903). See especially Lectures XVI and XVII.

[111] *Religious Systems of the World*, 1905, pp. 120-1, 'Hinduism', by Sir A. Lyall: 'The true goal and final purpose of passing through all these worlds and existences is to get finally beyond the power that afflicts men with sensation. ... The Hindu thinks it safest to travel beyond all possible vicissitudes of joy and sorrow into a state that is likened to dreamless sleep.'

[112] *Die Welt als Wille und Vorstellung*, bk. IV, §§ 67-8; *Ergänzungen*, ch. xlvii; *Grundlage der Moral*, § 18; *Parerga und Paralipomena*, § 115. These passages give Schopenhauer's altruistic code; the following ones give his theory of escape from the pressure of the will through the study of art:—*Die Welt*, &c., bk. III, *passim*; *Ergänzungen*, ch. xxxiv; and *Parerga*, ch. xix. § 205. 'Das eigentliche Problem der Metaphysik des Schönen lässt sich sehr einfach so ausdrücken : wie ist Wohlgefallen und Freude an einem Gegenstande möglich, ohne irgend eine Beziehung desselben auf unser Wollen ? ... Meine Lösung ist gewesen, dass wir im Schönen allemal die wesentlichen und ursprünglichen Gestalten der belebten und unbelebten Natur, also Plato's Ideen derselben, auffassen, und dass diese Auffassung zu ihrer Bedingung ihr wesentliches Korrelat, *das willensfreie Subjekt des Erkennens*, d. h. eine reine Intelligenz ohne Absichten und Zwecke, habe.'

[113] James, *Varieties*, p. 411.

[114] H. Heppe, *Geschichte der quietistischen Mystik in der katholischen Kirche*, Berlin, 1875, p. 2: 'Aber auch die Mystik des Mittelalters beruhte auf jenem unabweisbaren Drange des evangelisch-angeregten Herzens. ... Doch war der Gedanke der Rechtfertigung des gefallenen Menschen durch gläubige Aneignung der verdienten Gerechtigkeit Christi der katholischen Mystik im Allgemeinen fremd.' Heppe expounds the Roman mystics faith-

fully, but finds the ultimate repose of the mystical spirit in the Protestant churches, and has no notion of it as a radical element of secular human nature.

[115] For Madame Guyon and Fénelon, see Prof. L. Crouslé's elaborate *Fénelon et Bossuet*, 2 vols., 1894; and Heppe, *passim*. Miguel de Molinos, *Guida Spirituale*, 1675: Eng. tr., 1688 and 1699. Molinos merits dispassionate study; there is an interesting notice of his abjuration and fate in *Three Letters from Italy* (anon., 1688).

[116] *Des Angelus Silesius 'Cherubinischer Wandersmann'* (reprint of 1675 ed.), Jena and Leipzig, ed. Bölsche, 1905, bk. I, Nos. 8, 92, 293. Cp. bk. II, No. 200; III, No. 37 (' God perishes of anguish, because I do not belong to him '), &c., &c.

[117] See Locke's famous chapter, 'Enthusiasm', in his *Essay*, bk. IV, ch. xix—the challenge to a hundred battles.

[118] Görres, *Die christliche Mystik*, 4 vols., 1836–42. I have not seen the modern accounts (named by James, *Varieties*, p. 406 note) by Ribet and Vallgornera.

[119] 'Meister' Eckhart, who died about 1327, was the most pagan of all the great mediaeval mystics, and engrafted a pantheism, founded on the neo-Platonists, into the Christian faith. He was forced by the Inquisition into disavowal, but his work remained.

[120] *Inferno*, vii. 100–130.

[121] S. Juan de la Cruz: in *Bibl. de Autores españoles* (Rivadeneyra), vol. xxvii (1853). See *Subida del Monte Carmelo*, bk. I, ch. iii; bk. III, ch. v, and *Noche escura del Alma*, bk. I, ch. viii.

[122] *Grace Abounding to the Chief of Sinners.*

[122a] Tauler, *Sermons*, tr. Winkworth, p. 327: 4th S. after Easter.

[123] Hegel, *Philosophy of History*, Eng. tr. by Sibree, 1861 (Bohn), p. 177.

[124] W. R. Inge, *Christian Mysticism* (Bampton Lectures, 1899), pp. 19, 20. 'When Harnack says " Mysticism is nothing else than rationalism applied to a sphere above reason ", he would have done better to say that it is "reason applied to a sphere above rationalism "' (p. 21). Better say, the mystic reasons about irrationals, but refuses to reason about their reality.

[125] *Encycl. Brit.*, ed. ix, art. 'Mysticism'.

[126] See note 123 *supra*: *op. cit.*, p. 147.

[127] See note 112 *supra*. *Ergänzungen*, ch. xlvii: ' In Folge dieses

Egoismus ist unser Aller Grundirrthum dieser, dass wir einander Nicht-Ich sind. Hingegen ist gerecht, edel, menschenfreundlich seyn, nichts Anderes, als meine Metaphysik in Handlungen übersetzen.' Schopenhauer then repeats the 'Brahmanenformel, *tat twam asi*, "Dies bist Du"'.

[128] *Varieties*, Lectures IV and V.

[129] G. D'Annunzio, *Intermezzo*, Naples, 1894, pp. 63-76.

[130] 1900, reprinted 1905. The prefatory notes to each author represented are by many hands ; and, if they suffer here and there, as criticism, from personal piety and from the insular self-absorption of Ireland, they are done with scholarship and good taste.

[131] *The Need and Use of Getting Irish Literature into the English Tongue*, London, 1893.

[132] In the *Quarterly Review*, July, 1903 (*Sagas and Songs of the Gael*).

[133] *The Aran Islands*, Dublin, Maunsel & Co., by whom most of the plays and some of the poems named in this and the next section have been published. Others can be found in Mr. Yeats's annual, *Samhain*, 1904-7 ; or in *A Celtic Christmas*, the Christmas number of *The Irish Homestead*, 1905-7.

[134] *New Songs*. A Lyric Selection made by A. E. from Poems by Padraic Colum, Eva Gore-Booth, Thomas Keohler, Alice Milligan, Susan Mitchell, Seumas O'Sullivan, George Roberts, and Ella Young. Dublin, O'Donoghue & Co. ; London, A. H. Bullen. 1904.

Addendum to note [9]. I am indebted to Prof. A. J. Butler for another mention of Bruno by an Englishman of the day. This occurs in a MS. letter of Sir H. Cobham, ambassador in Paris, to Walsingham on March 28 (O. S.), 1583 :—' Il Sr Doctor Jordano Bruno Nolano, a professor in philosophy, intendeth to pass into England; whose religion I cannot commend.' The letter is in the Record Office.

ERRATA

P. 7, l. 18, *for* Sir Toby Matthew *read* Toby Matthew.
P. 18, line 8, *omit commas*.

INDEX

The small numerals refer to the numbers of the notes.

Z

INDEX

339

Marston, John, 148.
Martialis, M. V., [57].
Massinger, Philip, 144, 150-1.
Matthew, Toby, 7, 8, [8].
Maupassant, Guy de, 230.
Maurice, F. D., 183.
Mauvissière, Maria de Castelnau de, 5.
Mauvissière, Michel de Castelnau de, 3-5, 10.
Mazzini, Giuseppe, 217-20, 230, 252.
McIntyre, Mr. J. Lewis, 1, [1], [2], [20].
Meredith, Mr. George, 195-6, 228-44, 252: *The Amazing Marriage*, 240, 242; *Beauchamp's Career*, 233; *The Egoist*, 239-40; *Evan Harrington*, 239-40; *Emilia in England* (*Sandra Belloni*), 233; *Emilia in Italy* (*Vittoria*), 233; *On the Idea of Comedy*, 237-9; *Lord Ormont and his Aminta*, 229; *Odes*, 229; *One of our Conquerors*, 231; *A Reading of Earth*, 241; *Rhoda Fleming*, 235; *The Shaving of Shagpat*, 229, 242; *The Tragic Comedians*, 233.
Meredith, The Poetry and Philosophy of George: *see* Trevelyan, G. M.
Meres, Francis, 59, 149.
Meyer, Dr. Kuno, 294.
Michelangelo, 30, 85-6.
Middleton, Thomas, 148.
Millais, Sir John, 197.
Milnes, R. Monckton, Lord Houghton, 189.
Milton, John, 38, 66, 102, 129, 133, 137, 141, 147, 189, 197, 204, 223, 285, [93]; *Lines to Shakespeare*, 66; *Lycidas*, 66, 204; *Paradise Lost*, 102, 141, 147, 285; *Samson Agonistes*, 223, 285; *When the Assault was Intended*, 66.
Mirror for Magistrates, The, 56.
Misanthrope, Le, 239.
Mitchell, Miss Susan, 319.
Modern Language Review, 136.
Molière, J.-B. P., 239.
Molinos, Miguel de, 109, 160, [115].
Montaigne, Michel de, 27, 81, 86, 139.

More, Henry, 315.
Morehead, William, 8, 35.
Morris, William, 129, 211-13, 223, 225, 287, 299.
Musophilus, 63-4.
Mysticism, **156-82**, 293, 300, **314-20**.

Nash, Thomas, 25.
Nation, The, 290.
Neoplatonism, 159: *see* Plato.
New Songs, 319, [134].
Nietzsche, Friedrich, 7.
'Nirvana', 177.
Nola, 4, 6.
Norris, John, 161, 317.
'Nundinio', 16, 19.

Obscure Night of the Soul, 169.
Ode on Intimations of Immortality, &c., 210.
O'Grady, Mr. Standish, 296.
O'Grady, Mr. Standish Hayes, 295-6.
Oliphant, Mrs., 207.
O'Neill, Miss Maire, 312.
Orlando Furioso, 69-71.
'Ossian', 297.
Ovidius Naso, P., 40, 46, 49.
Owen, Mr. John, [1], [23].
Oxford, 5-10.

Pascal, Blaise, 36.
Pater, Walter, 139.
Paulus Jovius, 8.
Peacock, T. L., 231.
Peccato di Maggio, Il, 214.
Pennant's *London*, [3].
Pessimism, 109, 194.
Petit de Julleville, M., 135.
Petrarca, Francesco, 38, 42, **46-52**, 56, 141, [58], [79], [74-8]; *Ad Posteros*, 48; *Africa*, 41, 48, 50; *De Contemptu Mundi*, 50; *De Remediis Utriusque Fortunae*, 49; *Trionfo della Fama*, 48, 60, [87].
Philocosmus, 63-4.
Phthisical, 315.
Pico della Mirandula, 28, [35].
Pindar, 40-1, 209, [55].
Pinero, Mr. A. W., 308.
Plato, Platonism, and Neoplatonism, 6, 25-6, 28-30, 309. 60, 137, 141-2, 158-60.

Oxford : HORACE HART, Printer to the University

SELECTIONS FROM

MR. EDWARD ARNOLD'S LIST.

PROFESSOR RALEIGH'S WORKS.
MILTON.
By WALTER RALEIGH,
Professor of English Literature in the University of Oxford.
Second Impression. Crown 8vo. Cloth, 6s.
CONTENTS.
Introduction—John Milton—The Prose Works—Paradise Lost: The
Scheme—Paradise Lost: The Actors—The Later Poems—The Style of
Milton: Metre and Diction—The Style of Milton and its influence on
English Poetry—Epilogue.
'Admirably written. We congratulate Professor Raleigh upon what we
do not hesitate to call a beautiful as well as a stimulating book, one which
suggests high hopes for the future of English criticism.' —*Athenaeum*.

WORDSWORTH.
By PROFESSOR WALTER RALEIGH.
Second Impression. Crown 8vo. Cloth, 6s.
CONTENTS.
Introduction—Childhood and Education—The French Revolution: Cole-
ridge—Poetic Diction—Nature—Humanity—Illumination—Conclusion.
'Since Matthew Arnold's famous essay on Wordsworth, there has been
none so illuminating as this of Professor Raleigh's.'—*Daily Telegraph*.

STYLE.
By PROFESSOR WALTER RALEIGH.
Sixth Impression. Crown 8vo. 5s.
'Mr. Raleigh's volume is the fruit of much reading and more thinking.
It is informed by the true literary spirit; it is full of wisdom, inclining now
and then to paradox; and it is gay with quaintnesses and unexpected
epigrams.'—*The Times*.
'In our judgment Mr. Raleigh's volume on "Style" is an amazingly
good and pre-eminently interesting and suggestive book. His whole treat-
ment of his subject is vigorous, manly, and most sensible.'—*The Speaker*.

ROBERT LOUIS STEVENSON.
By PROFESSOR WALTER RALEIGH.
Third Impression. Crown 8vo. 2s. 6d.
'A capital piece of work, written with great life, and curiously Steven-
sonian in mood and style, though by no means unpleasantly imitative.'—
Manchester Guardian.

LONDON: EDWARD ARNOLD, 41 & 43 MADDOX ST., W.

SELECTIONS FROM
MR. EDWARD ARNOLD'S LIST.

SIX RADICAL THINKERS (BENTHAM, MILL, COB-
DEN—THOMAS CARLYLE—MAZZINI—T. H. GREEN). By
JOHN MACGUNN, LL.D., Professor of Philosophy in the University of
Liverpool. Crown 8vo. 6s. net.

THUCYDIDES MYTHISTORICUS. By F. M. CORNFORD,
M.A., Fellow and Lecturer at Trinity College, Cambridge. Demy 8vo.
10s. 6d. net.

'An exhaustive and fascinating study. Mr. Cornford has made a contribution not merely to the interpretation of Thucydides, but to the understanding of ancient thought in general, of great originality and of permanent
value.'—*Manchester Guardian.*

STUDIES IN VIRGIL. By TERROT REAVELEY GLOVER,
Fellow and Classical Lecturer of St. John's College, Cambridge; Author
of 'Life and Letters in the Fourth Century.' Demy 8vo. 10s. 6d. net.

'Mr. Glover has achieved a real triumph; he sends his readers away
longing to take up their Virgil again.'—*St. James's Gazette.*

TRANSLATIONS INTO LATIN AND GREEK VERSE.
By H. A. J. MUNRO, sometime Fellow of Trinity College, and Professor
of Latin in the University of Cambridge; with a Prefatory Note by
J. D. DUFF. Medium 8vo. With a Portrait. 6s. net.

STUDIES IN EARLY VICTORIAN LITERATURE, 1837–
1870. By FREDERIC HARRISON, M.A., Author of 'The Choice of
Books,' &c. Fifth Impression. Large Crown 8vo. 3s. 6d.

MEMOIRS OF MISTRAL. Translated from the French by
CONSTANCE MAUD, Author of 'An English Girl in Paris,' 'Wagner's
Heroes,' &c. Demy 8vo. With Portraits. 12s. 6d. net.

SELECT ESSAYS OF SAINTE-BEUVE. Chiefly bearing
on English Literature. Translated by A. J. BUTLER, late Fellow of
Trinity College, Cambridge. Crown 8vo. 3s. 6d.

LONDON : EDWARD ARNOLD, 41 & 43 MADDOX ST., W.

Telegrams :
'Scholarly, London.'

41 and 43 Maddox Street,
Bond Street, London, W.,
March, 1908.

Mr. Edward Arnold's List of New Books.

———•—•—•———

NEW NOVEL.

By the author of 'The Jungle.'

THE METROPOLIS.

By UPTON SINCLAIR.

Crown 8vo. **6s.**

This is Mr. Upton Sinclair's first new novel since 'The Jungle,' wherein he startled the world with his lurid account of the iniquities perpetrated in the American canned meat trade.

In 'The Metropolis' he brings a scathing indictment against the vulgar element in New York Society, whose exotic and vicious lives are exposed with all that unrestrained and brilliant relentlessness of which Mr. Sinclair is a master.

It will be remembered that a few months ago a report went round to the effect that Mr. Sinclair had managed to get a situation as butler in the house of a prominent millionaire, where he was studying the occupants with the intention of describing them in a book. The report was unfounded, and was denied at the time; but it is quite clear from this book that he must have had opportunities of no ordinary character to have enabled him to handle the subject with such telling and convincing effect.

LONDON : EDWARD ARNOLD, 41 & 43 MADDOX STREET, W.

NEW NOVEL.

By the author of ' The House of Shadows.'

THE WAYS OF REBELLION.

By REGINALD FARRER.

Crown 8vo. **6s.**

Mr. Farrer has gained for himself a reputation as a writer of novels with fresh and original themes. In the present instance certain phases of modern life are hit off with great skill and incisiveness. The vacillating relations of a young married lady with a man who has divested himself of his wealth in order to devote his life to service among the poor, are handled in a manner extremely modern. Mr. Farrer knows his world, and provides much crisp dialogue and clean-cut phraseology.

FROM THEIR POINT OF VIEW.

By M. LOANE,

Author of ' The Next Street but One,' ' The Queen's Poor,' etc.

Crown 8vo. **6s.**

Miss Loane is a district nurse ; she has lived among the poor and for the poor ; she knows the society of the poor from the inside, yet she comes in from the outside, consequently she sees closely enough to descry details accurately.

This new book, full of real knowledge, common sense, and robust humour, is urgently recommended to the attentive perusal of all men and women who are interested in the problem of life among the poor. The following are among topics discussed in it : The Manufacture of the Tramp, The Cost of Food, Mental and Moral Characteristics, Why the Poor prefer Town Life, What is Charity ? Miss Loane has a great gift for telling anecdotes, and employs it with effect in the present instance.

NEW AND CHEAPER EDITION.

THE NEXT STREET BUT ONE.

By M. LOANE.

Crown 8vo. **3s. 6d.**

GEORGE RIDDING, SCHOOLMASTER AND BISHOP.

Forty=third Head Master of Winchester, 1866—1884. First Bishop of Southwell, 1884—1904.

By his Wife, Lady LAURA RIDDING.

With Illustrations and a Plan. Demy 8vo. **15s. net.**

Whilst appealing especially to Wykehamists, this valuable and interesting biography claims the attention of the larger public that enjoys reading about the careers of successful and distinguished people.

The volume is roughly divided into three sections, the first telling of Dr. Ridding's early days at Winchester and Oxford. After this comes the account of his notable headmastership—notable because during it was evolved the Winchester known to most of her sons now living. So many buildings were added and so many improvements made that Dr. Ridding, the prime mover in it all, came to be known as 'the second founder.' The third section describes the formation of the Diocese of Southwell, and is a remarkable revelation of the successful application of exceptional administrative ability.

PICTORIAL ART IN THE FAR EAST.
By LAURENCE BINYON.

With Coloured Frontispiece and numerous other Illustrations beautifully reproduced in collotype. Crown 4to. **21s. net.**

This important work, which is only rendered possible by the immense additions to our knowedge of Far Eastern art during the last decade, brings out and establishes the high interest of Chinese painting, hitherto practically unknown in Europe, and of the older schools of Japan, the subsidiary schools of India, Persia and Tibet being also glanced at. The author's aim has been to treat his subject not merely from the technical historical side, but as a theme of living and universal interest, with its background of Oriental thought and civilization.

MINES AND MINERALS OF THE BRITISH EMPIRE.

Being a Description of the Historical, Physical, and Industrial Features of the Principal Centres of Mineral Production in the British Dominions beyond the Seas.

By RALPH S. G. STOKES,

Late Mining Editor, *Rand Daily Mail*, Johannesburg, S.A.

Demy 8vo.   With numerous Illustrations.   **15s. net.**

This work is the outcome of a careful and exhaustive inspection of the mines all over the Empire, covering a considerable period, on the part of the author, who has visited personally the places he describes, and who has brought much practical knowledge to bear upon his subject.   A moment's consideration enables one to realize the great amount of romance there is attached to this prosaic-sounding industry : the histories of some of the mines are capable of filling volumes by themselves.   On the other hand, the book is indispensable as a work of reference for capitalists, investors, and many others interested in the different aspects of mining.

TURKEY IN EUROPE.

By SIR CHARLES ELIOT, K.C.M.G.

('Odysseus').

A New Edition, with Additional Chapters on Events from 1869 *to the Present Day.*

Large Crown 8vo.   **7s. 6d. net.**

Although the identity of 'Odysseus' has for some time been an open secret, it is satisfactory to be able at length to reveal definitely the authorship of this important work.   The additional chapters contain a valuable review of the present position of the Turkish question, and bring up to date a book that is already regarded as a standard authority on its subject.

BOOKS RECENTLY PUBLISHED.

FROM THE NIGER TO THE NILE.

By BOYD ALEXANDER,

LIEUTENANT, RIFLE BRIGADE.

Two volumes. Large Medium 8vo. With Illustrations and Maps.

36s. net.

'This is a great book on a great subject. The expedition of which it tells the story was by far the most remarkable feat of recent African travel, the greatest feat of endurance since Mr. Grogan's memorable journey from the Cape to Cairo, and more fruitful in scientific results than any expedition since that of Stanley. Mr. Alexander modestly disclaims literary skill, but we know few books of travel written in purer English.'—*Spectator.*

'It is a book which is worthy to be ranked with the classics of Stanley, Speke, and Livingstone—a book that deserves to, and assuredly will, take rank as one of the most fascinating revelations of savage Africa. We have seldom read a better book of travel, never a more deeply interesting one.'—*Country Life.*

MEXICO OF THE TWENTIETH CENTURY.

By PERCY F. MARTIN, F.R.G.S.,

AUTHOR OF 'THROUGH FIVE REPUBLICS OF SOUTH AMERICA.'

Two volumes. Demy 8vo. With Illustrations and Map. **30s. net.**

ACROSS PERSIA.

By E. CRAWSHAY WILLIAMS.

Demy 8vo. With Illustrations and Maps. **12s. 6d. net.**

RAILWAY ENTERPRISE IN CHINA.

An Account of its Origin and Development.

By PERCY HORACE KENT.

Demy 8vo. With Maps. **12s. 6d. net.**

MODERN STUDIES.
By OLIVER ELTON, M.A.,
PROFESSOR OF ENGLISH LITERATURE IN THE UNIVERSITY OF LIVERPOOL.
Large Crown 8vo.   **7s. 6d. net.**

MEMOIRS OF MISTRAL.
Rendered into English by CONSTANCE ELISABETH MAUD,
AUTHOR OF 'WAGNER'S HEROES,' 'AN ENGLISH GIRL IN PARIS,' ETC.

Lyrics from the Provençal by ALMA STRETTELL (MRS. LAWRENCE HARRISON).

Demy 8vo.   With Illustrations.   **12s. 6d. net.**

THE
GROWTH OF MODERN NATIONS.
A History of the Particularist Form of Society.

Translated from the French of HENRI DE TOURVILLE
by M. G. LOCH.

Demy 8vo.   **12s. 6d. net.**

AN INTRODUCTION TO CHILD-STUDY.
By W. B. DRUMMOND, M.B., C.M., F.R.C.P.E.,
AUTHOR OF 'THE CHILD: HIS NATURE AND NURTURE.'

Crown 8vo.   **6s. net.**

THE CHILD'S MIND: ITS GROWTH AND TRAINING.
By W. E. URWICK, M.A.
Crown 8vo.   **4s. 6d. net.**

THE MYSTERY OF MARIA STELLA, LADY NEWBOROUGH.

By SIR RALPH PAYNE-GALLWEY, Bart.

Demy 8vo. With over 20 Illustrations and a Photogravure Frontispiece. Second Impression. **7s. 6d. net.**

MY ROCK-GARDEN.

By REGINALD FARRER,

Author of 'The Garden of Asia,' 'The House of Shadows,' 'The Sundered Streams,' etc.

Large Crown 8vo. With Illustrations. Second Impression. **7s. 6d. net.**

THE LIFE OF THE SALMON.

With Reference more especially to the Fish in Scotland.

By W. L. CALDERWOOD, F.R.S.E.,

Inspector of Salmon Fisheries for Scotland.

Demy 8vo. With Illustrations. Second Impression. **7s. 6d. net.**

IN OUR TONGUES.

Some Hints to Readers of the English Bible.

By ROBERT H. KENNETT,

Canon of Ely Cathedral; Regius Professor of Hebrew in Cambridge University, etc.

Crown 8vo. **3s. 6d. net.**

THE GOLDEN PORCH.

A Book of Greek Fairy Tales.

By W. M. L. HUTCHINSON.

Crown 8vo. With Illustrations. **5s.**

A GALLERY OF PORTRAITS.

Reproduced from Original Etchings.

By HELLEU.

With an Introduction by FREDERICK WEDMORE.

Crown Folio. **25s. net.**

FAMILIAR FACES.

By HARRY GRAHAM,

AUTHOR OF 'RUTHLESS RHYMES FOR HEARTLESS HOMES,' ETC., ETC.

Medium 8vo. With 16 *Illustrations by* GEORGE MORROW. **3s. 6d. net.**

OUT OF CHAOS.

A Personal Story of the Revolution in Russia.

By PRINCE MICHAEL TRUBETZKOI.

Crown 8vo. **6s.**

RECENT FICTION.

Crown 8vo. **6s.** *each.*

HIS FIRST LEAVE.

By L. ALLEN HARKER,

AUTHOR OF 'THE INTERVENTION OF THE DUKE,' 'WEE FOLK, GOOD FOLK,' 'CONCERNING PAUL AND FIAMMETTA,' ETC.

Second Impression.

THE ELECTION OF ISABEL.

By RONALD MACDONALD,

AUTHOR OF 'A HUMAN TRINITY,' 'THE SEA-MAID,' ETC.

THE DESERT VENTURE.

By FRANK SAVILE.
